The Humanities "Crisis" and the Future of Literary Studies

The Humanities "Crisis" and the Future of Literary Studies

Paul Jay

palgrave
macmillan

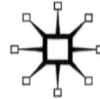

THE HUMANITIES "CRISIS" AND THE FUTURE OF LITERARY STUDIES
Copyright © Paul Jay, 2014.

Softcover reprint of the hardcover 1st edition 2014 978-1-137-40330-8

All rights reserved.

First published in 2014 by
PALGRAVE MACMILLAN®
in the United States—a division of St. Martin's Press LLC,
175 Fifth Avenue, New York, NY 10010.

Where this book is distributed in the UK, Europe and the rest of the world, this is by Palgrave Macmillan, a division of Macmillan Publishers Limited, registered in England, company number 785998, of Houndmills, Basingstoke, Hampshire RG21 6XS.

Palgrave Macmillan is the global academic imprint of the above companies and has companies and representatives throughout the world.

Palgrave® and Macmillan® are registered trademarks in the United States, the United Kingdom, Europe and other countries.

ISBN 978-1-349-48696-0   ISBN 978-1-137-39803-1 (eBook)
DOI 10.1057/9781137398031

Library of Congress Cataloging-in-Publication Data

Jay, Paul, 1946–
   The humanities "crisis" and the future of literary studies / by Paul Jay.
      pages cm
   Includes bibliographical references and index.

    1. Humanities—Study and teaching (Higher) 2. Literature—Study and teaching (Higher) 3. Humanities—Philosophy. 4. Education, Higher—Philosophy. 5. Humanities—Political aspects. 6. Education, Higher—Political aspects. I. Title.

AZ182.J38 2014
001.3071'1—dc23   2014001798

A catalogue record of the book is available from the British Library.

Design by Newgen Knowledge Works (P) Ltd., Chennai, India.

First edition: July 2014

10 9 8 7 6 5 4 3 2 1

Contents

Acknowledgments	vii
Introduction	1
1 The Humanities Crisis Then and Now	7
2 Professionalism and Its Discontents	33
3 Humanism, the Humanities, and Political Correctness	55
4 Getting to the Core of the Humanities, or Who's Afraid of Gloria Anzaldúa?	83
5 Aesthetics, Close Reading, Theory, and the Future of Literary Studies	115
Conclusion: The Humanities and the Public Sphere in the Age of the Internet	143
Notes	173
Works Cited	195
Index	203

Acknowledgments

This book could not have been written without the support and enthusiastic encouragement of my friend and department chair Joyce Wexler, and to her I express my deepest thanks. I also owe a debt of gratitude to my colleagues in the English department, a fabulous group of scholars and teachers who create a warm and intellectually exciting environment in which to work. One could not ask for a scholarly environment more conducive to original and innovative research than the one in my department, and in Loyola's College of Arts and Sciences. I also want to express my thanks to the university for generously granting me research leave in the spring of 2011 that allowed me to draft much of this book. Whenever I have been at a crucial juncture in writing a monograph the university has been there to provide time for research and writing, and for that I am truly blessed. Without that support, there simply would not have been time to write this book.

    I also want to thank my students at Loyola, both undergraduate and graduate, for helping to create an environment in which I could test, question, refine, and rethink the scope and aim of this book and the arguments I wanted to make in it. Many of the historical explanations in this book, and the claims about critical theories and methodologies it makes, were worked out over a number of years in English 354, Introduction to Contemporary Critical Theory, and I owe a debt of gratitude to the students who have worked with me in that course over the last decade. I also owe particular thanks to the graduate students in my fall 2011 course in Contemporary Literary Criticism. They read a number of the key texts I discuss in this book and a range of essays and articles about the issues I cover here, and their ideas, responses, questions, and feedback were absolutely crucial in helping me rethink the analyses and arguments that finally made their way into this book. I want to particularly thank Sean O'Brien, a student in that course who later served as my research assistant on the project and who did an extraordinarily effective job finding and reviewing materials for me. His concise, intelligent synopses of a whole range of books and articles were simply invaluable.

This book also benefited from constructive discussion and intelligent feedback from audiences at invited lectures at Texas Tech University, Whittier College, and the University of Alberta. In addition, portions of this book were presented at conferences including The Making of the Humanities III, in Rome, Italy, and again in Rome at a conference on the Humanities, Society, and Business. The exchanges I had with colleagues at these and other conferences helped enormously in shaping my thinking about the claims and arguments I make here.

I also want to thank friends and colleagues who read earlier drafts of some chapters and provided me with extraordinarily helpful suggestions. Gerald Graff generously read early versions of the first chapter and his encouragement and concrete editorial suggestions were invaluable. It was his idea, after reading the draft of that chapter, that we collaborate on the article that became "Fear of Being Useful." That collaboration was a rich experience that became a turning point in my work, and I cannot thank him enough. As always, I benefitted from hours of discussion and exchange with Gregory Jay about the issues in this book over the course of many years. Greg also was particularly helpful in providing critical feedback on chapter 3, as was Jane Gallop with regard to chapter 5. Jaap Maat prodded me to make some valuable clarifications to my argument in the same chapter, and I thank him for taking the time to do that. I also want to thank my colleague in the history department Anthony Cardoza, for coauthoring with me a formal exchange for *Loyola Magazine* on some of the issues touched upon in this book. Thanks as well to Leonard Cassuto from whom I have learned a lot about the institutional challenges of graduate education in the humanities. Our televised appearance together on Higher Education Today provided the venue for a very valuable exchange and led to fruitful collaboration on a forthcoming essay on the topic. This book also benefitted from both formal and informal discussions with Marjorie Garber and Terry Eagleton, who contributed to Loyola University's series of lectures on the future of the humanities. I also would like to thank the anonymous readers who reviewed different versions of this book for Palgrave Macmillan. Their observations and suggestions made this a much better book. I also want to thank Sarah Nathan, my editor at Palgrave Macmillan, for her invaluable support and advice. And finally, I thank my wife and partner, Lynn Woodbury, chairperson of the department of English at Oakton Community College, for her love, devotion, and support during the years I worked on this book. I marvel at her ability to balance a busy professional life with the one we share together in our wonderful home, a place where the bulk of this book was written. The space she helps shape for us to live in made this book possible.

And finally, I would be remiss if I did not thank all of my friends on Facebook who, over the last three years, have posted links to important articles about the state of the humanities I might otherwise have missed. In particular I want to thank Cathy Davidson, Richard Grusin, Teresa Mangum, Hugh Miller, Bruce Robbins, Eric Schuster, Phoebe Stein, and Siva Vaidyanathan.

Introduction

This is a book about how to defend the humanities in general—and literary studies, in particular—at a time when there are shrinking resources to support them, and growing skepticism about their worth. The humanities today seem the victim of a perfect storm. Budget cuts stemming from a persistent recession, accompanied by the defunding of public institutions of higher education through shrinking tax revenue, have threatened humanities programs everywhere. The corporatization of higher education has increasingly turned university presidents into CEOs, and academic administrators into upper management. The decisions they make regarding academic programs are increasingly driven by boards of trustees dominated by businessmen, bankers, and financial consultants whose bottom-line methods of operation are taking precedence over the traditional role faculty have played in determining academic and curricular programs. In this context, higher education is increasingly seen in sheerly instrumental terms, with courses and programs judged in terms of their pragmatic and vocational value. Education that ends in credentializing seems to be trumping education as an end in itself. For many, the teaching of practical skills is becoming more important than making sure students have a basic knowledge of history, philosophy, literature, and the arts. With the value of education being measured more and more by the economic payoff that comes after graduation, it is becoming difficult for many to understand the value of a humanities education.

While this book takes the current "crisis" of the humanities as its point of departure, it places that crisis in a larger historical context and questions whether the term "crisis" is even appropriate for characterizing the historical stresses and strains that have characterized their place in higher education. Indeed, I argue that what many commentators see as a perpetual humanities crisis is fueled in part by the rhetoric of crisis itself. Toward this end, I identify a set of recurring issues that seem to always come up in debates about the nature and value of the humanities. They include arguments about the practical utility of a humanities education, about the value of knowledge for its own sake versus knowledge that has a clear utilitarian value, debates about the role of professionalized theories and methodologies in the undergraduate classroom, and arguments about the right balance between traditional knowledge and a healthy critique of tradition. One of the problems with the perpetual rhetoric of crisis surrounding these issues is that the term "crisis" suggests a dramatic turning point at the brink of catastrophe, a decisive moment of instability portending collapse, yet the humanities have gotten along just fine in US higher education for nearly a hundred years. While concerned critics in the 1920s, 1940s, 1960s, and, increasingly, in the 1980s, 1990s, and in our own time have invoked the rhetoric of crisis to characterize the state of the humanities, what they are in fact talking about are largely structural issues about pedagogy and the production of knowledge that are inherent to the questions humanities students and their professors explore together in the first place.

Take, for example, the debates about theory and political correctness that have been at the center of the current humanities crisis since the 1980s. There is nothing new about the core of this debate except its politicization by conservative defenders of a static, traditional version of the humanities. In reality, arguments about the role that professional theories and methodologies ought to play in the undergraduate humanities classroom have taken place over the whole course of the twentieth century, a point I explore at length in chapter 1. There is nothing particularly alarming about these debates. They certainly do not suggest that there is a "crisis" in the humanities. Rather, they suggest that those who teach and do scholarship in the humanities are continually thinking in a productively self-reflexive way about what they do in the classroom and in their own research. What could be better than that? We want coherence across the disciplines, but coherence is a fluid and changing thing, the product of continual debate, innovation, and change. Whenever people are worried that the study of English, history, or philosophy is becoming "fragmented" you can be sure these disciplines are simply rethinking how they define coherence.

The same is true when it comes to questions about the social, cultural, and political character of a humanities education. As we will see in chapter 4, the humanities core curriculum at Columbia University in fact had its origins in the development of a program of instruction organized not around a study of the classics, but around a study of contemporary social and political problems related to the First World War and its aftermath. People in history, philosophy, and English have perpetually argued about the extent to which students ought to study great works for their own sake because they contain universal truths, or whether they should study texts for how they reflect, and reflect on, social and political problems that are related to the past or to our own time. These are decidedly healthy debates, and they ought not to be reduced to a simple-minded either/or approach to knowledge. As I point out in chapter 3, humanism itself was a movement connected to defining and insuring human rights, agency, justice, and power for all citizens, so it is difficult to see how the humanities could *not* be about power, agency, justice, and human rights. The only time that theory or politics cause a crisis in the humanities is when critics argue that theory and politics ought to be banished from the classroom and played down in scholarship. This is what happened, of course, in the heyday of the so-called culture wars in the late 1980s and 1990s, when critics devoted to a conservative political ideology argued that the humanities were in crisis because professors and students with other political ideologies were raising questions they didn't like and using theories they didn't understand. But that is not a crisis. That is innovation, the continuation of a thoroughly humanist tradition of exploring ideals about human rights, human agency, and the nature of social justice that have always been at the center of humanist inquiry. While critics fond of dismissing a focus on such issues as "political correctness" have fought a pitched battle against post-structuralist, new historicist, feminist, queer, and postcolonial theory, and while they have worried over the marginalization of canonical humanist texts by new attention to multicultural and non-Western texts and authors, professors and students in these fields have been busy reinvigorating and expanding the scope of humanism and the forms of knowledge it represents, and doing so in ways that are extraordinarily valuable for twenty-first-century students.

Because I believe the humanities have been significantly enhanced by the theoretical work informing these schools and movements, I stress throughout this book the value for humanities students of studying critical theory. Indeed, I argue that courses teaching critical theories and methodologies provide students with a set of practical skills that are transferable to a wide range of careers outside the academy. This makes such courses extremely relevant to the currently heated debate about the practical value of a humanities education. Critics inside and outside of the academy who bemoan the rise of theory and complain about the professionalization of humanities faculty, who even blame these developments for the crisis in the humanities, are doing a serious disservice to the very institution they are seeking to protect. Why? Because their argument ignores the fact that courses putting a stress on critical theories and disciplinary methodologies are some of the best ones we have for teaching critical thinking, and for training students to think ethically about social justice, both of which nearly everyone agrees are central to any conception of a humanities education. Courses in critical theory teach students to read rigorously, closely, and skeptically, to explore the underlying assumptions behind the positions others take, to understand the larger historical and ideological frameworks in which knowledge is presented and arguments are made, and to develop their own critical perspective on the claims with which they are confronted. Theory is about learning how to question commonsense assumptions and dig down to the foundations—or the absence of foundations—informing claims about value, meaning, and truth. What could be more valuable than that? And what could be more important than developing an ability to track how history, philosophy, literature, and art represent the world of human experience in ways that reflect, perpetuate, or critique uneven forms of power related to gender, sexuality, class, and race?

We ought, then, to be skeptical about the rhetoric of crisis in the humanities when people announcing that crisis blame it on innovation and change. Doing so makes the humanities look static and moribund, trapped in a curatorial mode in which the preservation of a fixed group of authors, texts, philosophical positions, historical events, and works of art are asserted to be their primary concern, where vague pronouncements about timeless value and universal truth trump the expansion of knowledge and critical inquiry. The increasing rigor and sophistication of work in the humanities are not to be blamed for the plight of the humanities. That plight has more to do with economic and institutional changes related to the corporatization of higher education I referred to earlier. I believe humanists and their supporters must take a pragmatic and nuanced approach to articulating the value of the humanities in the context of these changes. For this reason, I will be arguing throughout this book that while the humanities play an important role in maintaining an institutional space for thinking critically about the increasingly pragmatic and utilitarian orientation of our culture, it is a mistake for humanists and their supporters to resist the need to articulate the practical value of a humanities education. In an era of tightening budgets and demands that academic programs articulate their value, I believe it is important that we respond to the questions students, their families, college and university administrators, and the wider public have about why a humanities education matters, and that the response ought to focus not just on the value of humanistic knowledge for its own sake, but also on the value of the skills humanities students develop through exposure to disciplinary (and interdisciplinary) theories and critical methodologies in the courses they take. The questions raised by those who are skeptical about the value of investing in a humanities or liberal arts education are not going to go away because the institutional restructuring of higher education as it streamlines its budgetary and administrative operations in order to fit a new business model in an era of shrinking resources is going to continue. This means that defending the humanities must be a two-pronged effort, insisting on the important role the humanities play in fostering critical thinking about bottom-line values and the instrumentalization of everyday life, *and* articulating the value of a humanities education in concrete terms that stress the practical skills humanities students learn.

While this book has much to say about the history and future of the humanities, it is particularly interested in exploring what is at stake here for the future of my own field, literary studies. For this reason, my discussion in chapter 2 regarding debates about professionalization draws heavily on examples of how that debate has played out in the fields of English and comparative literature, and chapter 5 is devoted entirely to a discussion of various proposals regarding the direction literary studies ought to take in the twenty-first century. Similarly, my concluding chapter is concerned with the specific impact the rise of the digital humanities and the movement toward online education will have on the teaching of literature. Thus, as its title indicates, much of this book looks at the future of literary studies through the lens of the so-called humanities "crisis." Although there clearly are major differences between the disciplines of literature, philosophy, history, theology, and the fine arts, I think the case of literary studies is to some degree paradigmatic, especially with regard to debates about the impact of theory, which is of course a profoundly interdisciplinary field. That is because while much critical theory today has its origins in philosophy, political science, history, and literary criticism, it is fair to say that what we call "theory" has coalesced—and gotten much of its traction—in literary studies. This book grows out of my own experience teaching and writing about theory for over 30 years, a professional life that has spanned the whole era of theory, from its inception through debates about its value to a literary education, through the 1990s culture wars and into our own time when debates about its coherence and its future continue unabated.

The changes I have witnessed have been dramatic, and salutatory. The protocols of close reading and textual analysis developed by the

American New Critics, which dominated literary study for decades, have been become much more sophisticated through the incorporation of structuralist and deconstructive modes of reading, and the exploration of narrative and poetic structures has become remarkably more sophisticated with the rise of narratology, poetics, and semiotics. The historical study of literature has been utterly transformed during the years I have been in the profession, under the aegis of the New Historicism and influenced by the rise of African American, Chicano/a, and multicultural studies. What counts as literature has changed dramatically, canon formation has been subjected to much-needed and systematic rethinking, and the scope and range of the texts and authors students read has been dramatically expanded. The canonical works of the Western tradition continue to have a strong presence in the literature curriculum, but students now have the opportunity to read and study a much fuller range of literary expression on a multicultural and global scale that is profoundly inclusive. Given these changes, of course, the topics, issues, and subjects covered in literary studies have also broadened dramatically. The new critical focus on form which required focus on the text itself and the bracketing off of historical, critical, and cultural context has given way to forms of reading that reinsert literary and other texts in those contexts (without, on the whole, sacrificing attention to form and language). Issues central to what it means to be human, related to gender, race, sexuality, class, subjectivity, and the politics of cultural belonging have become central in literary analyses. These developments should not be viewed as a turn away from the traditional interests of the humanities, but rather, as an important expansion and deepening of those interests. As contemporary humanists rise to the challenge of explaining what gets studied in the humanities and why it is valuable, they need to find a way to stress the value of these changes, to emphasize how they expand and deepen the study of what it means to be human.

CHAPTER 1

THE HUMANITIES CRISIS THEN AND NOW

Nearly everyone seems to believe the humanities are in crisis. Hardly a week has gone by since I began research for this book late in 2009 without an article in the *Chronicle of Higher Education, New York Times, Wall Street Journal, Inside Higher Ed*, or *Washington Post* about the declining prestige of the humanities, the defunding of its programs, and the poor employment prospects of its students. The supposed causes of the crisis are by now familiar. Students and their parents have increasingly come to see a college or university education as vocational training. They want maximum value for the high cost of higher education, and that value is increasingly measured in utilitarian terms. Courses in the humanities seem of little practical use at best, and, at worst, like a waste of time. The intangible value of an education in history, philosophy, literature, and the fine arts is of decreasing interest to families worried about their children's employment prospects. Study in the humanities disciplines seems backward looking and without any utility in an age of exploding technology. For this reason students are flocking to the science, technology, engineering, and mathematics (STEM) disciplines because, unlike the humanities, they are forward looking. Add to all of this the pressures of a sustained economic recession and the increasing corporatization of higher education, where the bottom-line mentality of boards of trustees dominated by executives from the business community tends to dominate budget priorities, and you have something like a constellation of forces that, worse than a crisis, seem to portend the very end of the humanities.

The only problem with this dire scenario of the contemporary plight of the humanities is that there is little that is new about it at all. The humanities have *always* been in a state of crisis. As Frank Donoghue has shown in *The Last Professors: The Corporate University and the Fate of the Humanities* (2008), the educational value of humanities courses has regularly been questioned by business elites who worried about their practical value. From this point of view contemporary debates about the practical value of the humanities seem nearly as old as the humanities themselves. As Donoghue observes, "The terms of the so-called crisis, from the academic humanist perspective, are always the same: corporate interests and values are poised to overwhelm the ideals of the liberal arts and to transform the university into a thoroughly businesslike workplace" (1). From early in the twentieth century, Donoghue observes, "the great capitalists...saw in America's universities a set of core values and a management style antithetical to their own" (2). "America's early twentieth-century capitalists," he demonstrates, "were motivated by an ethically based anti-intellectualism that transcended interest in the financial bottom line," for it had its ultimate origins in a "distrust of the ideal of intellectual inquiry for its own sake" (3). From this point of view questions about the utility of a humanities education do not seem part of a contemporary crisis, but rather, are a structural character of higher education.

The perennial nature of the rhetoric of crisis surrounding the humanities also becomes clear by simply searching "crisis of the humanities" in the Humanities Citation Index. That search will turn up nearly 20 articles dating back to 1990. According to these articles the humanities have fallen into crisis because of the emergence of cultural studies, a new focus on canons and culture, the influence of Nietzsche, political and economic forces, or simply because they're becoming irrelevant. In 2010, Wayne Bivens-Tatum, the philosophy and religion librarian at Princeton University, searched "crisis in the humanities" in JSTOR and found articles on the topic dating from 1922. He notes that by the 1940s "a steady stream of complaints" about the state of the humanities had developed. Indeed, his essay is full of quotes from scholars in the 1940s, 1950s, and 1960s (1965 saw the publication, for example, of a book titled *Crisis in the Humanities*) decrying the crisis in the humanities. And, as he points out, the reasons for that crisis are nearly always the same. "Not only is the sense of crisis decades old and persistent," he observes, "but for the most part the causes are as well. Students are choosing professional programs over the humanities; the sciences have the most authority and get the most funding; there are too many humanities PhDs; they're evaluated by standards appropriate to the sciences but not the humanities. Every generation of scholars wakes up afresh, looks about, and thinks the sky is falling." The sky may be falling, he dryly points out, "but if it is, it seems to be falling *very* slowly."

One of the big problems with the current rhetoric of crisis in the humanities is that much of the evidence cited to document that crisis has increasingly proved to be inaccurate. Take what has become the nearly axiomatic idea that the crisis in the humanities can be measured by falling enrollments and decreasing majors. This is a recurrent point made by those who argue the humanities are in crisis. Let's look at a couple of examples. The first is an autumn, 2009, essay in *The American Scholar* by William M. Chace called "The Decline of the English Department." Chace calls attention to the drop in students majoring in English between 1970–1971 and 2003–2004, noting that majors declined from 7.6 percent of students receiving the bachelor's degree at the beginning of this period to 3.9 percent at the end. Chace's assertions recall similar ones made earlier that year by the literary critic John M. Ellis in "Why Students Flee the Humanities." Ellis, a founder of the National Association of Scholars, is the author of *Literature Lost: Social Agendas and the Corruption of the Humanities* (1999). Ellis laments a drop in English majors and blames it on the rise of critical theory and political correctness (an accusation I will explore in much more detail later in this book).

> As the economy improved dramatically during the 1980s the figure for English majors rose with the economy, reaching 4.7% by the end of the decade. But now the familiar pattern broke down: as the economy continued to get stronger, the figures for English majors began to go in the opposite direction, the first time this had happened. By 1995, English majors had declined to 4.3% of all bachelor's degrees, and by 2005 they had gone down to 3.7%, the same figure that was seen at the economy's bottom in the early 80's—except that the economy had now been booming almost continuously for 20 years.[1]

As a number of commentators have pointed out, these claims are based on very misleading data. Much of the problem stems from the fact that critics such as Chace and Ellis date the decline they lament from 1970, an unprecedented high point in humanities enrollments. The truth is that humanities enrollments have held remarkably stable. According to Ben Schmidt the percentage of humanities majors has held steady between 1984 and 2010, measuring 6.5 percent at the beginning and ending of this period, with some upticks between 1988 and 1996. As Schmidt points out, "That overall pattern gives the lie to any arguments that claim the humanities are being eroded by things like ethnic studies or a departure from the classics. Students aren't any less interested in majoring in history or English now than they were at the moment deconstructionism hit American shores." The big decline, his analysis shows, was between 1970 and 1980, when humanities majors fell from a high of about 17 percent to 8 percent. However, they moved up again beginning in 1985, reaching a peak in the mid-1990s of about 10 percent, then settled back to around 8 percent until the 2008 recession when they slipped down to 6 percent.

Michael Bérubé draws on Schmidt's work in a July 1, 2013, article to make the same point: arguments that humanities enrollments have declined due to the rise of theory and political correctness have no basis in fact (a point he has been making since 2002).[2] "There was a decline in bachelor's degrees in English," he points out, "just as there was a drop-off in humanities enrollments more generally. But it happened almost entirely between 1970 and 1980. It is old news. Students are not 'now making the jump' to other fields, and it is not 'getting worse.' It is not a 'recent shift.' There is no 'steady downward spiral.' It is more like the sales of Beatles records—huge in the 60s, then dropping off sharply in the 70s." And, he continues, "because the real lament is almost always about recent intellectual and curricular developments in the humanities," the enrollment numbers are "little more than a pretext for jeremiads."

Scott Saul also throws some cold water on the idea that the humanities crisis can be demonstrated by falling enrollments. In a July 2013 article in the *New York Times* titled "The Humanities in Crisis? Not at Most Schools," Saul, like Bérubé, points out that the "downward trajectory" of the humanities looks "striking" only if you use the 1960s as a benchmark. But from this point of view the so-called crisis in the humanities "is a half-truth." It is true, Saul points out, that humanities majors have dropped at elite universities such as Cornell, where, between 2006 and 2011, the number of history majors dropped 49 percent, and the number of English majors dropped 37 percent, and Yale, where "the number of English majors plummeted more than 60 percent between 1991 and 2012."[3] Yet, the humanities are doing much better at many other colleges and universities that have a more diverse student body. He points out that nationwide, enrollment in what he calls the "softest" humanities disciplines, English, foreign languages and literatures, and the arts, "has been remarkably steady over the last two decades, hovering between 9.8 percent and 10.6 percent of total bachelor's degrees awarded." At the University of California, Berkeley, for example, "the English department this year graduated 375 majors, or 5 percent of the class." Like Schmidt, Saul notes that according to Humanities Indicators, a project of the American Academy of Arts & Sciences, the share of bachelor's degrees earned in the humanities has stayed remarkably steady between 1987 and 2010 (10% in 1987, and about 11% in 2010, with some brief fluctuations up during the overall period).[4] And Saul makes the same point Bérubé does about the claim that critical theory and political correctness have damaged humanities enrollments: "Here we must straighten out one of the great misconceptions that has circulated around humanities professors: that we are a trendy lot, 'tenured radicals' wrenching the curriculum into irrelevance as we impose the latest theoretical paradigm upon it. Yet 30 years from the culture wars of the 1980s, what is remarkable is the continuity with the curriculum of old."[5]

Enrollment figures, then, do not bear out the claim that the humanities are in crisis, that students are fleeing the humanities because they've been ruined by critical theory and political correctness. The simple truth is that humanities enrollments have fluctuated for a range of reasons between the late 1960s and the present, but they do not justify in themselves the claim that the humanities are in crisis.[6] The emergency in the humanities looks overblown, as well, if we examine employment figures. While critics of the humanities claim that students do themselves a financial and vocational disservice by majoring in the humanities (so much so that Florida recently entertained the idea of charging humanities majors higher tuition than STEM majors), the facts are not nearly as alarming as these critics make them out to be. Jordan Weissmann, in an *Atlantic* magazine article titled "The Best Argument for Studying English? The Employment Numbers," has recently pointed out that "according to the most recent survey of the college graduate labor market by the Georgetown Center on Education and the Workforce...recent humanities and liberal arts majors had 9 percent unemployment" (in 2010–2011). He notes that his is "right about on par with students in computer and math fields (9.1 percent), psychology and social work (8.8 percent), and the social sciences (10.3 percent). And it's just a bit above the average across all majors of 7.9 percent." A close look at the statistics (from a survey done by the Georgetown Center on Education and the Workforce) reveals that immediately after graduation the 9.8 percent and 9.5 percent unemployment rates for English and History majors, respectively, were lower than those for economics majors (10.4 percent) and political science majors (11.1 percent). For the computer science major, he points out, "which is regularly talked about as if it's the single most practical major a young person can choose these days, graduates are still staring at 8.7 percent joblessness." While it is true that students who major in health, business, education, the hard sciences, and engineering have lower unemployment rates and higher salaries, Weissmann notes that humanities students have gravitated to the humanities in part because they do not consider earning high salaries as their top priority.[7]

Arguments that the humanities crisis can be measured by falling enrollments and are increasingly caused by poor employment opportunities for humanities graduates are nearly always tied to the idea that the humanities have no practical value. The skills students need to get ahead, so the argument goes, are taught in business schools and the STEM disciplines. However, this argument is also belied by the facts. Increasingly, employers in the business and corporate world are expressing an enthusiastic interest in hiring students with the capabilities humanities students obtain. Take, for example, Edward B. Rust Jr., chairman and CEO of State Farm Insurance Companies, who observes that "at State Farm, our employment exam does not test applicants on their knowledge of finance or the insurance business, but it does require them to demonstrate critical thinking skills" and "the ability to read for information, to communicate and write effectively, and to have an understanding of global integration."[8] And in an essay whose title asks, "What Can I Do with My Liberal Arts Degree?" Diana Gehlaus notes that "surveys by the National Association of Colleges and Employers (NACE) show that most hiring managers care more about a job candidate's skills than they do about a college major. And the skills employers say they want most in a candidate, such as communication and critical thinking, are precisely those for which liberal arts students are known."[9] Then there is Google, which more than any other company has sung the praises of humanities students and intends to recruit many of them. "We are going through a period of unbelievable growth," reports Google's Marissa Mayer, "and will be hiring about 6,000 people this year—and probably 4,000–5,000 from the humanities or liberal arts."[10]

This evidence regarding the marketability of humanities students belies Frank Donoghue's assumption (in *The Last Professors*) that the "the corporate world's hostility" (xiii) toward humanistic education remains as intense today as it was a century ago when industrialists such as Andrew Carnegie dismissed such an education as "literally, worthless" (xiv). Donoghue ignores changes in the global economy, the culture, and the humanities themselves since Carnegie's day that have given employers in a range of fields—corporate, technological, nonprofits, arts foundations, and so on—a dramatically more favorable view of the humanities' usefulness based on the range of transferable skills they teach. When students in the humanities acquire literary, philosophical, historical, and artistic knowledge they also develop an impressive range of workplace competencies: the ability to read and analyze information and arguments, summarize the positions of others and think critically about their underlying assumptions, and to develop in writing their own analyses, arguments, and recommendations. These core competencies are supplemented by a range of more general capabilities fostered by courses in fields such as rhetoric and composition, literary criticism and critical theory, philosophy, history, and theology, which include the ability to confront ambiguity and think imaginatively about complex problems, and to reflect skeptically about received truths, abilities that are increasingly sought for in upper management positions in today's information-based economy. Even more important for operating as global citizens in a transnational marketplace, studying the literary, philosophical, historical, and theological texts of diverse cultures teaches humanities students to put themselves in the shoes of people who see and experience the world very differently from their own accustomed perspectives. For an increasingly globalized workforce these skills are not incidental. They are central. In fact, students today who don't major in the humanities may well be relegating themselves to less ambitious career options than those who do.

It is becoming increasingly clear that narrow training in the STEM disciplines is simply not enough to meet the challenges of the twenty-first-century workplace. This recognition recently moved Damon Horowitz, director of Engineering at Google, to return to Stanford to pursue a PhD in philosophy. Explaining his decision, Horowitz wrote, "If you are worried about your career...getting a humanities Ph.D. is not only not a danger to your employability, it is quite the opposite. I believe there no surer path to leaping dramatically forward in your career than to earn a Ph.D. in the humanities."[11] "You go into the humanities to pursue your intellectual passion," he explains, "and it just so happens, as a by-product, that you emerge as a desired commodity for industry." Horowitz, a leading figure in artificial intelligence and the head of a number of tech startups, ought to know. He took a break from his lucrative career to enroll in Stanford's

PhD program in philosophy because, like Steve Jobs before him, he figured out that in order to do his job in technology well he needed to immerse himself in the humanities.[12] "I realized that, while I had set out in AI to build a better thinker, all I had really done was to create a bunch of clever toys." Horowitz came to realize that the questions he was "asking were philosophical questions—about the nature of thought, the structure of language, the grounds of meaning." Returning to the humanities, Horowitz took time out from the world of artificial intelligence to study "radically different approaches to exploring thought and language," such as philosophy, rhetoric, hermeneutics, and literary theory. As he studied intelligence from these perspectives he "realized just how limited my technologist view of thought and language was. I learned how the quantifiable, individualistic, ahistorical—that is, computational—view I had of cognition failed to account for whole expanses of cognitive experience (including, say, most of Shakespeare)."

Horowitz here is getting at something essential about what a humanities education can provide that students do not get enough of in the natural and social sciences, as crucial as they are. First of all, the humanities offer students engagement with a diverse range of aesthetic materials, works of art that can surprise and move them through lyrical language, drama, and sheerly formal beauty played out across a variety of times, places, and cultures. Students cannot nurture these crucial—and uniquely human—capabilities in any other set of disciplines. The quality of the mind's engagement with art, philosophy, and religion is fundamentally unlike what happens in the natural and social sciences, as exciting and even moving as they can be. For the humanities shifts their attention from quantification, measurement, calculation, and formulas to affect, interpretation, ethical and moral thinking, dramatic representation, and the kinds of emotional and intellectual experiences they shape. The literary and visual arts in particular engage the emotions as well as the minds of readers and viewers, creating an intersection—along with philosophy, history, and religion—between the emotions and the intellect.

It would be a mistake, of course, to separate these kinds of experiences from the development of what we usually think of as "practical" skills. Indeed, one of the problems with our increasing emphasis on the practical and the utilitarian is that it simplifies, and even distorts, the relationship between skills, knowledge, and experience. Certainly we trivialize learning by reducing value in education to the question of whether or not students are learning practical skills. However, it is also important to recognize that when students engage the subjects covered in humanities courses they are learning how to *do* something. They learn to sharpen the quality of their affective, imaginative engagement with complex artistic, philosophical, and historical materials, capabilities that have value in their own personal lives, *and* in their work lives as well.

The practical value of a humanities education for employers was underscored more recently in a 2013 survey of business leaders conducted by The Association of American Colleges and Universities. Their report, titled "It Takes More than a Major: Employer Priorities for College Learning and Success," made it clear that employers are less interested in narrow knowledge in a specific field than they are in broad knowledge and a set of transferable skills.[13] The survey reported that 93 percent of employers believed that a demonstrated capacity to think critically, communicate clearly, and solve complex problems is more important than a candidate's undergraduate major. More than 75 percent want higher education to place more emphasis on critical thinking, complex problem solving, written and oral communication, and applied knowledge. In a survey of employers' key priorities, it is striking that "quantitative reasoning and knowledge about science and technology" ranked at the very bottom, at 55 percent and 56 percent respectively, while humanities and liberal arts related competencies ranked at the top. For example, "problem solving in diverse settings" generated the largest consensus, at 91 percent. The other qualities most highly valued by the business leaders surveyed included the "ability to consider ethical issues" (87%), "critical thinking and analytic reasoning" (82%), "civic knowledge, skills, and judgment essential for contributing...to our democratic society" (82%), and "written and oral communication" (80%). This consensus translated into a broad-based vision of higher education priorities informed by just those qualities humanities and liberal arts students are associated with. They include knowledge about "human diversity, and global cultures," the ability to perform "evidence-based reasoning...including analysis, communication, critical and creative thinking," a facility for "ethical reasoning, civic and democratic knowledge and engagement, global acumen...the capacity to work productively with diverse people and perspectives," and, finally, the "ability to apply knowledge, skills, and responsibilities to complex problems and new settings."[14]

The consensus among these business leaders about the value of a humanities education is clear, and it ought to give us pause in simply repeating the idea that the humanities are in crisis or that they are useless. The social, cultural, and communication skills business leaders highlight are all hallmarks of an education in philosophy, literature, history, and the arts. Indeed, there is recent evidence that the only students who are learning much in American colleges and universities are students in the humanities and liberal arts because they are required to think critically and write clearly and persuasively. This was one of the key findings in an otherwise bleak book called *Academically Adrift: Limited Learning on College Campuses*, by Richard Arum and Josipa Roksa (University of Chicago Press, 2011). Their book cited dismal figures on the lack of learning in higher education today. However, the liberal arts were a notable bright spot in the study. Arum and Roksa studied scores by students taking the Collegiate Learning Assessment test. The test, widely used in higher education by colleges and universities, provides a means for measuring an institution's success in enhancing curricula and programs in ways that support the teaching of concrete cognitive, analytical, and communication abilities. The test presents students with realistic, hands-on problems that require them to analyze complex materials and make recommendations to a fictional employer. Students' written responses to the tasks are evaluated to assess their abilities to think critically, reason analytically, solve problems, and communicate clearly and cogently. Scores are then compared across institutions to provide information to a particular school about how their students as a whole are performing.

When Arum and Roksa analyzed these scores they found little improvement among most students as they worked their way through college, except among liberal arts students. Liberal arts students had markedly higher scores compared to those in non-liberal arts programs such as social work, communications, engineering, computer science, and business. Indeed, business students had the lowest scores and showed the least improvement.[15] Why? Because the test assesses forms of critical thinking that include analytical, reasoning, and evaluation skills demonstrated through close reading and effective writing. Students on these tests have to evaluate documents, critique the arguments of others, and make their own arguments. Since these are the primary skills humanities and liberal arts students develop, it's not surprising they do much better on this test than non-liberal arts majors. Indeed, the authors of the book write that students from the liberal arts see "significantly higher gains in critical thinking, complex reasoning, and writing skills over time than students" in other fields of study (112). Why is this significant? Because students who score high on the CLA test have a much, much higher employment rate than those who score low. Even during the current economic recession, they report that only 3.1 percent of students who scored in the top 20 percent on the CLA test were unemployed. Students with low CLA scores were much more likely to be unemployed, another indication that humanities and liberal arts students are getting jobs, and they're getting jobs because employers value the capabilities the CLA tests for.[16]

As the evidence I have been discussing suggests, if there *is* a crisis in the humanities it has less to do with their inherent lack of practical utility and more to do with the reticence of humanists to emphasize their usefulness and take advantage of it.[17] Defending the humanities by proudly declaring their impracticality to *be* their virtue, insisting that the humanities are simply about exploring big, vague questions about the meaning of life, and insisting that their primary value can be narrowly defined in terms of exposing students to traditional masterpieces in literature, philosophy, and history for their own sake both does an injustice to the deeper value of the humanities and exacerbates the very crisis such defenses are attempting to thwart. The false assumption in both anti-utilitarian defenses of the humanities and pessimistic predictions of their extinction is that humanists have to choose between a credentialing and a humanizing view of higher education, between practical vocational utility and knowledge, and high-minded humanistic study as an end in itself. They don't. As I insisted earlier, this either/or way of thinking about the humanities—either they exist solely for their own sake or they have no justification at all—is a trap, leaving humanists unable to argue for the value of their work in terms of the transferable skills it teaches, an argument that inevitably has to be made in the changing marketplace of higher education. What is ironic about these debates is that, in the final analysis, there is no defense of the humanities that is not ultimately based on the usefulness of what it teaches. The very argument that the humanities help students to resist our culture's investment in practical utility is itself an argument for the practical utility of the humanities.

Of course current arguments about the usefulness of a humanities education, and indeed, whether their value should even be measured by the skills they teach, are not rooted in purely intellectual debates. They have their immediate roots in the economic recession that began in the fall of 2008 and that continues to persist. That downturn, the result of ten years of deficit spending combined with tax cuts, the cost of two wars (in Iraq and Afghanistan), and rampant deregulation in financial and lending markets, combined to dramatically reduce the current budgets of both public and private universities. College and university presidents—and boards of trustees—had to scramble to manage significant reductions in private university and college endowments, and in the state financing of public universities. Citizens have been increasingly reluctant in this environment to have their taxes raised to pay teachers and keep a broad range of courses afloat, so cuts have had to be made. It is not at all clear that these conditions will be temporary, of course. This may well result in significant, structural, long-term changes in the shape of higher education. The current humanities crisis, then, was not caused by theory, political correctness, or the uselessness of its subjects. It has been produced by the convergence of an increasingly technological and instrumental age with the demands of a global economy, a convergence that coincided with an economic collapse that drove unemployment up and university budgets down, and all at the very moment in which the managerial values of higher education were becoming increasingly corporate.

For all of these reasons, the pressure to make cuts in order to maximize revenue flows and keep college and university budgets robust, and to retain what academic administrators like to call the core academic mission of colleges and universities, has fallen disproportionately on the humanities.[18] While these forces had been threatening the humanities for some time, the *New York Times* columnist Stanley Fish was probably right in arguing that the current crisis in the humanities began on October 1, 2010.[19] That was the date George M. Phillip, president of the State University of New York, Albany, announced that, for financial reasons, his university was shutting down five program areas in the humanities division, Classics, French, Italian, Russian, and Theatre.[20] Facing a reduction of nearly $12 million in state assistance, President Phillip explained, "it is critically important for the University to rethink, balance and reallocate resources to support its core academic and research mission." Phillip was quick to insist that while these programs were deemed to fall outside that mission, "this action does not reflect" negatively on "the value of these subjects to the liberal arts." The University, he assured everyone, "will continue to offer a broad array of arts, humanities, and language courses in its curriculum." This was not enough to satisfy Fish, who wrote on October 11 that the decision by Phillip was a clear sign that the "crisis in the humanities" had "officially" arrived.[21]

News of President Phillip's decision became a defining moment in the country's realization of how the economic collapse that had begun in the fall of 2008 was taking a toll on higher education in general and on the humanities in particular.[22] The Phillip decision, however, was only the latest in a series of highly public news reports and columns in the *Times*, *The Chronicle of Higher Education*, and elsewhere reporting on the tenuous state of the humanities in the United States. Carolyn Foster Segal, for example, writing many months before Phillip made his announcement, observed in a *Chronicle of Higher Education* article called "Chiseling Away at the Humanities," that for many the humanities have become "dessert," a "nonessential decadent luxury."[23] The year before, writing in the *New York Times*, Patricia Cohen observed that "in this new era of lengthening unemployment lines and shrinking university endowments, questions about the importance of the humanities in a complex and technologically demanding world have taken on new urgency."[24] The point here couldn't be clearer: in a time of jobs scarcity, and when the demand for technical capabilities is increasing, the humanities, which do not teach students skills, seem increasingly marginalized. Another article in the February 28, 2010, *Chronicle* examining enrollment trends and bachelor degrees in the humanities (which were down) wondered whether or not the humanities are "on the ropes."[25] All of these developments led Martha Nussbaum to gravely observe, "The liberal arts" themselves "are being cut away in both elementary and secondary education and in universities. Indeed, what we might call the humanistic aspects of science and social science—the imaginative, creative aspect, and the aspect of rigorous critical thought—are also losing ground."[26] A sinking economy makes the humanities seem like dessert because the main course is increasingly thought of in terms of concrete capabilities that translate into skills-based jobs.

The concerns about the value and utility of a humanities education I have been reviewing, of course, need to be viewed in the context of a longer narrative about the humanities being in crisis that runs back to the so-called culture wars of the 1980s and 1990s. Then the humanities crisis had less to do with economic pressures or questions about practical skills than with the intellectual and even moral tenor of the humanities. For traditional humanists the humanities were falling into crisis due to the rise of critical theory and the politicization of both the research and teaching agendas of so-called tenured radicals. These concerns, articulated by a range of conservative critics from Dinesh D'Souza and Roger Kimball to Lynne Cheney and William Bennett, were largely ideological.[27] This narrative dates to the 1984 publication of William Bennett's "To Reclaim a Legacy: A Report on the Humanities in Higher Education."[28] Bennett's particular concern—that the humanities had strayed from its traditional focus on the great, canonical texts of Western civilization—narrowed and politicized a century-long debate about the value of the humanities. Joined by Kimball, Cheney, D'Souza, and others, Bennett helped establish the idea that the humanities were being ruined by the professionalized interests of the faculty, that theory and political correctness were beginning to displace the traditional focus of a humanities education. As we will see in a later chapter, this conservative critique of theory, along with the specter it raised of political correctness, helped fuel broader (and in my view, counterproductive) concerns about professionalization among humanities faculty, concerns that theory, and methodologies associated with research and graduate education, were infecting the undergraduate classroom.

While arguments about theory, multiculturalism, gender, and the politics of humanities research launched during the early 1980s continued to play some role in general debates about the nature and value of the humanities well into the twenty-first century, they fell-off pretty quickly in the mid-1990s, giving way in the early twentieth century to a return to broader, pre-1980s questions about the practical value and utility of the humanities, especially when measured in sheerly economic terms. For example, while articles continued to appear in the *Chronicle of Higher Education* about political correctness in the humanities through the mid-1990s, they largely disappeared from its pages after 1993. While Scott Heller wrote in that year how "bruised after years of attack, professors in the humanities and related fields are working to answer their critics and to speak and write in a public voice,"[29] by April the *Chronicle* was reporting a "lull" in the political correctness debates.[30] By this time a new narrative in the crisis of the humanities was beginning to take hold, one that was organized around meeting the challenges of globalization. Writing in 1993 as he was about to take stewardship of the National Endowment for the Arts, Sheldon Hackney identified the challenges the humanities faced in broad structural terms that do not mention debates about political correctness and the culture wars at all, but instead begin to focus on the role a humanities education can have in educating citizens to participate in a global economy:

> The country has never needed the humanities more. We not only face the challenges of a new geopolitical situation and the problems of adjusting to economic competition in a new global marketplace, but we face a crisis of values at home. What is happening to family and community? Who are we as a nation and where are we going? What holds us together as a nation and what do citizens owe to each other? What is the relationship of the individual to the group in a society whose political order is based upon individual rights and in which group membership is still a powerful social influence?[31]

Hackney's remarks represent the beginnings of a crucial shift in debates about the challenges the humanities face, away from narrow, politicized arguments about the relationship between tradition and theory punctuated by accusations that work in the humanities has been hijacked by political correctness, and toward the idea that the humanities must redefine itself in relation to the challenges of globalization. In Hackney's view the humanities need to balance an investment in the past with an investment in the future. Hackney was not concerned, as Bennett was, with reorganizing the humanities around a historical canon of traditional works, but rather, with training students for the future. He rejects the narrow, either/or choice between tradition or politics, between a vision of the humanities as the static preserve of timeless cultural value, on the one hand, and a hotbed of critique and revolt, on the other. By insisting the humanities must face the broader "challenges of a new geopolitical situation and the problems of adjusting to economic competition in a new global marketplace," Hackney, in effect, shifts the conversation about a humanities education to the question of what role the humanities can play in helping new generations of American students deal with a dramatically different marketplace. To be sure, the questions he insists the humanities can help students explore—the changing nature of family and community, who we are as a nation and where we want to go, what "holds" Americans together, how we balance individual rights with broader social needs—seek to keep the humanities focused on a range of perennial questions, but it is remarkable how the culture wars are no longer writing the script of "what's wrong with the humanities." Hackney stakes out the terms of debate about the fate of the humanities very differently than they had been a decade earlier: How will the humanities justify its existence and value in an era of dramatic globalization in which marketplace values dominate?[32]

At this point general questions about the utility of the humanities, which have now become routine, begin to reemerge. More and more the key question became: Are the humanities important because they constitute a body of knowledge to be preserved, or because they foster a valuable set of skills? Are the humanities an essentially historical and moral enterprise, or one centered on fostering rhetorical, analytical, reading, and critical abilities? These are the terms in which Marjorie Perloff approached the debate in 1997:

> The what of literature...doesn't matter nearly as much as the how. This is why the canon wars of the 1980s have proved to be such a

colossal distraction. For even as we have endlessly debated what authors to read or not to read in a given course, we have rarely discussed what "reading" is or does. If a stiff course on the practice of reading and writing—known, once upon a time, as rhetoric—were the prerequisite for all further work in the English or literature department, I believe we would see much more interest in our discipline...I believe that taxpayers would be much more inclined to vote for funds for the humanities if they felt that their children were accumulating such cultural capital.[33]

Like Hackney, Perloff wanted to shift debates about the humanities away from political issues central to the culture and canon wars of the early and mid-1980s toward a focus instead on the practical skills taught in humanities courses, those that in her view have less to do with preparing students for life in a global economy than with accruing "cultural capital" (of course, characterizing rhetorical skills as cultural "capital" is a way of articulating the practical, even economic value of study in the humanities). In her view the whole debate set off by conservative critics is, in the end, a misguided, politicized distraction from the real task of literary studies in particular and the humanities in general: fostering reading, critical thinking, and rhetorical skills. And this way of valuing a humanities, of course, works in synch with calls such as Hackney's for a humanities remade to serve students who need skills that will enable them to function in a twenty-first-century global marketplace.

We can observe the cyclical nature of debates about the humanities in the shift of emphasis in Hackney and Perloff. As timely as it seems, there is nothing particularly new about Perloff's call for a return to rhetoric as a way to reground literary studies. Terry Eagleton had made the same argument 14 years earlier in the conclusion to his widely read 1983 book, *Literary Theory: An Introduction*.[34] Prior to that rhetoric had a passionate advocate in the American critic, Kenneth Burke,[35] and rhetoric, of course, has always had a strong if vexed presence in literary studies through the field of rhetoric and composition. However, as this skills-based defense continued to gain attention it also became specific in ways neither Perloff nor Eagleton had in mind. One striking example can be found in an April 23, 2001, *Chronicle* article titled "Making English Majors marketable," in which Tim Swartzendruber writes about a set of proposals made by Philip Cohen, the former chair of the English department at the University of Texas, Arlington, aimed at making "English majors more attractive to business and industry."[36] Cohen does not have in mind the general rhetorical abilities Perloff foregrounds, nor does he have anything to say about globalization. Rather, he wants to see English departments and the humanities in general teaching "technology skills" that in turn translate into internships in the business world: "If we continue ruling out the business world for our majors...we may find that there is precious little for them—and eventually us—to do with their sheepskins." Here, unfortunately, the teaching of literary history or forms of interpretive analysis gives way completely to the sheer utilitarian potential the study of English has in the business world. And of course, this is as far away from Fish's vision of the beautiful uselessness of the humanities as one can get. It also represents the worst fears of humanists who are rightly wary of calls for a skills-based approach to valuing the humanities that reduces "practical" and "skills" to sheerly economic, business skills.

The history I have been tracing is one in which debates about cultural literacy, the teaching of practical skills, and the effects of professionalization keep recurring. It has a kind of deep structure that continually pits cultural literacy against critical literacy. The cultural literacy defense of the humanities is wary of the practical skills defense, and vice versa. Both traditional and liberal or progressive humanists worry about an overinvestment in practical skills, traditionalists because this will divert attention from the core mission of the humanities, which they believe is cultural literacy, and liberals and progressives because they fear an emphasis on practicality aligns the interests of the humanities with those of big corporations. The problem here, as I have been stressing, is that both positions have significant legitimacy and so an either/or way of framing the argument fails both sides. This is a particular problem in our own time, when the pressure on the humanities to justify themselves in a time of economic scarcity has, for better or worse, become paramount. As Patricia Cohen wrote in 2009, "In tough times the humanities must justify their worth," and she meant it literally.[37] Education in the twenty-first century is technology driven, vocational, and corporate. These forces have converged with shrinking economic resources to put the squeeze on the humanities, which, more and more, are being asked to prove their utility and value when measured against the natural and social sciences. The demand that college and university programs and curricula prepare students for jobs, that they have a practical, vocational utility, *is* the crisis in the humanities, and it is only going to accelerate in an age of dramatic technological innovation in which instrumental learning has become paramount. Particularization, specialization, and utility have become key values in an age when students have increasingly complex demands on their time. The more the business of higher education continues to become a business, the more it reshapes its programs and curricula to reflect corporate interests, a process that only works to accelerate the vocationalizing of higher education.

A central feature of the either/or approach I've been discussing is the scapegoating of critical theories and methodologies linked to the professionalized interests of humanities faculty. The problem with scapegoating theory in the blame game about what is wrong with the humanities is that theory provides much-needed rigor not only to graduate, but to undergraduate courses as well. It is ironic that the field of critical theory has taken a beating from the same critics who tout the humanities for their ability to train students in critical thinking. What too often gets missed here is the fact that critical theory courses are some of the most effective courses we have in higher education for teaching critical thinking. Seeing critical theory as training in critical thinking not only emphasizes the general utility of such courses, but it also helps add substance to the concept of critical thinking itself, which is often invoked but rarely defined in discussions about higher education. For example, the benefits of an education in contemporary critical theory align quite neatly with those the Foundation for Critical Thinking associate with critical thinking. The foundation's website (http://www.criticalthinking.org) outlines an approach to critical thinking that links it both to disciplinary practices in general, and to the kind of theoretical thinking associated with structuralism, deconstruction, and other social, cultural, and political theories that challenge received dogmas and entrenched assumptions. The foundation's mission statement declares that critical thinking cultivates "intellectual discipline...self-reflection and openmindedness," insisting that it requires a break with "automation and fixed procedure" and embraces "radically different" forms of "thinking...adaptable, more sensitive to divergent points of view." Critical thinking is also tied explicitly to social changes under globalization. "The world in which we now live requires that we continually relearn, that we routinely rethink our decisions, that we regularly reevaluate the way we work and live. In short, there is a new world facing us, one in which the power...to regularly engage in self-analysis, will increasingly determine the quality of our work, the quality of our lives, and perhaps even our very survival."

This approach to critical thinking underscores its roots in professional, disciplinary forms of thinking, but also to challenging, resisting, and rethinking those forms in the very act of using them. From this point of view you cannot have critical thinking without professionalization, for what's being subjected to critical thinking here are entrenched, naturalized professionalized assumptions and protocols. Critical thinking involves asking challenging questions about ways of thinking and conceptualizing problems that have become automatic and fixed. According to the foundation this approach to critical thinking deals with received concepts "openmindedly within alternative systems of thought, recognizing and assessing, as need be, their assumptions, implications, and practical consequences," and in this sense is thoroughly in synch with the shorthand definition of theory Jonathan Culler provides in his book, *Literary Theory: A Very Short Introduction*. "The main effect of theory," he points out, "is the disputing of 'common sense': common-sense views about meaning, writing, literature, experience" (4). Theory, from this perspective, is a form of critical thinking that in challenging old, naturalized orthodoxies gets us to see that what we take to be "common sense" explanations and assumptions are in fact theories. For "theory," Culler explains, is an "attempt to show that what we take for granted as 'common sense' is in fact a historical construction, a particular theory that has come to seem so natural to us that we don't even see it as a theory" (4).[38]

There is a deeper irony in traditional humanists scapegoating critical theory for what they believe is wrong with the humanities, for theory, in the form of critique, has been central to humanism since its inception in the late nineteenth and twentieth centuries. From this point of view, theory is not a contemporary aberration in the humanities but a continuation of one of its most important traditions. The problem with contemporary complaints about theory is that they tend to elevate subjects of knowledge over learning how to think critically about systems of thought, ideologies, and authority. One of the most significant drawbacks of this position is that it too often sees objects of knowledge and the practice of critique in either/or terms. This problem is exemplified by Andrew Delbanco's distinction between *curation and criticism*. According to Delbanco, the humanities went astray when criticism overwhelmed curation, when the teaching of theory and critique took the place of the humanities' responsibility to preserve and venerate a traditional body of knowledge (and the seemingly timeless authority it had). What this point of view misses, of course, is the *reciprocal* relationship between curation and criticism, for to a significant degree the act of curation *requires* criticism, and criticism is itself a form of curation.

A curator does not just make decisions based on quality and distinction. He or she is also critically and imaginatively involved in putting together objects in ways that produce new relations between things and new forms of knowledge. Humanities scholars and educators curate *by* being critical in this more capacious sense of the term. Contemporary work in the humanities is therefore curatorial in the best sense of the word. It both reorganizes old materials and gathers them together with new materials to create new perspectives on both the past *and* the present. This means theory is not a threat to the curatorial enterprise, but rather, is central to its intellectual and pedagogical vitality.

Because these enterprises are at the center of forms of critique central to the traditions of humanism, the distinction between preservation and critique simply does not hold up. Delbanco wants the great texts or art works in literature, philosophy, art history, or religious studies to be the primary focus of attention, but in a way that runs the risk of separating them off—even protecting them—from criticism. In his view the act of curation must always take precedence over what he takes to be the counterproductive practices of criticism. My point, of course, is not to argue that Delbanco gets it backward—that the humanities ought to be all about criticism and that they ought to put curation on the back burner. My point is that the two activities are interdependent. When we articulate the value of the humanities we need to emphasize not only the body of knowledge they preserve but also the value of the forms of critique they teach, and to underscore that critique is a practical skill integral to both scholarly work and critical citizenship.

Now, what do I mean when I invoke the word critique, and how has critique been central to the making of the humanities? By critique I mean the practice of systematically analyzing and interrogating the constitution of conceptual categories and the sources of their authority. Critique explores historically and conceptually the development of norms that regulate our personal, social, and political lives together (for that matter, it explores the historical constitution of the very "we" these norms are supposed to protect). It is important to stress here that there is such a thing as critique *itself*—separable from *particular* critiques of particular discourses. And critique can be taught, not just particular critiques, but the activity of critique per se. Indeed, this is what those of us who teach theory teach when we teach theory. Judith Butler, writing about Foucault's conception of critique, has observed that critique "will be dependent on its objects, but its objects will in turn define the very meaning of critique."[39] "Further, the primary task of critique is not to evaluate whether its objects —social conditions, practices, forms of knowledge, power, and discourse—are good or bad, valued highly or demeaned, but to bring into relief the very framework of evaluation itself." This meta-level in critique, this bringing "into relief the very framework of evaluation itself" is at the heart of the activity we call critique.

Critique is, in this sense, at the very heart of the humanist enterprise. It involves the kind of abstract, systematic thinking we associate with Kant's theory of the aesthetic, Hegel's dialectic, Marx's analysis of the class structure or the operations of ideology, Nietzsche's idea of the death of god, or Freud's work on the unconscious, or his great work, *Civilization and Its Discontents*. But it also involves our evaluating the very frameworks of evaluation that have been employed to think about those critiques, including our own evaluation of those evaluations. Indeed, it's quite impossible to think about humanism, and thus the humanities, without thinking of the primary role that dissent and critique played in the development of Enlightenment thought, especially in terms of its radical proposals about human liberty and agency, about the primacy and autonomy of the individual, and about the natural or human rights to which everyone is entitled (a topic I will pursue at greater length in chapter 3). All of these ideas involved a theoretical critique of the status quo. It was what humanism, at its very foundations, was all about. From this point of view, the criticism of theory by traditional humanists makes no sense. Worse still, it seems to strike at the very heart of the humanist enterprise, relegating its critical vitality to the past. Seen this way, humanism is over, fixed, curated, and sanitized. It is worthy of historical study, but not something that still lives.

One thing that is particularly interesting about Butler's discussion of Foucault's approach to critique is her focus on how he associates critique with *virtue*, the cultivation of which—along with an ethical sensibility—we like to associate with a humanities education. About his idea that "there is something in critique that is akin to virtue" she observes, "virtue is most often understood either as an attribute or a practice of a subject, or indeed a quality that conditions and characterizes a certain kind of action or practice. It belongs to an ethics which is not fulfilled merely by following objectively formulated rules or laws. And virtue is not only a way of complying with or conforming with preestablished norms. It is, more radically, a critical relation to those norms."[40] This critical relation to norms, Butler emphasizes, involves "a resistance to authority," something Butler points out Foucault saw as absolutely central to Enlightenment critiques of the status quo.[41]

Critique, in the sense Foucault and Butler invoke the term, is not only intimately related to theory but helps inform a deeper and more complex understanding of critical thinking, which, as I pointed out earlier, is all too often invoked without much specificity. The value of teaching critical theory, then, is that it teaches the broadly useful skill of critical thinking, the skill most employers put at the top of their list of qualities they are looking for in college graduates. Theory in the humanities, then, is not a distraction from what the humanities ought to be doing. Theory is central to what everyone believes the humanities ought to be doing. Critical theory challenges students to think open-mindedly in the context of divergent points of view about their core beliefs, to rethink and reevaluate their values, and to entertain different ways of thinking about how meaning is produced; about the relationship between art, philosophy, and power; and about the relationship between class, gender, race, sexual orientation, and social justice. From this point of view theory, as it challenges professionally entrenched ways of doing intellectual work across the disciplines, is an important vehicle for critical thinking and thus central to the core mission of the humanities. Indeed, it is one of the most concrete examples of teaching critical thinking we have in higher education.

The teaching of theory, then, adds much-needed rigor to work in the humanities. However, as I pointed out earlier, scholars in the humanities are caught between a rock and a hard place when it comes to rigor. Too much loose talk and exploration make the humanities seem to have no rigor, but too much rigor seems to spoil the value of loose talk in the humanities. Scholars and students in the humanities benefit enormously from asking basic theoretical questions about the nature and function of literature, philosophy, and history; about the textual and ideological nature of ideas about truth and meaning; and by exploring how assumptions about things such as identity, race, class, sexuality, and gender operate both in the literary, philosophical, historical, and religious texts they study and the approaches they take to read them. The humanities, after all, are not simply about the exploration of specific literary, philosophical, theological, and historical texts. They explore the very meaning and status *of* the literary, the philosophical, the theological, and the historical. The humanities are not just interested in meaning, but in the nature and production of meaning, and in how readers ought to go about verifying the meanings that they propose the texts they study have.

The intellectual and critical rigor inherent to these kinds of enterprises go a long way toward teaching students the kinds of transferable skills we like to talk about when we talk about the general utility of a humanities education. Studying the technical mechanics of a text with a focus on how it uses language and rhetorical devices, and how it is structured in formal ways to produce effects (the kind of thing Perloff has in mind) is central to teaching students analytical capabilities that push beyond the pedestrian to the complex. Such approaches have the attraction of avoiding the mushy subjectivity that often gets associated with humanities courses loosely organized around exploring "big ideas," "the meaning of life," and "universal truths." Theorized, technical, and formalist approaches have the look of rigor and objectivity because they mirror the protocols of disciplinary work across the humanities. Every discipline in the humanities has a set of research and critical methodologies they use to find, analyze, historicize, and interpret the materials they study. They also have *critical* theories, theories about both the materials themselves—what literature is, what constitutes history, how art works communicate their power—and how to study them, theories about how to *do* criticism. For this reason, basic beginning level courses in literary, historical, religious, or art studies, of course, usually introduce students to the range of its basic theories and methodologies in just the kind of way students would expect from a social or natural sciences course. The deep irony here, as I've already indicated and will explore in more detail in the next chapter, is that attacks on specialization and professionalization in the humanities take aim at all of this. When critics of the humanities complain they've become too research oriented, theoretical, and esoteric, they are taking aim at the very intellectual and methodological infrastructure that gives the humanities disciplines academic rigor in the first place.

If the humanities always seem to be in a state of crisis it is because they are caught in a paradox. To the extent they define themselves in contrast to the rationalist, productive, data-driven, scientific, methodical protocols of the sciences, the humanities become associated with subjective speculation and imaginative interpretation, all geared toward the necessarily general exploration of questions having to do with the meaning of life or what it means to be human, important questions, to be sure, but vague enough to raise questions about the academic rigor—and practical utility—of the humanities. But then, to the extent scholars in the humanities emphasize rigor— the role that theory, methodology, criticism, and scholarship play in their professional work—the more they open themselves up to accusations they have strayed from their core mission, letting their own specialized professional interests trump the value of a general undergraduate education. This is particularly the case in my own field, literary studies, where the embrace of theories and methodologies like those regularly used in the natural and social sciences often lead critics to insist on a return to the study of something called literature itself. Indeed, one of the reasons why the humanities always seem to be in a state of crisis is because they continually have to negotiate the terms of this paradox. Crisis seems deeply structured into the disciplines of the humanities because they inhabit a curricular and scholarly world constantly pulled between an imaginative, speculative engagement with art and abstract ideas, *and* the need to shore up their credentials as academic fields of specialization with the theoretical, methodological, and research apparatuses that are associated with them.

In the face of arguments that the humanities are becoming irrelevant, I have been insisting that they *do* teach practical, transferable skills, that they are taught in courses that feature professional approaches to knowledge, that courses on critical theories and methodologies are central to teaching them, and that humanists and their supporters should not to be embarrassed to defend the humanities in terms of the skills they teach. As we have already seen, business and corporate leaders who are recruiting humanities students in large numbers are increasingly making that argument for them. For this reason, humanists and their supporters need to stop the ritualized lamentation over the crisis in the humanities and get on with the task of making them relevant in a twenty-first-century world.[42] Such lamentation only reveals the inability of many humanists to break free of a nineteenth-century vision of education that sees the humanities in narrow terms as an escape from the world of business and science. As Cathy Davidson has forcefully argued in her 2012 book, *Now You See It*, this outmoded way of thinking about the humanities as a realm of high-minded cultivation and pleasure in which students contemplate the meaning of life while others toil away in mechanized factories is a relic of the industrial revolution, one that will serve students poorly in meeting the challenges of the twenty-first century. Ultimately, to take advantage of the vocational potential of humanities study is not to sell out to the corporate world, but to bring the critical perspective of the humanities into that world. And as the experts I have quoted illustrate, it is a perspective many employers are searching for. Humanities graduates are trained to think both critically and imaginatively, and they bring mastery in research, conceptual analysis, and communication to the table. In addition, they help forge much-need links between scientific and humanistic thinking, and they have learned to look at the world from diverse perspectives. To those who worry that such a move would blunt the humanities' transgressive power, I would reply that it would actually increase the skills of students who want to challenge the status quo.

Chapter 2

Professionalism and Its Discontents

I pointed out in the last chapter how deeply ironic it is that when critics both inside and outside of academia lament the state of the humanities, they put the blame on the over professionalization of faculty. Of course this point of view reflects a more general belief outside the academy that professors in general—and humanities professors in particular—speak an arcane language, deploy overly complicated methodologies, and indulge themselves in research topics nobody else understands. If professors of English, so the argument goes, would just spend more time in the classroom exploring literature itself with their students in commonsense language uncontaminated by their professionalized discourses, we would all be better-off. I think this argument is, by and large, misguided. In fact, as I will be arguing in this chapter, the transferable skill students learn in humanities courses are largely the product of their engagement with the professional training they receive from their professors.

Blaming the professionalization of the professoriate for the shrinking relevance of the humanities is, of course, paradoxical, for one can hardly profess without being a professional. After, all, a profession is a paid occupation requiring formal qualifications and highly specific training. The word professing has, in its older form, a deep connection with professionalism, of course, for it implies a kind of public claim to knowledge and a set of skills, along with a commitment to teaching (or professing) that knowledge and those skills. A professional, it seems, can hardly profess without being professional, which is to say, teaching a branch of knowledge in an expert way. It seems, then, that the essence of being a professor is to be professional, so the idea that professionalization is harming the humanities seems counterintuitive.

Professors who blame professionalization for a significant share of the humanities crisis do so because they believe that a focus on critical theories and methodologies distracts students' attention from the core authors and subjects that ought to be at the center of a humanities education. We saw an example of this in the last chapter when Andrew Delbanco complained that critique had trumped curation in the humanities. Delbanco's argument is based on the idea that if the general population is becoming more and more skeptical about the value of the humanities it has to do with a historical conflict in the United States between "a genuine yearning for enlightenment" and an "ingrained distrust of eggheads."[1] For this reason, Delbanco insists, the humanities have to find a way to earn back the public trust: "Academics concerned with the life of the mind generally, and the academic humanities in particular," will be well "served by looking inward and asking what we can do to earn public trust." Delbanco, to his credit, insists the humanities can only earn this trust if they can find a way to demonstrate their practical value. "Most Americans," he insists, "are neither anti nor pro-intellectual but bring to the question the same pragmatic attitude they bring to everything else: a desire to see results." "Those who believe in a broad liberal education for all Americans," he continues, have a "demand for some demonstrable utility in what we teach: literature, history, philosophy, the arts." However, the "utility" Delbanco has in mind is not related to the kinds of critical thinking, analytical, or rhetorical expertise I discussed in the last chapter, but rather, one related to what E. D. Hirsch called cultural literacy, with its emphasis on a canonical body of texts and ideas all students should know.[2] As we have already seen, in Delbanco's view the skills associated with critical inquiry have usurped the centrality of cultural literacy, and for this reason he insists we need a dramatic recalibration of the balance between the "curatorial" and the "critical" functions of the humanities.

The main lines of Delbanco's analysis reflect the more traditional approach to the humanities we explored in the last chapter. It pits a commitment to cultural literacy (defined narrowly as familiarity with canonical Western texts) over-against the proficiencies associated with criticism, theory, and professionalization. If the humanities have lost the trust of the public, it is the fault of over professionalization, an emphasis on critical and theoretical skills at the expense of cultural literacy. The crisis in the humanities, then, becomes the fault of professionalization, and the cure for professionalization is a return to curation, the reading and appreciation of key canonical texts and ideas largely unmediated by criticism and theory. This is a soft version of more openly hostile attacks on the role of theory and historical, social, and political forms of criticism in literary studies among critics who argue the field has suffered a dramatic falloff not only in its engagement with literature itself but also in its ability to attract students to the English major. Literary studies since the late 1960s, so the argument goes, have become increasingly distracted from what ought to be their core focus on literature by theories from other disciplines (philosophy, psychoanalysis, linguistics, history, and the social sciences), theories shot-through with the kind of irony and iconoclasm Delbanco alludes to. From this point of view, the study of literature itself has been transformed into the study of theories about literature. Worse still, literary studies have become politicized. Professors and critics seem more interested in using literature as a pretext for discussing forms of social injustice than studying the formal qualities of literature. The new, highly professionalized theories and methodologies informing these critical discourses make literary studies look more sophisticated and rigorous, boosting their profile as academic disciplines within the university. But critics argue that in replacing literary questions with professional questions about political power—and about theories and methodologies themselves—they alienate students and drive down the number of students who major in English. Here we have the paradox I featured in the first chapter: too little professionalization makes the humanities look soft, too much professionalization makes them look like they've lost sight of their core mission.

Lisa Ruddick, in a 2001 article that argues professionalization is the "near enemy" of the humanities, also worries that critical theories and methodologies have the kind of alienating effect on students Delbanco alludes to.[3] Too much theoretical thinking, especially about identity and authenticity, has contributed in her view to something approaching nihilism in the humanities, fostering a belief that all meanings and values are socially constructed and relative, making it impossible to make claims about authentic truths. As she puts it, questions about "what's the point" have animated a "conversation that has been taking place in English departments for years." For her the problem is "how to sustain a human connection" in the classroom, a challenge that seems to be undermined by the forms of criticism she finds in scholarly journals in her field, which she feels are "stepping away from humane connection." This means, Ruddick insists, that many students find "literary studies dry and unnourishing." The dominance of a kind of pervasive philosophical skepticism underlying post-structuralism meant that she increasingly felt she had to "hide or smuggle in my convictions about what sustains people—my faith, for example, in some quality of shared humanity that makes literary experience meaningful." In a theoretical environment that questioned the very possibility of innate, universal, and essential truths, she felt increasingly constrained from what she believes ought to be a key feature of humanism, "supposing that there are shared features that constitute the essence of being human." The turning point, for her, was a course she offered on "the social construction of authenticity," a course she later came to regret teaching. In retrospect, Ruddick came to believe that teaching her students to think critically—and even skeptically—about the nature and meaning of "authenticity" put instruction in "the norms of the profession" above identifying and valuing authenticity itself. In this she expresses sympathy with Jeff Schmidt's idea that "professional training" in the disciplines "has something in common with brainwashing," and that students exposed to professional protocols need "deprogramming." One of her big worries is that an "obsessive objectivity" in professionalism puts students "out of touch with their own emotional and spiritual reserves." In her view, "professional training" can lead to "systematic demoralization," and such demoralization is "a hidden feature of many kinds of professional training."

There are two big problems with Ruddick's argument. First of all, it is overly bleak and pessimistic in the way it devalues the importance of critical thinking and analytical skills associated with philosophical skepticism. The second, perhaps worse, is that her argument is wholly anecdotal and lacks any empirical evidence whatsoever. Regarding the first problem, it is worth noting that Ruddick is not really dealing with professionalism per se in its myriad forms—research methodologies, approaches to the authentication of textual versions and authorship, methods of critical analysis and interpretation, and protocols regarding the presentation of evidence—but with post-structuralist theory narrowly defined as philosophical skepticism. But philosophical skepticism is not the same thing as professionalism. Philosophical skepticism can of course inform one's professional work, but it is not professionalism itself, so dissatisfaction with philosophical skepticism should not be the basis for criticizing professionalism. But of course there is a deeper problem here, and it is that there is nothing wrong with teaching students to think in a systematically skeptical way about truth claims and the arguments that put them forward. Indeed, that ought to be central in any humanities classroom. The point is not that students should leave our classrooms believing there is no such thing as authenticity, or that all values are relative. The point is that they benefit greatly from learning how to develop a historical and conceptual analysis of truth claims, and to present that analysis and think through its implications in their own writing. The ability to do this will play an important role in improving their odds of success in whatever they do.

Ruddick's conclusions would be alarming if they had any basis in fact. But they do not. Critics who have insisted that the professional dominance of critical theory has had a negative impact on humanities enrollments have been proven wrong. Arguments such as Ruddick's, it is worth noting, are often tied to the long-standing claim that the research agendas of graduate faculty infect the undergraduate classroom. For example, Geoffrey Galt Harpham, in his book, *Humanities and the Dream of America* (2010), recently traced contemporary problems with literary study back to a historical tension between undergraduate and graduate programs, and thus, to the increasing professionalization of literary studies fueled by research faculty working with graduate students. Because I believe this argument leads to some alarming, and unwarranted conclusions, I want to explore it in more detail. Contemporary literary scholars, according to Harpham, have "exacerbated an already problematic structural division within literary studies between the undergraduate and graduate programs" in their effort to "convert themselves into engines of research" in a discipline increasingly "requiring professional training" (100).[4] Harpham makes the familiar claim here that this has the effect both of elevating research over teaching (100) and alienating students from the experience of literature itself, the study of which should simply function to "open oneself to the experience of literature" (101). I think this is a misguided, counterproductive argument, and I want to explain why.

Harpham's argument is based on a questionable set of assumptions about literary studies. While he acknowledges that theories, methodologies, and research may be central in other disciplines outside the humanities, he insists literary studies are a different matter. Thus, while "the standard 'Intro' class in a given discipline will have undergraduates reading basic or classic texts in the field, learning how and why the subject is important, and acquiring some sense of methodology" in order to communicate "the impression that there is a certain order and sequence to the way one acquires an understanding of the field," he insists that "literary study is different" (101).

Why are literary studies "different" from the other disciplines Harpham cites? The obvious answer is that they aren't, or at least they shouldn't be. His description of the standard introductory class in most disciplines is in fact absolutely appropriate for an introductory course in literary studies. If such a course would not "have undergraduates reading basic or classic texts in the field," if it would not have them learn "why the subject is important," if it would not help them to acquire "some sense of methodology," and, finally, if it would not "attempt to communicate the impression that there is a certain order and sequence to the way one acquires an understanding of the field," what else would it do? According to Harpham, students study literature "not to learn about it but to enjoy it...to open" themselves "to the experience of literature" (101). This vague and idealized account of what a literature course ought to do verges on old forms of anti-intellectualism that, as we have already seen, often creep into debates about the value of the humanities. It sets aside the kind of intellectual rigor most introductory courses have in favor of vague references to enjoyment and experience, insisting the humanities are mostly about pleasure and getting a break from the rigors of reason, criticism, and methodology (i.e., from the practical, pragmatic, and utilitarian expertise Perloff and Eagleton value). It insists that the problem with what Graff called professing literature is professionalism itself. This kind of defense has the unfortunate effect of touting the humanities because they do not have professional standards of rigor like other academic disciplines.

In the final analysis, Harpham confronts us with an example of the humanities paradox I discussed earlier: too much disciplinary or professional rigor is seen to ruin the humanities, but the lack of disciplinary rigor or professional methodologies threatens to turn classroom inquiry into the kind of subjective mush that undermines the rigor of its disciplines as seen in the wider context of college and university learning. For this reason, the approach Harpham sketches out is exactly the wrong way to argue for the value of the humanities in general and for literary studies in particular. Any course introducing students to the study of literature ought to have the professional dimensions he rules out. It ought to introduce students to key literary and critical texts in the field, get them to see why the field is important, and introduce them to the basic theories and methodologies that have historically guided literary scholarship, providing some order and sequence to the field. The study of literature is a professional field, no less than the other disciplines Harpham mentions, and it ought to be approached as such without embarrassment.

The quickest way to make sure literary studies lapses into insignificance is to defend it to professors, students, their parents, and administrators, as simply enjoyable. Hiking in the mountains is enjoyable, but in colleges and universities we don't teach students how to enjoy hiking in the mountains. And what, we might ask, does it mean to "open oneself to the experience of literature?" Simply put, it means reading and thinking. What else could it mean? There is no experience of literature outside of reading and thinking about it, and part of what is taught in literary studies is how to read; how to become more critically self-conscious of how we read; to learn about reading as a cognitive, analytical, and interpretive process; to learn how other readers, including professional readers, read; and to see how the way we read is determined to a significant extent by how we've been taught to read, which means there are different approaches to reading that produce different interpretations of texts, different experiences of literature. Ironically, the problem with Harpham's invocation of "literary experience" is that the concept is not theorized. He simply begs the question of what "literary experience" is, as if one's own commonsense assumptions will do just fine. However, we don't just have literary experiences when we take a literature course, we study those experiences and the complex technical devices that help produce them. The whole point of a rigorous, academically sophisticated study of "literary experience" ought to be to understand both historically and theoretically how "literary experience" has been constituted in the first place (both the concepts of "literary" and "experience" have been the subject of exciting conceptual inquiry over the last 40 years). We shouldn't just have literary experiences in literature courses. We should also research, and think critically about, what a "literary experience" is, how such experiences became constituted as such, and for what purposes. The same holds for the experiences we have reading philosophy or history or looking at works of art.

Harpham's argument about what ought to go on in the introductory classroom is tied later to his discussion of the larger impact of professionalization in the humanities, especially at research universities. The problem, for Harpham, is that "professors who theorized rather than illuminated, who published rather than taught, who gravitated toward social science and away from the humanities, generally had a strong professional and disciplinary self-conception" (106). This kind of professionalism, Harpham alleges "fails to solicit, and even actively suppresses, undergraduate enthusiasm that is the focus of the undergraduate English program and the basis for the argument that English is an important discipline" (107–108). The idea that the "focus" of undergraduate English programs is student "enthusiasm" is both vague and puzzling. The problem is not that enthusiasm isn't important to the study of literature, but that it cannot be the end goal determining how literary study ought to be organized. Of course any academic program wants to instill enthusiasm in the students it educates, but enthusiasm is not the "focus" of academic programs anywhere. I have yet to see an English department mission statement that claims its aim is to tap into, and increase, its students' enthusiasm. Enthusiasm is a good thing, but enthusiasm is not a rigorous intellectual concept. Enthusiasm itself cannot replace substantive and academically rigorous goals, nor has it ever been the focus of undergraduate English programs or the basis of their importance.[5] Even if we grant that getting students to experience enthusiasm about the study of literature is a good thing, Harpham cites no evidence to prove his argument that professors who publish or do research or teach theories and methodologies commonly used in the study of literature today suppress their students' enthusiasm. Indeed, one could argue just the opposite, that when students become more critically sophisticated and are able to deploy a variety of theories and methodologies in their reading and writing they become more deeply engaged with the intricacies and the wonder of literary texts, and so their enthusiasm actually increases.[6]

The key terms in Harpham's characterization of a professionally engaged faculty member's "disciplinary self-conception"—*theorize, illuminate, teach, publish,* and *social science*—are all coded in obvious ways to question the value of professional expertise. This verges on the kind of anti-intellectualism Delbanco was talking about in the essay I cited earlier. Theoretical sophistication, the ability to produce publishable scholarship, and the ability to develop discussions of literary works that underscore their social significance, should all be seen as virtues in academia, not as vaguely suspect or actually detrimental to the interests of students. Worse still are the not-so-subtle suggestions here that people who publish aren't good teachers, that theories do not illuminate, and that illumination can't have a theoretical basis. All of these suggestions are simply wrong, and, as we shall see in a moment, they recirculate a vaguely anti-intellectualist critique of literary studies that has a very long history. By needlessly reducing, even trivializing, undergraduate literary studies as simply the pursuit of enjoyment and pleasurable experiences, inexplicably ruling out the kind of rigor he associates with other disciplines, Harpham creates a false dilemma for literary studies in particular and for the humanities in general. They are, in his view faced with "an exquisite, almost perfect, incoherence: embracing theory and research, as it was virtually forced to do, English has undercut its own intellectual and even moral foundation and alienated its most reliable customers, undergraduates; but by retaining, as it must, the high value placed on literary experiences of the kind that once excited them and continue to excite their students, English has made itself an outlier in the research environment of the modern university" (108). This assertion presents humanists with a false dilemma. Having already ruled out for English the kind of disciplinary coherence he rightly associates with other academic departments (covering basic texts, having methodologies, making clear why the discipline is important, providing order and sequence to the acquisition of knowledge, etc.), Harpham leaves the reader with incoherence. By drawing an absolute line between undergraduate and graduate studies in English, then insisting that all of the disciplinary rigor inherent to literary studies—a basic understanding of how literary history was invented, the key theories and methodologies that have shaped literary interpretation and the production of literary knowledge, how protocols of reading are shaped, what the relationship is between aesthetic production and social and political life, and so on—must be relegated to the graduate classroom, nothing is left for the undergraduate classroom besides the vague categories of pleasure and literary experience.

Besides presenting the reader with a false dilemma, Harpham's position is based on a number of questionable assertions. First of all, it is not at all clear why, in "embracing theory and research, as it was virtually forced to do, English has undercut its own intellectual and even moral foundation." Since when were having theories about literature and its analysis, and doing research, not part of the "moral foundation" of literary studies? Is there something immoral about having theories and doing research? Of course not; both are fundamental in any discipline. And why should placing a "high value" on "literary experiences of the kind that once excited" professors and which "continue to excite their students" make "English...an outlier in the research environment?" There is no obvious logical justification for this argument (professors who were excited as students, of course, were often excited by critical, interpretive, and analytical theories and methods as well as by the literature they read), nor does Harpham cite any empirical evidence for his position.

In the end, as I have been arguing, Harpham simply presents us with a false dilemma. There is no reason in the world why literary studies cannot maintain the rigor of an academic discipline at both the graduate and undergraduate levels *and* sustain students' excitement and interest, and why it cannot articulate its value as an academic discipline in these terms.[7] What is most striking about Harpham's treatment of professionalization in the humanities is that it rehearses a long-discredited vision of higher education that ought to be set aside once and for all. This vision has a cyclical history. Just as debates about the value and utility of the humanities in general run all the way back to the beginning of the twentieth century, the arguments made by critics such as Harpham, Chace, and Ellis recall earlier and often hostile responses to the professionalization of literary studies that run back in the United States at least to the 1920s (something we will see in more detail in chapter 4 when we look at the historical development of core curriculums). Concerns that literary studies have drifted away from the reading, enjoyment, and appreciation of literature itself in their preoccupation with developing the kind of theoretical, methodological, and critical scaffolding associated with the "harder" disciplines in higher education are not new. Nor are they a response to something new in literary studies. In fact, they have been a regular feature of debates about the nature and role of literary studies almost since the day they became a part of the curriculum in US colleges and universities.

Since all of the arguments I have been reviewing are based on the distinction between literature *itself* and professional theories and methods used to study literature, it is worth our taking a few minutes to review how untenable this distinction actually is.[8] Indeed, it has been debunked so thoroughly for so long that one wonders why it keeps getting invoked. Take, for example, Gerald Graff's thorough treatment of the question in his 1987 book, *Professing Literature: An Institutional History*. Briefly reviewing Graff's treatment of the debates I have been discussing will help us to see how they largely rehash old ones that have dogged literary studies for most of their history (in this sense Graff performs the same historical service for literary studies Donoghue performs for the humanities in general). Graff's book abundantly documents how arguments being made in the late 1970s and early 1980s against professionalization—that is, criticism, theory, and an emphasis on methodology—(arguments that are being recycled in our own time) have a long history running back to the very inception of literary studies. His book ought to have put to rest altogether the simplistic idea we can solve the problem of literary studies by returning to "literature itself." He points out that during the 1930s and 1940s research and scholarship in literary studies were routinely criticized as being "antihumanistic" (248) because they separated students from literature itself. A key example for Graff is Douglas Bush's 1948 attack on the New Criticism for its supposed "aloof intellectuality," "aping" of science, and rejection of the "common reader," criticisms that parallel attacks on theory in the early 1980s when Graff is writing and those I have been reviewing from the early 2000s. By the early 1980s, however, this kind of scholarship and criticism had become thoroughly naturalized in literary studies and "theory" had come to bear the brunt of such attacks: "[T]oday, when the words 'scholarship' and 'criticism' no longer denote incompatible or even necessarily distinguishable activities, critical explication has in its turn become a 'traditional' method, and it is forgotten how recently explication was thought to be almost as much a threat to traditional literary studies as literary theory is felt to be today" (249). When, Graff points out, "current traditionalists urge that we put theory behind us and get back to studying and teaching literature itself" (249) they are repeating the same kind of tired argument Bush circulated in 1948 (and that we have seen critics such as Ellis, Delbanco, and Harpham circulate in our own time). Of course, these critiques of criticism, scholarship, and theory are critiques of professionalization. They continue to get recycled as each new innovation in theory or literary criticism takes hold in the discipline. Calls for a return to "literature itself," or "literariness," then, are almost always a thoroughly predictable response to theoretical and methodological innovation, to professionalization.

Graff's discussion of what he calls "The Return of Literature Itself" could have been written today by any commentator writing about contemporary calls to stop with all the theorizing and get back to literature. Again, keep in mind Graff is writing in 1987. "[T]oday," he insists, "many humanists have decided that the literature department can right itself only if it desists from theoretical chatter and puts literature itself back at the center of its concerns... let literature speak for itself so that we do not need a theory of how to organize it institutionally" (254). This summary anticipates just the kinds of arguments we've seen Delbanco, Harpham, Chace, and Ellis make, and it underscores how the overly simple, even ideological distinction between "theory" and "literature itself" is not only a cyclical but also a structural one in debates about literary studies. Behind the idea that literature can speak for itself, of course, is the idea that "literature *teaches* itself" (Graff, 9–10, italics in original). The main feature of such arguments, and it is a feature I have been highlighting in current debates about literary study, is the distinction between literature itself "and commentary about literature" (10). This distinction is central, we have seen, to Harpham's discussion of what is wrong with literary studies. The problem here, however, is the utter banality of the very idea of "literature itself."[9] Is there such a thing as literature itself? Of course there is, but the only thing it could possibly reference is the object of the book itself. Once a particular reader picks up a book and begins to read it the text ceases being *itself* in the narrow sense of being print on a page and becomes something performed by the reader. These individual performances, of course, are shaped by the reader's experience, disposition, beliefs, and capabilities as a reader (what critical theorists call literary competence). They make it impossible to have an unmediated experience of the text itself. There is no readerly encounter with a text that can in any sense be said to be an encounter with the text itself.

The idea that we should seek to be in contact with "literature itself," of course, is used to defend the assertion that theories and critical approaches get in the way of some kind of primary, precritical contact with literature. But one cannot possibly study literature in any responsible way without thinking theoretically about the very object we call "literature" and about "literariness."[10] Literature is not a natural object, but a historically invented and ever changing one. It refers to a category that has always been theorized. Such questions are nearly perennial: What kind of writing is literary? What texts should we teach when we teach it? How is literature related to, and different from, other kinds of writing? What are its elements, purposes, and effects? What is literary experience? These are all theoretical questions, and you cannot have literature without answering them, which is to say, you can't have literature without theorizing about literature.[11] Moreover, you cannot have literature without politicizing the topic, since it is nearly always people in power who decide what literature is, which literary texts with which messages are important, and which ones ought to be taught (or kept out of) the classroom. There is nothing apolitical, for example, about insisting literature professors only teach great works, canonical texts, or the best that has been thought and said, eschewing political issues in sticking to aesthetic analysis and appreciation. Why? Because this involves choices about the perpetuation of certain authors and their ideas over others, the valuing of certain aesthetic forms and subject matters over others, and the valuing of certain social and political methods over others. That is fine, even inevitable. But it is wrong for traditionalists to claim that when they make these choices they are not political, but that when others make them, they are. Even the question of how one teaches literature verges into the realm of power and so is political as well. Certainly when a professor declares that he or she is going to lead the class through a sustained inquiry into how issues related to class, gender, or race are treated in a set of assigned literary texts that professor can be thought of as being political. However, when another professor declares that a class reading the same texts will not be looking at political issues but instead will stick to "literature itself," to studying a text's formal, linguistic, or aesthetic qualities as literary texts, that decision is also political to the extent it rules out of bounds the discussion of social, cultural, and political issues. The explicit inclusion and the explicit exclusion of politics in the classroom are equally political. This means that the very insistence one is going to focus on "literature itself" is a political one.

One way to think about the differences I have been discussing is in relationship to contextualization. The approach advocating attention to literature itself, and which complains that theories and methodologies—the whole professional apparatus of criticism—get in the way of that attention, is based on the idea that too often contextualizing literature displaces literature itself. This is an argument Marjorie Garber cogently makes, for example, in the introductory chapter to her 2004 book, *A Manifesto for Literary Studies*. Titled "Asking Literary Questions," the chapter argues literary studies have suffered from too much contextualization and that by asking literary questions about literature we can avoid putting context ahead of literature itself and get back to the proper activity of literary study—which is studying literature. How did context displace literature, according to Garber? Not surprisingly, by putting theoretical and methodological approaches to literature ahead of literature itself. She presents a cogent overview of how structuralist, post-structuralist, and historicist approaches to literary study came not only to dominate literary studies in the last decades of the twentieth century, but also how those approaches came to be extraordinarily influential in other disciplines of the humanities, particularly history.[12] She joins critics such as Harpham in complaining that theory, politics, and historical contextualization had the effect of marginalizing literature, that teachers and scholars in the field had, in effect, stopped asking literary questions. Under the aegis of theory, sociology, and historicizing, she concludes, "literary study was in the process of disowning itself.... Genteelly, professionally, persuasively, and without an apparent consciousness of what might be lost in the process, departments of literature and literary study have shifted their emphasis" (11). In her view, the turn to history, in particular, shifted attention "from text to context, from author or artist to historical-cultural surround" (11). In particular, the New Historicism represented a return to the empirical after the "heady attractions" of theory (8), an emphasis on historical and institutional contextualization that had the effect, however, of further marginalizing or demoting attention to the aesthetic qualities of literary texts as the "mere products" of culture and broadly related to the production of "social meaning" (9). The "literary" thus lost its privileged status and became "one realm among many" in an increasingly cultural and historical approach to its study. The aesthetic gave way to an interest in the materiality of culture and literature's involvement in the social construction of identities and ideologies (9). Literary critics, she laments, had become "scholars of material culture" (10).

Sympathetic as she is to all of these developments, Garber still regrets that their collective effect was the marginalization of literature itself. "Some literary historians and historicist critics within departments of literary study," she writes, "are in danger of forgetting, or devaluing, the history of their own craft and practice, which is based not only on the contextual understanding of literary works but also on the words on the page" (12). Literary studies, she insists, will make a "contribution...to intellectual life" only if it returns to a focus on "literariness," a focus on "style, form, genre, and verbal interplay...elements like grammar, rhetoric, and syntax; tropes and figures; assonance and echo" (12). The position she takes here gets elaborated in a 2010 essay on the importance of close reading, "Shakespeare in Slow Motion," where asking literary questions gets positioned quite specifically as a response to theoretical and historical contextualization. "My objective," she writes, "is to slow down the move to context, if not reverse it altogether, by redirecting attention to the language of the plays [of Shakespeare], scene by scene, act by act, moment by moment, word by word" (151). Here the notion of "slow motion reading," borrowed from a 1959 essay by the literary critic, Rueben Brower, reads like the prescription for a return to the methods of the American New Criticism, which famously bracketed off all extrinsic contexts in order to pay attention to the intrinsic qualities of the text itself. Here is Garber's injunction: "Let us not speculate on [Shakespeare's] personal or professional motives his inner thoughts, his relationships with his wife or children, his cultural aspirations, his finances, his religion, or his attitude toward the reigning monarch...but rather the text of the play and what it tells us" (151). Garber underscores the pre-professional nature of the reading practice she is endorsing here by calling it "mere reading" (152). Garber wants to ask "what does it mean to close read Shakespeare in the twenty-first century, after the most recent period of attention to historical, cultural, and religious context?" (152). The aim, here, is to focus on "the way meaning is conveyed rather than on the meaning itself" (the words here are quoted from an essay about Brower by Paul de Man) (152).

Garber here is calling attention to a reading practice that is absolutely essential to the study of literature, and we will have occasion to return to an in-depth discussion of reading practices in a later chapter. And she is certainly right that this kind of careful, word-by-word reading of a literary text is basic and foundational. The problem is that it's based on the idea there is such a thing as "mere reading," and that mere reading is presented as an antidote to the forms of theoretical and historical contextualization she discusses in "Asking Literary Questions." Here "slow motion reading" is presented as a way of asking literary questions that will help reverse the tendency to ask non-literary questions. This of course begs the question of what a "literary question" is (more about that in a minute), but here I want to focus on the issue of contextualization I highlighted a moment ago. Garber's position turns on the rather dubious distinction between "mere reading" and contextualized reading. Mere reading can constructively slow down the move to contexts, of course, but in her view it ought to reverse it altogether. However, this glosses over the simple fact that slow-motion reading—indeed, any mode of reading, whether one is self-conscious about its operations or not—is a contextualized reading. As I argued earlier in my discussion of Harpham's position regarding literary experience, reading is a practice that we learn, and learn to do in different but highly sophisticated ways. There is no such thing as mere reading, that is, if we define "mere" as over-against trained or learned reading (the word "mere" has its roots in the middle English sense of pure and the Latin word "merus," which means undiluted). Mere has the virtue of sounding modest and unpretentious; it seems calibrated to avoid the professional forms of theoretical and historical contextualization she believes need reversing.

The problem with context is that it is everywhere. As Jonathan Culler has pointed out, "meaning is context bound, but context is boundless" (*Literary Theory*, 67). Indeed, I would argue that there are in fact no meanings produced with regard to literary texts that are not mediated by context of some kind, even the kind of word-for-word slow-motion reading Garber endorses. Indeed, so-called slow-motion reading is just as liable to distort a text as to illuminate it. For example, I once encountered a film called "24 Hour Psycho," made in 1993 by Douglas Gordon, consisting of Hitchcock's film slowed down to run over a 24-hour period, and it was quite clear to me that viewing the film this way was a context that dramatically affected is meaning. If we are worried, along with Garber, that the kinds of theoretical and historical contextualizations she reviews in the opening chapter of her *Manifesto* are problematic, we would do well to recall Gerald Graff's insistence that "the remedy for a poor contextualizing of literature is not no contextualizing but better contextualizing" (11). Too often calls for a return to the nebulous or even dubious categories of "literature itself," "literary experience," and "mere reading" can seem less like no contextualization than bad contextualization, bad because they refuse to recognize that they *are* contextualizations. Contextualization, of course, gets conflated here with professionalization, as if contexts that are grounded in theory, methodologies, and professional practices are somehow worse than contexts that do not even recognize themselves as such. The cure for bad professional practices is better professional practices, rather than no professional practices at all.

One of the recurrent complaints about the kinds of contextualizations Garber worries over—and they reflect concerns I have been discussing throughout this book—is that they widen the gulf not only between the academy and mainstream culture but between professionalized and ordinary experience. Rita Felski takes up this problem in a thoughtful 2008 essay, "Remembering the Reader." Like Garber, Harpham, and many other critics I've been discussing, Felski worries that what she calls "high theory" in literary studies has separated academic readers and their concerns from ordinary readers and their concerns (what we might call, after Garber, mere readers). After all, as Felski points out, theory is committed to revealing ordinary beliefs, interpretations, and assumptions about texts as in some sense naïve or deluded. This split between ordinary and theoretical readings is, she insists, central to the current "legitimation crisis" in literary studies, and in the humanities in general. The more complex the critical theories humanists use, the more difficult it is for them to explain to the general public what they do. "How," she asks, "do we come up with rationales for reading and talking about books without lapsing back into the canon worship of the past," on the one hand, or drawing on the kind of complex, highly theorized contextualizations Garber discusses? Such theories, she observes, tend to displace literature, which becomes secondary and recedes into the background.... Literature, in becoming an "object of knowledge," ceases to be a "source of knowledge."

Like Garber, Felski is tempted to take recourse to something like mere (or ordinary) reading to bridge this divide. However, she resists the impulse to turn this into an either/or problem and instead considers whether there might not be a middle way between, on the one hand, naïve or ordinary reading, and, on the other, forms of professionalized reading that make the meaning of texts seem undecidable or produce "ideological readings that reduce literature to its political functions." Attracted to the idea that reading ought to involve something like the kind of close or slow-motion reading Garber endorses, reading that focuses on the words on the page and brackets extrinsic contexts, Felski rightly balks, worried that by "separating literature from everything around it, critics are unable to explain how it moves in and through the world. Highlighting literature's uniqueness, they overlook its equally salient qualities of commonality and connectedness." Interestingly, Felski insists that in order to work out this middle vantage point "demands that we reassess our ways of talking about 'use.'" In doing so she exhibits just the kind of nervousness about labeling literature useful we have observed in all of the commentators who have engaged this question: "Clearly, literature is not useful in the same way as a toolbox or a train schedule. Indeed, the word 'useful' radiates a host of unhappy undertones, conjuring up images of drab practicality, of shapeless overalls and sensible shoes. We tend to equate the useful with what is practical, rational, and charmless, opposing utility to the lure of pleasure or surprise." Felski proposes we get around this problem by thinking of literature as "usable" rather than "useful." "Usable," she argues, is "a word that better captures its chameleonlike ability to speak to diverse interests and desires, to morph into different roles and functions." Since, she insists, "use is not always strategic or calculating, manipulative or grasping," it does not "have to underwrite instrumental thinking or imply indifference to beauty or complex form."

Literature, it turns out, can be useful in Felski's view by helping us to see how structures of language and thought in literary texts actually produce things such as pleasure, something I explored a little earlier in this chapter. Linked loosely to methods drawn from phenomenology, the approach to reading she sketches out is characterized by an "intense curiosity about structures of thought, perception, and emotion that are often so close to us as to be invisible. Its aim is to describe rather than prescribe, to be patient rather than impatient, to look rather than overlook, allowing us to see for the first time what we thought we already knew." Such an approach to literary analysis, she insists, "invites us to explore the relations between form and feeling and to delve into the mysteries of our many-sided attachments to texts," but with the important recognition that our "aesthetic experience is shaped by salient and often sobering differences of education, class, and culture." Unlike Harpham, Felski does not invoke the vague category of "literary experience" as an antidote to cultural and historical contextualization, valorizing ordinariness over-against professional forms of reading. Rather, she wants to link theorized approaches to reading that recognize the inevitable priority of context to forms of literary analysis that focus on the ordinary affective emotions we experience when we read, and she does so while underscoring the important difference that class, race, education, and culture make in how we read, and even in what we think we are reading.[13]

The debates about theory, reading, enjoyment, and political correctness I have been exploring are all related both to the question of how literary studies—and other disciplines within the humanities—are organized, and how teachers articulate its value. Indeed, the two are inextricably related, since what we most value is what we want to preserve and pass on. We have seen that the value of literary studies can be articulated in various and often contradictory ways. From one point of view the value of literary studies is grounded in knowing a literary heritage, in being exposed to the best that has been thought and said. From this point of view aesthetic and moral quality are paramount. These qualities are defined and circumscribed by a classical canonical tradition that it is the responsibility of literature professors to curate. This approach to the value of literary study is primarily grounded in history, moral edification, and a desire for cultural literacy. Students should know the great texts of Western civilization because these texts constitute their history and will edify their minds and their souls. This way of valuing literature is grounded in the idea that if we have an unmediated experience with "literature itself" we will experience its aesthetic quality *and* become morally edified by it. However, while this point of view has a historical orientation it often eschews historical contextualization and scholarship because they supposedly get in the way of what Harpham calls "literary experience," which is connected in turn to the idea Graff alludes to that literature teaches itself. The other way to value literary studies is the one endorsed variously by critics such as Perloff, Eagleton, and Nussbaum, who insist that the study of literature fosters a set of concrete skills central to what Nussbaum calls global democratic citizenship. Perloff and Eagleton, we have seen, go so far as to argue it does not matter what literature students read so long as they engage with texts in a way that expands their rhetorical and critical capabilities. On the one hand, is the traditional notion of literature as an idealized aesthetic and moral universe, on the other, the pragmatic idea that reading, thinking, and writing about literature sharpens practical skills generally applicable across the disciplines and in the public sphere as well. This narrow debate about the orientation of literary studies—perpetual as it is—reflects the more general debate I have been tracking about how to value the humanities in general, as a collective cultural heritage whose value is that it has no practical value, or as a set of disciplines that teach students particular forms of expertise they do not get in the natural and social sciences.

I have been arguing, of course, that in current debates about the value of the humanities the criticism of professionalization and the scapegoating of contemporary theory are both misplaced and counterproductive, and they are rooted in an either/or mentality the humanities ought to reject. There is no reason why the two philosophies of a humanities education I just sketched out ought to be seen as incompatible. Not only are courses in contemporary literary and critical theory *not* to blame for what's wrong with the humanities, they are some of the best courses we have for teaching critical thinking, but that thinking can be foregrounded in any literature course. The last thing humanists and their supporters ought to be doing, however, is blaming the so-called "humanities crisis" on the professional protocols of work in their disciplines, since these protocols in fact provide students just the kind of discipline they need as readers, analysts, thinkers, and writers.

In the final analysis, how we organize literary study depends upon the way we value it. If we value literature primarily in terms of its aesthetic and formal properties, the experience it facilitates when we get swept away in it, and the moral edification we might believe it produces, we will organize literary study around literature itself and some notion such as Harpham's of literary experience and the pleasure of reading. The problem, I fear, is that neither will be theorized because that just gets in the way of both the literature and the experience. And we will not politicize the literature we study or the way we analyze it because that would void the requirement developed by Kant, popularized by Arnold, and fostered by the New Criticism that we approach reading in a disinterested way, suspending our subjective or political biases. If, on the other hand, we value literature not only for its aesthetic and moral dimensions, but also for the analytical, critical, rhetorical, and research skills its study facilitates, we will organize literary study in a very different way, creating requirements and courses that insure students develop those skills. And if we value the diversity of literary production over time and want to foreground for students how canons are constructed in a context in which people in authority are exercising power, then we will value a diverse range of texts in the courses colleges and universities offer, texts that engage the experience of diverse people with diverse cultures and beliefs.

The challenge of organizing literary studies has become particularly difficult because we live in a time when the category of the "literary" has become a contested term connected to larger debates about the democratic nature of culture and about social justice. Literature originally entered the curriculum of US colleges and universities more or less as a body of works identified with a particular class and its socialization, and, as Graff points out, it was less difficult then than it is now to organize its study. "To 'organize literature' is difficult under any circumstances," he observes, "but particularly when it means reconstituting as a curriculum under more or less democratic conditions something that had previously been part of the socialization of a particular class" (2). Humanist educators following Arnold largely organized the study of literature around a set of canonical texts that were class and gender bound, and tied to the socialization of young men being groomed to enter the professional classes. Literature socialized students and solidified the values of the dominant class. To the extent it shaped the intellectual lives of students those students were nearly wholly male and white. The reorganization of literary studies that began in earnest in the 1970s took place under significantly more "democratic conditions" in the sense that the demographics of the university, and then, of the professoriate, began to change dramatically with the civil rights movement, the women's movement, and The Immigration and Nationalization Act of 1965, all of which had the result of radically transforming the demographics of higher education, first in terms of students and then the professoriate itself. What Perloff refers to as the canon wars were a result of the reorganization of the curriculum in literary studies under the "democratic conditions" Graff alludes to. Female, African, Asian, and Hispanic American professors and their students began to insist on a more representative body of texts and authors, one that embodied the broader literary history of the United States and Britain, changes that accelerated with the rise of postcolonial studies. The older, narrower, class- and gender-bound literatures taught under the rubric of "English" gave way to a much more heterogeneous set of texts, reflecting a diversity of social and cultural experience so striking that traditionalists pushed back, often in anger and frustration. These welcome changes underscore the value of professionalization in the sense that they were the direct result of dramatic theoretical and methodological changes related to the ways in which humanists approached knowledge and its production.

The question of disciplinary coherence might be a lot easier if there were such a thing as literature itself, and if literary studies could operate without professional protocols to direct the work students and faculty do. But as we have seen, there is no such thing as "literature itself," and as an academic discipline literary studies cannot be either non- or anti-professional. "Literature itself" suggests a self-evident category, one that isn't shaped by history, social ideals, cultural values, and politics. But these are precisely the forces that do shape our notion of what literature is. And while it might seem disciplinary coherence would be easier if we could focus our attention on the experience of literature itself without the seemingly elaborate contextualizations theory and critical methodologies provide, that would simply mean the discipline would have no coherence at all. It wouldn't be a discipline, wouldn't be *professional*. There is no form of reading or analysis or study that is not theoretically driven and shaped by a methodology. This means, of course, that the divide between literature as a romanticized, aestheticized ideal, a set of texts that float above history, culture, and methodologies of reading is an illusory one, as is the dream of literary studies as a de-professionalized discipline. In the final analysis, one can't make anything like a coherent distinction between literature itself, on the one hand, and the analytical capabilities and practices students who study literature learn, on the other, since the two are codependent and co-productive. It is a simple fact that literary study depends upon practices and skills; indeed, the very concept of "literature" we operate with is the product of those practices and skills. From this perspective, it makes little sense to shrink away from articulating the value of literary studies in terms of the practical competencies it provides students, and pointing out the link between them and the professional work of the faculty who teach both the works their students read and the skills they learn. For this reason it makes little sense to vilify theory or criticism, since the analytical expertise literary studies helps students learn are grounded in their practices.

CHAPTER 3

HUMANISM, THE HUMANITIES, AND POLITICAL CORRECTNESS

> *What happens when the guardians of culture reject the authority of the philosophical, historical, and literary traditions that defined a cultural consensus and made its transmission possible? How can we teach when there is no more "we," meaning a group of people who, whatever their differences, agree to respect a certain inherited body of knowledge and the traditional valuations accorded it? How, indeed, can the humanities exist at all without respect for tradition, since the humanities have always been—at least since the great Renaissance humanists—essentially about preserving and transmitting tradition?*
>
> —Peter Brooks, "The Humanities as a Cultural Combat Zone," 1992[1]

I have been arguing that one of the ironies about current debates regarding the practical utility of a humanities education is that the very courses that most effectively teach students the critical-thinking skills they need—courses that stress theory and methodology—are routinely disparaged by those who claim the humanities have become marginalized and irrelevant. In fact, as we have seen, theory courses can play a central role helping to train students in just the kind of critical-thinking they will need no matter what career they choose. In this chapter I want to expand my discussion of the impact critical theory has had on the humanities by exploring how it has productively transformed the way we think about humanism. While many traditional humanists complain bitterly about the critique of humanism mounted by contemporary critical theory, dismissing it as "political correctness," and while many theorists themselves present that critique as anti- or post-humanist, I want to argue that theory's critique of humanism ought to be seen as part of the long history of humanist thought and therefore as part of the ongoing attempt to expand the inclusivity both of its characterization of the human and the rights it advocates. In doing so I do not want to downplay the significance of theory's critique of traditional humanist thought. On the contrary, I want to underscore how dramatic it has been, and to insist that we cannot articulate the current value of the humanities without foregrounding that critique. We ought not to be defending an old, outdated humanities in debates about their future. Instead, humanists and their supporters need to articulate the value of a *contemporary* humanities, one based on a more expansive, inclusive, and historically and theoretically more sophisticated understanding of the human. It is one thing to defend the humanities; it is another thing to defend a historically and theoretically transformed humanities based on what Jeff Noonan and others have called a critical humanism.[2]

Contemporary structuralist and post-structuralist theories about art, culture, and power have transformed the way humanists think about nearly everything associated with humanism, especially the way in which we think about human agency, the formation of subjectivity, and individual rights. Moreover, our increasing recognition that what counts as history, philosophy, literature, or art has itself been socially and historically shaped through a complex set of discourses and ideologies has challenged our understanding of how such disciplines came about in the first place. We no longer think of either the history or the ideals of humanism as fixed and given, grounded in something universal or transhistorical, but rather as socially and historically constructed and continually refined in the interested exercise of social and political power. For all of these reasons, we cannot talk about the contemporary role of the humanities in higher education without considering how recent theory has productively altered our understanding of human nature and the rights and responsibilities it entails. Defending the humanities today requires that we explain our contemporary understanding of what it means to be human.

What happened to alter this understanding? We can return to Brooks for a concise answer. First of all, recent theoretical work in the humanities insisted that tradition is not "something fixed and rigid" but is in fact shaped by "individual interpretations" that are "themselves the product of interpretations." For this reason, scholars who were "largely responsible for new thinking in the humanities over the past two or three decades have made us acutely aware that traditions are really constructions that we both continue and modify." To say this, he continues, "is, of course, to undermine any unproblematic notion of 'intellectual authority': We are forced to ask where traditions came from, who formed them, what interests they have served, and, not least, whether they are the right traditions for future scholarship." Brooks was keen to call attention not only to "the problems encountered when a cultural tradition created by and for a social elite comes under increasing pressure to make good on the democratic and egalitarian claims of American society," but also to stress the paradoxical situation this creates for the humanities, for all of "this leaves humanists in a peculiar situation. They cannot simply blaze a trail backward to some lost world of fundamentalist intellectual authority located in a great tradition or a fixed canon, nor can they simply slough off tradition. Rather, they have no choice but to accept the discomfort of working from traditions that no longer appear adequate to the work to be done."[3]

Brooks presents here a strikingly concise characterization of the predicament the humanities were in by the early 1990s. Unlike the recurrent concerns we saw Donoghue catalog, which over the whole course of the twentieth century revolved around complaints about the uselessness of the humanities, this one comes not from outside academia but from within academia. And it doesn't turn on the question of whether or not studying the humanities is a waste of time. Rather, it focuses on the challenges new theories about art, literature, power, and human agency present to business as usual in the humanities. Brooks calls attention to how theory in general has produced what Martha Nussbaum has called a "culture of dissent" within the humanities. This culture of dissent is still prominent, of course, and how it is managed will help determine their future. To be sure, the future of the humanities is tied to the fate of the economy and to the choices administrators and boards of trustees make in prioritizing the competing demands of departments and programs, but where the humanities come out in this process will depend to a large degree on how humanists themselves characterize the nature and value of the work they do (the particular challenge this holds for literary studies will be the focus of my final two chapters). Whether humanists take a stand for the value of their various areas of study by reaffirming their traditional interests and practices, or whether they can find a way to articulate a twenty-first-century version of the humanities expanded and revised to include the new work Brooks alludes to, will be crucial in determining their future.

In my view, the humanities have no choice but to make the second case. They must rise to the challenge of teaching a tradition they also constructively critique, balancing a responsibility to explore with students the historical, social, cultural, and political construction of humanism with a form of critical inquiry that forces it to make good on both its claims and its advocacy of rights in an increasingly broader and global way. From this point of view the culture of dissent Brooks catalogues ought to be seen as a positive, not a negative force, an expansion of humanism's ideals, not an attempt to move beyond them to some post- or even antihumanism. This culture of dissent should strengthen, not weaken humanism, allowing it to, as Brooks puts it, "make good on the democratic and egalitarian claims of American society."

While we cannot talk about the shape of the humanities in the twenty-first century without recognizing the extent to which contemporary theory developed a complex critique of humanism, we also need to recognize that when theory exercises dissent it is exercising a kind of power at the very center of humanism itself.[4] New ways of thinking about the human subject, the role that language plays in constructing reality and shaping meaning and value, and how gender, sexual orientation, race, ethnicity, and class both shape identity and enable or limit agency, all contributed during the period I have been discussing to calls for a post- or antihumanism, to be sure, but also to calls for a constructive expansion and rethinking of traditional humanist ideas about individuality, autonomy, liberty, and rights.[5] While the concept of *antihumanism* helpfully emphasizes how theory during this period fostered the kind of dramatic break in traditional humanist discourses about individuality, autonomy, values, and rights Brooks references, I believe it is more constructive to see this work as an attempt to think critically about humanism in a way that has helped extend, broaden, and diversify its claims, to make the discourse of humanism more, not less legitimate.

Theory during this period, then, was not engaged in political correctness so much as in political *correction*. Although in its most radical moments theory seemed to be announcing the end of man or the beginning of a posthumanist age, it actually represented constructive, forward-looking dissent from the historical and ideological limits of humanism, dissent that sought to expand, correct, and broaden humanist ideals.[6] There is, after all, nothing wrong with political correction if it is aimed at expanding the social contract humanism offered to everyone in principle, but limited to too few in practice. And of course if it was anything, humanism was political in the sense that it was centrally about the right of individual humans to exercise power and agency in their own interests and through representative forms of government. The idea that the humanities ought to simply deal with a set of abstract, universal ideals that transcend history and politics is misguided, for humanism was itself a historical intervention; it was all about overcoming inequality, achieving agency, and the legitimate exercise of social power. To seek the expansion of equality, rights, agency, and social power, associated with humanism, to make them truly inclusive ("universal" was the word humanists most often used to get at this idea), is to engage in constructive forms of political dissent in ways thoroughly consistent with humanism. What conservative critics called political correctness was actually an extended (if sometimes messy and controversial) exercise in just the kind of cultural dissent Nussbaum has in mind. For this reason it really never made any sense to complain that the humanities had suddenly become politicized, for both humanism and the humanities have *always* been political.

Indeed, one of the ways in which contemporary theory sought to usefully complicate our understanding of humanism and the humanities was to underscore the extent to which they were both about power. As far back as 1987, Terry Eagleton observed that the humanities in the age of theory had "lost their innocence," that "they could no longer pretend to be untainted by power. If they wanted to stay in business," he insisted, "it was now vital that they paused to reflect on their own purposes and assumptions. It is this critical self-reflection that we call theory. Theory of this kind comes about when we are forced into a new self-consciousness about what we are doing" (*After Theory*, 27). For Eagleton, theory is disciplinary self-reflection, not in the interests of undoing disciplines but in becoming more self-conscious about what disciplines *are* doing. Thinking theoretically about the humanities in the kind of way Eagleton has in mind begins by recognizing that the humanities (and the concept of humanism that authorizes them) are not a *thing* so much as a *discourse*. Theory questions both the historical narrative and the metaphysical essentialism informing approaches to humanism that often underwrite the traditional project of the humanities in the first place. This was the point Brooks was attempting to make in reminding us that traditions are constructed, that they have institutional histories within which traditional ideals are conceived, modified, naturalized, and disseminated. The problem with thinking of the humanities as a *thing* is that it makes them seem fixed and timeless, comprising universal truths about human nature, truth, being, meaning, and reality.

To think of the humanities as a discourse, on the other hand, is to think of them as reflecting a socially and historically constructed way of talking about human nature, truth, being, meaning, and reality, one that changes and can be refined—even improved—over time. If we approach humanism as a thing, truth is understood as transcendental and thus universal. If we approach humanism as a discourse, however, truth is seen as historical and contingent. Such a distinction is fundamental to the linguistic turn that, beginning with structuralism, ushered in the critical approach to humanism associated with postmodern critical theory. The point is not that there is no such thing as human nature, being, truth, or reality, but that we only have access to these things conceptually through language. Each is a historically and linguistically contingent way of representing a concept. Humanism is a way of talking about human nature, being, truth, and reality, one that is contingent upon a whole set of power relations that are obscured if we think of them as simply given and universal. Key concepts such as "man," "rights," and "self-evident truth," for example, once understood as discursive in nature, are arguments in defense of a certain kind of status quo related to institutional and ideological forms of power (and to the extent they represent a break from business as usual they represent just the kind of dissent Nussbaum invokes). Of course, it is precisely this talk of power, institutions, and ideologies that put off conservative critics, who want to insist that these concepts somehow float above power, institutions, and ideologies. That, after all, is precisely what makes them seem universal and transcendent. But they don't.

Contemporary critical theory since the late 1960s has contested key elements of both the philosophical premises of humanism and the historical narrative of its emergence. These two projects are of course intimately connected. The collective effect of the successive "turns" associated with critical theory (the linguistic turn associated with structuralism, semiotics, and deconstruction, the cultural turn reflected by the emergence of cultural studies, the materialist turn connected to post-structuralist Marxism, and the historical turn associated with the work of Michel Foucault and the New Historicism) involved the simultaneous rethinking of concepts, ideals, and assertions about "Man," human nature, truth, and meaning associated with humanism in the West, and the emergence of a new historical genealogy of its development. I use the term "genealogy" quite purposely here to evoke the kind of theoretical/historical projects Foucault outlines in "Nietzsche, Genealogy, History."[7] Contemporary critical theory has produced, collectively, a genealogy of humanism that counters both the traditional historical narrative of humanism's origins and explores the philosophical and ethical logic of its central ideals. Humanism, from this point of view, is seen as both metahistorical and metaphysical, metahistorical because the traditional story of its origins has a kind of mythic element, and metaphysical because, philosophically, humanism's conception of "Man," human nature, being, and truth are presented as a set of transcendental ideals attributed in essentialist ways to all humans and to the very nature of "humanness" itself.

Foucault's distinction, following Nietzsche, between history and genealogy (or, between traditional and "effective" history) is fundamental if we want to grasp how contemporary critical theory rethinks humanism and the humanities in both historical and philosophical ways. To think of humanism in genealogical terms is to study its development as a discourse. This involves a form of historical thinking that rejects "the metahistorical deployment of ideal significations, and indefinite teleologies. It opposes itself to the search for 'origins'" (77). Why? "First," because the traditional search for origins is "an attempt to capture the exact essence of things, their purest possibilities, and their carefully protected identities; because this search assumes the existence of immobile forms that precede the external world of accident and succession" (78). The genealogist, rejecting the search for universal essences, "refuses" to rely on a "faith in metaphysics" in his or her development of a historical understanding of particular discourses (78). A genealogy of knowledge, madness, or sexuality, to recall some of Foucault's own projects—or of humanism—does not look for "a timeless and essential secret" that stands "behind things," but rather, "the secret that they have no essence or that their essence was fabricated in a piecemeal fashion" (78). Furthermore, this form of historical inquiry "fragments what was thought unified; it shows the heterogeneity of what was imagined consistent with itself" (82). In Foucault's schema (following Nietzsche) a traditional history, concerned with origins, is metaphysical in its orientation because it looks for the persistence of transhistorical, timeless, universal principles. In this sense, paradoxically, traditional histories can be ahistorical. A genealogical study, on the other hand, aims to be materialist, paying attention to multiple beginnings that exfoliate in rhizomorphic kinds of ways. "In placing present needs at the origin," Foucault explains, "the metaphysician would convince us of an obscure purpose that seeks its realization at the moment it arises. Genealogy, however, seeks to reestablish the various systems of subjection: not the anticipatory power of meaning, but the hazardous play of dominations" (83).

Post-structuralist theory since the late 1960s has, in effect, supplemented the history of humanism with a genealogy of humanism, one that helped foster the critically productive rethinking of both humanism and the humanities we saw Brooks allude to earlier. For a textbook example of such a genealogy we can turn, for a moment, to Tony Davies's *Humanism* (1997).[8] Davies explores the historical invention of humanism and the concept of humanity it advocates in a way that is consistent with Eagleton's observation that theory functions as disciplinary self-reflection and in so doing helps uncover the relationship between abstract ideals and the exercise of ideological and institutional power. Humanism, Davies points out, did not have its origins in Greek or Roman culture, or in the Renaissance. It was, rather, a nineteenth-century invention, one that did not emerge fully formed as a theory of "Man" in classical culture but as a curriculum in nineteenth-century German high schools and universities. The English word "humanism" is derived from the German, humanismus, a term that was initially used by nineteenth-century German scholars to simply refer to the Renaissance emphasis on the importance of a classical education.[9] He reminds us that there was no humanism as such in Greek or Roman culture, and humanism in the Renaissance, to the extent we can even talk about such a thing, consisted not of a general theory of "Man" or human nature, but a narrow insistence on the importance of an education in the classics.

From this perspective, then, humanism is a historical invention retroactively projected back in the nineteenth century onto Greek and Roman Culture, and the Renaissance. And its aims, Davies stresses, are nothing if not political. It develops first in Germany (most famously in the work of Jacob Burckhardt), and then takes root in England under the auspices of the educator, Thomas Arnold, his son Matthew, and the poet and literary critic John Addington Symonds. Burckhardt was less interested than some of his contemporaries (such as Winckelmann and Humboldt) in humanism's relationship to Greek culture than he was in how Italian Renaissance writers dealt with "the political and military necessities of independent Italian cities" and how those writings could be brought to bear in thinking about the contemporary emergence of Germany as a unified national state.[10] Burckhardt's interest in ideas about the state developed by Renaissance writers draws our attention to the relationship between humanism and nationalism, a relationship connected to his other passion, secular individualism, which Davies points out, is tied to Burckhardt's interest in the emergence of that new population, the "middle-class citizen" (Davies, 15)—a population that will later capture the attention of Matthew Arnold. The idea of the individual, we need to remember, is an invention of modernity, not of the Renaissance, and certainly not of Greece or Rome. It is not until Burckhardt's time that we get "the development of a universal capacity to think of yourself, in a fundamental way, as an individual...as a free-standing self-determining person with an identity and a name that is not simply a marker of family, birthplace or occupation but is 'proper'—belonging to you alone" (16).[11] Although we can observe what Davies calls "heroic individuality" evoked in Machiavelli's *Prince* or Vasari's *Lives of the Painters*, Burckhardt's more generalized notion of secular individual autonomy is a completely modern invention, and it will come to have tremendous influence on educational theory in both Germany and Britain.[12]

Of course given the disparate, competing versions of humanism that developed over the course of the nineteenth century it makes more sense to think about humanism in multiple terms, for it took a variety of forms. Where, for example, Gobineau's humanism denotes a heroic individuality asserting the racial superiority of the Teuton, for Marx humanism "underwrites the necessity of revolution and the dream of a humanity emancipated from inequality and exploitation" (Davies, 19). Meanwhile T. H. Huxley champions an atheistic, Darwinian notion of humanism (along with Charles Bradlaugh, who founded the National Secular Society). Arnold, of course, sees the culture of humanism (and literature in particular) as a new form of religion, and he intercedes to invoke "an eirenic humanistic 'culture' to arbitrate and unify the divisive anarchy of politics and class" (19). Crucial to the modern development of literary studies in the humanities, these disparate humanisms come to a head in Arnold's attempt in England to pull together various approaches to the classics, and the Renaissance fascination with Greek and Roman literature, into a single, unified humanist notion of a "truly human point of view," one that "stands for something essential, above and beyond the accidents of historical or national difference...visible in Homer and Sophocles no less than in Shakespeare or Goethe twenty or more centuries later" (Davies, 19). For those of us thinking about the humanities in its British and American context, of course, Arnold's intervention is crucial, for it represents the cultural tradition we saw Brooks refer to, the one humanists have had the responsibility to perpetuate. For Davies, Arnold's discovery of the "central, truly human point of view" in Chaucer's *Canterbury Tales* ("The Study of Poetry," 1888) is striking because it underscores the invention of humanism out of a British literary tradition. For Arnold, Chaucer's is the voice of secular humanism, cut loose from the church and from the authority of an aristocracy or professional elite, and embedded, instead, in the "voice of secular individuality...people with recognizable names and real occupations" living in places "you can actually find on a map" (21). Experience here is thought of both as human in its unique individuality, and as it invokes an "all-embracing humanity, a 'human condition,' to which the great poets of the European tradition, Homer and Dante and Chaucer and Shakespeare and Milton and Goethe can give us the key" (21–22).

This is an absolutely pivotal—yet paradoxical—moment in the history of literary humanism in the West, pivotal because it links the invention of humanism to a canonical tradition of literary texts and authors, and paradoxical because it is grounded in a double gesture, one that puts the stress on everyday human experience in its ordinariness, triviality, and uniqueness while at the same time postulating a single, essential, universal, transhistorical condition said to be "truly" human. One emphasis gestures toward material experience and the real, the other toward a metaphysical condition that, in effect, reinvests a monolithic, universalized humanity with the very form of transcendence that was supposed to mark off a secular conception of humanity from a religious one in the first place. "Man" here is reinvested with the very form of transcendence humanism ought to have once and for all buried, especially in the insistently secular and materialist forms it was taking in thinkers such as Huxley and Marx. Arnold takes the notion of secular individualism from the German tradition of humanism,[13] deifies it, then reinserts it in a Western classical literary tradition that is supposed to fill the void of waning religious commitment. In one bold move we get the British invention of what we can call, for shorthand, metaphysical humanism, and "the humanities" as characterized by a curriculum that marries the study of Greek and Roman classical literature to a canon of early modern and Renaissance literary texts thought to embody a universal humanity, one that can authorize a certain notion of cultural and political citizenship in nineteenth-century England, roiled as it had become by economic and social change driven by an increasingly mobile working class. In a single gesture, the study of what we now think of as "the humanities" gets organized around a fixed set of canonical texts and a thoroughly idealized, transcendental notion of "Man," one that universalizes a culturally elite, scholarly, patriarchal, Western notion of human nature meant to stand for *all* human nature at all times and in all places, and which is calibrated quite explicitly to shape the cultural and social identity of the working class.[14]

Davies's genealogy of humanism is important both as a model of how theory has come to operate in the late 1990s with regard to the analysis of humanist ideals about individuality, agency, value, and culture, and because it underscores the historically invented nature of humanism and its relationship to power. It also—and this is crucial, it seems to me—emphasizes the roots of humanism in what Nussbaum calls a culture of dissent and what Graff identifies as theory. I want to stress that there is nothing sinister at all in thinking about humanism in this way. Indeed, it has the great value of demystifying humanism and underscoring some of its key paradoxes, for stressing how humanism emerged as a nineteenth-century intellectual and political discourse in the West emphasizes its roots both in the need to theorize and consolidate a certain notion of "Man" that authorizes a broad-based ideal of freedom, and its interest in consolidating and perpetuating particular forms of social and political power, the establishment of states defined along racial and ethnic lines, and the imperial project of "civilizing" large areas of the world that do not measure up to the notions of humanity and civilization that underwrite Western humanism. This way of thinking historically and theoretically about humanism is not part of a radical leftist plot to take over the university or overthrow democracy. It simply emphasizes the uneven, partial, and interested notion of "Man" and human rights that emerged in the nineteenth century and became solidified as "humanism." Analyses such as Davies's call our attention to two indispensable things about humanism and the humanities, then. The first is the socially and historically constructed, invented nature of "humanism" in all of its epochal guises—classical, Renaissance, Enlightenment, and modern—the central idea that what we think of as "Renaissance" or classical humanism was a nineteenth-century political invention projected back on these earlier periods.[15] The second key point is that nineteenth-century humanism invented what Davies calls a "myth of essential and universal man: essential, because humanity—humanness—is the inseparable and central essence, the defining quality, of human beings; universal because that essential humanity is shared by all human beings, of whatever time or place" (24). And the invention of this humanism was in turn central to the modern development of the humanities.

As I noted at the outset of this chapter, contemporary critical theorists questioned this limited view of the human not to do away with humanism but to make the case for expanding and diversifying humanism's conception of what it called "man." The use of "man" in humanist discourse was not simply a linguistic problem. "Man" in humanist discussions of rights often did mean white European men. Over the course of the last 40 years, this transcendent, universal "man" has become a contingent, historical, gendered subject, one who is the complex product, in different times and places, of very different languages, ideologies, and material forces. It is in this sense that recent theoretical work in the humanities, often broadly stigmatized by traditionalists as antihumanist, can be seen as developing a political correction to humanism from within the discourse of humanism itself. New work on the complex relationship between language, ideology, gender, race, ethnicity, sexual orientation, disability, and subjectivity has served to usefully complicate our notion of "man." It has also demonstrated how the conception of "man" informing humanist ideals of liberty has sometimes ended up circumscribing the social and political power of women and racial, ethnic, and sexual minorities. Exploring contradictions and gaps within humanist ideals, contemporary humanist theory laid the groundwork for applying those ideals in ways that expand what we mean by human nature and the forms of agency it guarantees.

This kind of critical engagement with humanism, of course, is not wholly a product of contemporary theory, for it has a long history running back at least to Marx, who was one of the first nineteenth-century humanists to call systematic attention to the need to expand the ideals of human liberty at the center of humanism to the working class. While many critics make a distinction between the early and late phases of Marx's career, often seeing the late phase as a break with his earlier humanism, it makes more sense to see the later period as a productive critique and extension of humanism, not an outright break with it.[16] During this period, Marx came to redefine universal "man" as a historical subject constructed by labor, class, and ideology, systems that tended to undercut abstract and idealist notions of human freedom and autonomy associated with humanist conceptions of the individual. In so doing he attempts not so much to reject humanism as to expand the promise contained in its conception of liberty. The idea that Marxism represented a break from humanism dates from the work of the French philosopher, Louis Althusser. In his 1964 essay, "Marxism and Humanism," Althusser insists on distinguishing between the young, pre-1844 Marx and the mature, scientific, materialist Marx of post-1844, one for whom all forms of humanist idealism were an anathema. Althusser stressed that Marx in this period tended to turn away from a notion of society based on abstract ideals of freedom and will, and began to pay systematic attention to how ideology, class, and modes of production shaped or restricted human agency. Althusser insists Marx's break with humanism is not a "secondary detail" but is in fact central to understanding his work:

> Marx broke radically with every theory that based history and politics on an essence of man.... This rupture with every philosophical anthropology or humanism is no secondary detail; it is Marx's scientific discovery.... The earlier idealist ("bourgeois") philosophy depended in all its domains and arguments (its "theory of knowledge", its aesthetics, etc.) on a problematic of human nature (or the essence of man).... By rejecting the essence of man as his theoretical basis, Marx rejected the whole of this organic system of postulates. ("Marxism and Humanism" first appeared in the Cahiers de l'I.S.E.A., June 1964)

In Althusser's view, Marx breaks with humanism because he rejects a metaphysical approach to human identity in favor of one that focuses on how social, economic, ideological, and class structures and systems construct our subjectivities. This shift from talking about identities to subjectivities was of course a crucial one. The human subject for Althusser is not defined by a set of abstract, psychological, or idealist notions of identity but concretely by social, economic, ideological, and material forces. Moreover, where humanism posits a fundamental sameness in human nature, Marxism (both classical and Althusserian) stresses the difference that material, class, and ideological forces make in constituting human subjectivity and enabling or restricting agency and autonomy.

One crucial thing about this approach to humanism is that it makes a distinction between essential or universal *being* and essential or universal *rights*. Marx may dissent from the kind of metaphysical idealism informing humanism's conceptualization of man's universal nature, but he is quite committed to the notion of universal rights, and to the extension of those rights to those who don't have them due to their class or economic status, or for reasons that are sheerly ideological. Of course this is how dialectical and historical materialism departs from essentialist humanisms, by focusing our attention on how material conditions determine the shape of both individual autonomy and social and political relations, and how they create uneven relations of power. It represents a critique of the metaphysical idealism behind humanism to the extent it universalizes the condition of "man" based on class- and gender-bound ideologies. But in postulating a set of rights formulated by the bourgeoisie that ought to be extended to the proletariat as well, and in arguing that the class and productive relations sustained by the division between the bourgeoisie and the working class may actually constrict the extension of those rights,

Marxist theory seeks to extend the universal rights associated with humanism to the working class.

This basic correction to humanism's conception of what we now call the human subject—one that rejects the flattening out of differences in the conception of an essentialized, universal "man" and instead focuses on rights that ought to be guaranteed for everyone—informs a variety of theoretical and critical approaches to thinking in a productively critical way about humanism in the last half of the twentieth century. Take, for example, the relationship between feminism and humanism. On the one hand, feminism dissents from humanism's notion of "man," based as it is on the universalizing of a version of human nature derived by, and largely based on, male experience, but, on the other hand, feminism is linked to humanism in its insistence that women be accorded the same set of rights and the same kind of autonomy and agency associated with traditional humanism. On the critical side, of course, feminist theory and history help foreground the patriarchal orientation of humanism. Not simply in the trivial and quite obvious sense that virtually all of the early thinkers and writers associated with humanism were males whose status as scholars and educators was predicated on all of the privileges that came with being male in a patriarchal system, privileges that were unavailable to women (who, more often than not, were treated as the property of men). The less obvious but perhaps even more important point is that the identity category of gender is altogether absent inside humanist thinking about the human. And, as I indicated earlier, we should not see this simply as linguistic hair splitting, believing that the great writers of Renaissance, Enlightenment, or modern humanism meant to include women when they wrote "man." Too often they did not. Humanist "man" was conceptualized from the experience of male human beings; it is about forms of power, thought, agency, and autonomy (not to mention access to education and therefore to the very activity of scholarship upon which humanism is founded) historically only accessible to men.

As critical as feminism is of how humanism's philosophy of man kept women disenfranchised, it is strategically important in terms of articulating a twenty-first-century humanism to see the women's movement as a struggle to expand humanism's ideals with regard to individual autonomy and liberty rather than as an attempt do away with humanist ideals altogether. Like Marxism, feminism has had a double relationship to humanism, simultaneously launching a critical dissent from, and insisting on the broad legitimating and application of, its central ideals about human individuality, autonomy, and agency. The work of early feminists such as Mary Wollstonecraft, Susan B. Anthony, and Elizabeth Cady Stanton constituted a collective form of dissent from the patriarchal ideology that helped inform humanism, for example, but a dissent aimed at insuring women the rights and autonomy humanists embraced (as in the suffrage movement, for example). This kind of productive dissent, of course, broadened with the advent of the contemporary women's movement and the rise of feminist theory in the early 1970s. The convergence of the women's movement and feminist theory spurred a wholesale academic and scholarly rethinking of knowledge in virtually every field of the humanities (and in the natural and social sciences as well). The timing of this collective critique is not surprising, for it coincided with a dramatic shift in the demographics of higher education as women were finally allowed into universities in great numbers, and then into the scholarly professions of the humanities where they found a dearth of scholarship on women in history, literature, philosophy, and the fine arts, and, more broadly, on the relationship between gender and the production and shape of knowledge itself in the humanities.

Of course it did not suffice to right this wrong simply by breaking down barriers that kept women out of higher education. The whole body of knowledge produced in each of the disciplines of the humanities (and in the social and natural sciences as well) had to be rethought from the ground up; histories, evaluative criteria, critical judgments, methodologies, and the very body of knowledge that had been marshaled and taught in each of the disciplines of the humanities had to be rethought.[17] This work collectively raised fundamental questions about the quality and the accuracy of the literary, historical, and philosophical knowledge produced in the humanities. If the humanist subject was not in fact a universal subject but the product of experiences, and a worldview, that were class- and gender-bound, then ideas about human nature and individual autonomy at the center of humanism had to be reconstructed, understood not as metaphysical truth but as social productions. The ideals of human nature and individual autonomy at the center of humanism's conception of "man" had to be conceived, and taught, not as metaphysical truth but as an interested discourse, a set of propositions about humankind produced under certain material, cultural, social, and political conditions, conditions that had begun to alter radically in the last half of the twentieth century.

The women's movement and feminist criticism and theory literally transformed the production of knowledge in the humanities and led to a wholesale and extraordinarily productive rethinking of what counts as literature, history, and philosophy. To call this a "crisis" in the humanities, as many traditionalists have, is a shame, for doing so fundamentally fails to recognize the living, fluid nature of humanism. Worse still, it implies the need for a return to outdated, mistaken, and discredited formulations about human nature, culture, truth, and history. The transformation of the canon in literary studies, and the new attention paid in history, the visual arts, and philosophy to women's experiences and the role and place of women in a radically revised sense of what constituted historical knowledge, were breathtaking and of course will never be rolled back. But even more important, perhaps, was the new theoretical focus, first on gender, and then on sexuality, that came with it. Humanist "man," simply put, was not gendered or sexed. Sexuality and sexual orientation played no part in the determination of his identity and values, or the positions that he took on social, cultural, and political issues. He was human in a way that ignored complicated biological, social, cultural, and political differences defined by gender and sexuality in ways that not only affected but aggressively policed behavior and opportunity at every social level, and in the cultural and political spheres as well. We now understand the extent to which power is regulated by gender and policed by normative attitudes toward sexual orientation, but the kind of power associated with the supposed agency of humanist "man" was not thought of or theorized in gendered or sexual terms at all. The whole conception of the human has had to be productively rethought top to bottom through the lens of gender, not as a biological category but as a socially constructed one. The very definitions of what philosophy, art, literature, history, and the classics are have had to be rethought not as universal categories but as interested, gendered, socially constructed bodies of knowledge that are the product of a particular set of material and social relations. And theory was largely responsible for doing that work.

The theoretical work among Marxian and feminist critics I have been surveying not only represents a kind of theorizing Graff rightly argues is consistent with the general enterprise of humanism, but it also marks a split with humanism deep enough to suggest the kind of break Brooks evokes in the passage I quoted at the beginning of this chapter. In both cases, the universality of humanist "man" comes to be seen as contingent as scholars and critics pay close, sustained attention to the differences that class, social relations, productive processes, and gender make in defining the human condition among individuals. Yet at the same time, the humanist ideal that there ought to be such a thing as universal rights is not only embraced but also pushed to the foreground by both theoretical discourses. From both these critical perspectives, the historical construction of humanism becomes as important as its ideals, indeed, the two become inseparable, and both are tied to the ends to which humanism is put, for humanism emerges from this point of view as something practical, even utilitarian, aimed at making change and acting in the world. Moreover, materialist and feminist approaches to the construction of human subjectivity, and to how power and agency circulate in social and political culture, link humanism to the exercise of political power, while at the same time seeking to expand the rights it defined in both natural and moral terms.

The same is true of postcolonial and critical race theory, which together developed a historical critique of nineteenth-century racial theories and the history of colonialism in a way that actually linked both to some of the key ideals of humanism. Here the paradoxes of humanism, its tendency to both articulate a revolutionary framework for thinking about individuality, autonomy, and the agency of humans while simultaneously making European man the norm for a universal notion of the human and of human civilization, are most clearly tied to the circumscribing of the very universal rights humanism claims to endorse.[18] Just as the rational, autonomous individual of humanism became universal "man," so too did the humanist ideal of civilization become a baseline by which the West measured forms of human organization and behavior everywhere they were encountered during the history of colonialism. There is, of course, a deep paradox here: The virtues of humanist civilization, codified during the Enlightenment and solidified in the nineteenth century, while they led to an explosion of positive social and political change in the West, also authorized imperial conquest and colonization in the Americas, Africa, and Asia. The slave trade, as Paul Gilroy pointed out in *The Black Atlantic*, is after all not an aberration of modern humanism. It was central to humanism because its view of human nature actually authorized imperial expansion and colonial domination.[19] In the final analysis, humanism developed and naturalized a set of distinctions—between the human and the savage, between reason and superstition, between civilization and barbarism—all wedded to a certain teleological notion of the West's inevitable expansion and domination of the globe—that formed the logical foundation for colonization and conquest.[20] It seems to me one cannot argue for the value of the contemporary humanities without underscoring the importance of such a perspective and the contradictions it reveals.

There is a paradox, then, at the very center of humanism, for it ushers in *both* a positive set of transformations for some, and a set of rationales for the subjugation and oppression of others. This focus on the paradoxes of humanism, of course, owes a lot to postcolonial studies, another contemporary form of cultural and critical theory that has transformed our understanding of humanist "man" and the social and political ideals of humanism. Postcolonial studies have had two principle effects on the humanities. The first was to call systematic attention to the extent to which the economic, political, and economic culture of Western, humanist modernity was both financed and shaped by colonialism, and the second was to systematically expand the geography and history of humanism to include the study of colonialism and its effects. Postcolonial studies have had the dramatic effect of underscoring how humanism served as the conceptual rationale for constructing the non-European as inferior other, which had the effect of normalizing the superiority of the European, a key move in humanism's theorization of universal "man." It has also turned our historical and critical attention to how a humanistic education was used in places such as India to subjugate foreign populations, to colonize their consciousnesses, eradicate their own cultural and social histories, and to consolidate their domination by the West. In literary studies, for example, this led to studies such as Edward Said's *Culture and Imperialism*, a work that systematically reads key nineteenth-century canonical English novels in terms of how they reflect—and reflect on—British imperialism. Postcolonial criticism—along with critical race theory, which helped debunk the idea there is a biological basis for "race" and has helped facilitate study of the interdependence between nineteenth-century race theories, humanism, and colonialism—have together served to constructively transform the way we think about humanism, the humanities, and human nature.

Contemporary theory, then, had the disruptive effect we saw Brooks allude to at the outset of this chapter because it confronted scholars and students with the conceptual inadequacies of traditional humanist formulations of human nature and individual autonomy. Perhaps the most dramatic disciplinary force working to complicate the discourse of humanism in our own time has been the much-maligned field of multiculturalism. There is a key link, of course, between multiculturalism and humanism: both are isms, both advocate something. As I indicated earlier, it is sometimes easy to forget that humanism does not simply describe a set of universal conditions. It also promotes a set of propositions. So thoroughly have humanism and humanity been conflated in the United States that it is easy to miss this point. One of the salutatory effects of the various critical theories I have been discussing is that they serve to foreground the social, political, and cultural elements of advocacy at work in humanism, and the powers this advocacy serves, usefully complicating the idea that contemporary theory politicizes the humanities, since, as we have seen, humanism has always been about social and political power. The study of humanism as a socially and historically invented discourse foregrounds this element of advocacy, countering the commonsense idea that the human in humanism has some kind of transcendental or universal status. The "multi" in multicultural has this affect as well, for it reminds us that whenever we talk about culture we are not talking about some pure, autonomous, transhistorical category but a set of contested beliefs, ideals, and practices that have been constructed over time from multiple sources.

However, as with all of the theoretical and critical fields I have been discussing, multiculturalism ought to be seen as seeking to broaden rather than delegitimize the claims of humanism, for it seeks to extend and diversify attitudes toward equal opportunity and social justice that have always been at the center of humanist discourse. What are the problems with traditional humanism multiculturalism seeks to address? In purely conceptual terms, late-nineteenth and early twentieth-century forms of humanism were increasingly based on and advocated racial and cultural similarity and conformity, where multiculturalism acknowledges and embraces multiracial and cultural diversity. Culture as it was understood by traditional humanists, tends to be monolithic, Western, and timeless. It has its origins in Greece and Rome, has a European Renaissance, deepens in Europe again during the Enlightenment, and has its full flowering in Germany, France, and Britain in the nineteenth century, profoundly affecting the construction of humanistic learning in the United States in the twentieth century.[21] The job of traditional humanists like those who derided political correctness in the humanities in the 1980s and 1990s is to preserve this culture, and so a multiculturalist impulse is perceived as a threat on a number of fronts. Most fundamentally, multiculturalism (beyond its banal, purely celebratory forms) usefully and constructively complicates the very theory of culture that authorizes humanism—and humanist "man"—in the first place. Culture under the rubric of multiculturalism has an expansively anthropological rather than a narrowly aesthetic and moral orientation. This anthropological approach is best glossed as "the whole way of life of a people," the well-known definition provided by the British cultural critic, Raymond Williams, one that offers a dramatic contrast to Matthew Arnold's "the best which has been thought and said." Arnold's "best" is based on aesthetic criteria embodied in what the British literary critic F. R. Leavis later termed a "great tradition" of Western texts (they also, of course, comprise the "tradition" side of T. S. Eliot's "Tradition and the Individual Talent"). It is based on the classic distinction between "high" culture and "popular" culture and runs from Shakespeare and Milton back through Dante to Greek and Latin literature, all of which, according to Arnold, contain touchstones for moral guidance and aesthetic edification in his and our own time (since the value of these works is, by definition, timeless). Culture, from the Arnoldian and humanist perspectives, is singular. It derives its quality, timelessness, universality, and transcendental character from its homogeneity within a narrow tradition of Western men and their ideals. Cultural forms produced outside of this stream are often perceived as a threat because they will contaminate, dilute, and corrupt the dominant, privileged culture of humanism. This is the case in Arnold's time, when popular cultural forms (and behaviors) associated with a rising urban working class represented a kind of "anarchy" that threatened culture, and it was true one hundred years later when, in the heyday of the US culture wars I discussed in chapter 1, conservative critics such as Bennett, Cheney, Hirsch, and Kimball, complained that multicultural learning constituted a central threat to the transmission of humanist culture, indeed, to cultural literacy itself. This critical perspective on culture and humanism has become broadly influential in the academic humanities, but it is rarely invoked in public debates about the value of a humanities education. That ought to change.

Perhaps the best recent analysis debunking traditional humanist conceptions of culture can be found in Kwame Anthony Appiah's 2006 book, *Cosmopolitanism: Ethics in a World of Strangers*. As I just indicated, Appiah's argument that there is no such thing as a pure, authentic culture is nearly axiomatic among contemporary cultural critics. According to Appiah, the whole effort to protect pure cultures from contamination is futile because cultures are always formed by contamination. Writing about African cultures by way of example, Appiah points out that

> trying to find some primordially authentic culture can be like peeling an onion [since] the textiles most people think of as traditional West African cloths are known as java prints, and arrived with the Javanese batiks sold, and often milled, by the Dutch. The traditional garb of Herero women derives from the attire of nineteenth-century German missionaries, though it's still unmistakably Herero, not least because

the fabrics they use have a distinctly un-Lutheran range of colors. And so with our kente cloth: the silk was always imported, traded by Europeans, produced in Asia. This tradition was once an innovation. Should we reject it for the reason it is untraditional? How far back must one go?... [C]ultures are made of continuities and changes, and the identity of a society can survive through these changes. (107)

From this point of view the phrase "cultural purity" is "an oxymoron" (113). While we might think of the "multicultural" as a new phenomenon, it is important to recognize that the processes Appiah describes above are not recent but in fact have a long history affecting all of the territories associated with the origins of humanism. The "migrations that have contaminated the larger world," he continues, "were not all modern":

Alexander's empire molded both the states and sculpture of Egypt and North India; first the Mongols then the Mughals shaped great swaths of Asia; the Bantu migrations populated half the African continent, Islamic states stretch from Morocco to Indonesia; Christianity reached Africa, Europe, and Asia within a few centuries of the death of Jesus of Nazareth; Buddhism long ago migrated from India into much of the East and Southeast Asia. Jews and people whose ancestors came from many parts of China have long lived in vast diasporas. The traders of the Silk Road changed the style of elite dress in Italy; someone brought Chinese potter for burial in fifteenth-century Swahili graves. (112)

Historical analyses such as these complicate the myth of a monolithic, universal, singular, classical, culture or kind of universal "man" traditionally at the heart of humanism. From Appiah's point of view culture is always already multicultural all the way down, and so, the humanities ought to be expanding its purview, especially in a globalizing age, to incorporate this more capacious approach to culture and identity. The only pure or authentic cultures are those that dub themselves pure and authentic and then actively work to protect and purge themselves of foreign cultures (or cultural forms) that might contaminate them.[22]

Like the other theoretical and critical movements I have been discussing, Western multiculturalism advocates an approach to the human condition that, while it challenges the traditional narrowness of humanism, evolves out of and seeks to expand it. Multiculturalism is not a form of political correctness. Rather, it attempts to correct—and update—the politics of traditional humanism through measuring humanism by its own ideals, asking whether or not the liberties guaranteed by humanism have in fact been extended to all humans. Humanists and their supporters should not shrink from underscoring the value of this multiculturalist approach to humanism. Indeed, it should be integral to defending the value of a twentieth-century humanities education. The emphasis ought to be on how work done under the rubric of multiculturalism, feminist, or postcolonial theory seeks to correct traditional humanist talk that defines humanity and its nature in overly narrow and restrictive ways. The contemporary theoretical critiques of humanism's construction of "man" I have been reviewing are nothing if not engaged with the subject of the human, for they attempt to expand, deepen, and demystify our understanding of what it means to be human and the diversity of behaviors and beliefs that constitute human nature. A critique of the historical discourse of humanism is not a critique of humanity itself. It is a critique of a certain way of talking about and formulating humanity.

From the point of view of traditionalists, of course, the critical work I have been reviewing is largely to blame for the crisis in the humanities. However, as we saw earlier, this is simply not the case. The humanities are on a much sounder historical, intellectual, and conceptual footing than they were just a few decades ago. Because the humanities have been enriched by this broad and productive critique of humanism, it makes little sense to think of this work as anti or post- humanist. It also makes little *strategic* sense to think of it this way. Humanists and their supporters ought to be defending a humanities transformed by theory, and in order to strengthen them they ought to avoid the polemical assertion that we are not working in a post- or antihumanist mode. That's the last way to convince college and university administrations, boards of trustees, and state legislators to continue to support the humanities financially. At a time when it is important to make a strong case for the role of the humanities in higher education, the rhetoric of "antihumanism" or "posthumanism" will not do. For both conceptual and pragmatic reasons, then, there is no getting outside the discourse of humanism, no rhetorically viable position from which to articulate an anti- or a post-humanism. It makes much more sense to see structuralist, deconstructive, feminist, postcolonial and even Marxist theory as having produced a more sophisticated and historically accurate understanding of the human, one that is vigilant in making sure that work in the humanities moves beyond a narrow and under-theorized version of the human, that it is humanist in a more capacious and diverse way. If we are going to defend the value of the humanities in the twenty-first-century we need to defend a twenty-first-century version of the humanities, but not in a way that claims it is anti- or post- humanist. As I have been arguing, that's a strategic mistake.

It is important to note that the changes I've been discussing were not simply born of esoteric theories developed inside academia but by larger social changes that unfolded *outside* academia. All of the theoretical approaches to study in the humanities I have been discussing have their corollary in key post–World War II social movements. The connections here are obvious, but they're worth recalling. Independence movements in formerly colonized areas of the world including the Caribbean, Latin America, Africa, Asia, and South Asia developed a rich vein of political and cultural theory that eventually entered the Western academy in the form of postcolonial studies.[23] The rise of African American criticism and theory is intimately connected to the Civil Rights movement. The same relationship is true of La Raza, the Chicano/a movement, and the explosive interest in Hispanic/Chicano/a/Latino/a literature and culture (along with the development of border studies as a new academic field) and the Native American liberation movement. The Women's Movement, which started on the streets, both entered the university and was fed by it in the form of feminist criticism and theory, the significance of which exploded beginning in the 1970s, transforming the way in which we think about identity and agency. The same is true of the gay and lesbian rights movements. They started out, like the others, as social justice movements. Both movements fed—and were fed by—new theories about gender and sexuality that have transformed the social and political landscape *and* the way identity, history, philosophy, literature, and religion are studied in the humanities. All of these social movements, and the new academic fields they were connected with, coalesced into the critical discourse of multiculturalism I have been discussing. Taken together these social movements have been nothing short of breathtaking, and they represent just the kind of critical expansion of humanist claims about rights and agency characteristic of the academic theories I have been discussing. The cultural and intellectual worlds students live in today are utterly transformed from the one I grew up in during the 1950s and 1960s, and their attitudes toward the whole range of social issues I've been discussing are, on the whole, dramatically different than they were then. Increasingly these students are multiracial in a country that will soon have a majority of citizens who are also multiracial, and they have largely rejected the old hierarchies and claims to superiority traditionally embodied in older conceptions of humanism. They understand that material forces that determine economic class, and ideologies about race, gender, and sexuality, shape our art and literature as well as our humanity, who we are as individuals, and how much autonomy and agency we have. And they make these connections not despite the prominence of theory in the humanities, but because of it.

These are not trivial changes that can be overlooked as we shift the humanities back to basics, returning to a narrow, supposedly depoliticized focus on what it is to be human. For as we have seen, the humanities have never transcended politics because they have always been about the study of power.[24] That is because, as we have seen, humanism was always about theorizing rights, liberty, and agency within a democratic framework. It wasn't just a set of abstract ideas about what it means to be human, but rather, it made claims about inherent, basic rights and about the moral responsibility humans have to empower one another. Humanism is full of contradictions, and a humanities education ought to focus students' attention on exploring them. On the one hand, by approaching human nature in terms of personal and social rights as natural, inherent, or self-evident, humanism became the philosophical rationale for the rise of increasingly democratic systems of political power in the West. On the other hand, however, theories about "man" developed under the rubric of humanism often worked against the broad, even, and systematic democratization of agency and political power. The humanist ideal of the rational, autonomous individual unfolded unevenly within a Eurocentric and patriarchal system that universalized a human nature that both unconsciously and consciously served to limit the rights of some, and worse, as a rationale for the military, political, and social domination of people who were defined within the very discourse of humanism as subhuman. Flawed as the history of humanism is, it is the history of a way of engaging human being that was always profoundly political. And so, to claim that contemporary work in philosophy, history, art, or literary studies has newly politicized the humanities is simply inaccurate. In my view, such a claim attempts to short-circuit constructive criticism in an effort to conserve a fixed, narrow set of ideals and the forms of power they protect. Humanism, especially during the Enlightenment and in the nineteenth century, developed as a culture of dissent, and its evolution since then, the expansion of its ideals in a more truly universal way, has also come out of dissent, dissent from some of the flawed and limited ways in which humanist ideals have been developed and applied. This means that when students learn about humanism in the humanities the ideal of constructive dissent we saw Nussbaum advocate ought to be at the very center of what they encounter. Likewise, when we think about the humanities as an institutional structure we need to realize that historically the humanities have fed off—and developed within—a context of constructive dissent. Without such dissent, the humanities would never have developed the breadth and scope they currently have.

For this reason, constructive intellectual or cultural dissent should not be seen as idiosyncratic and marginal to the humanities, but central to its continued invigoration and expansion. Humanists and their supporters need to develop a version of the humanities geared to the twenty-first century, one that is informed by the kind of constructive critique of traditional humanism I have been reviewing. The humanities should not simply tell us where we've been. They should help guide us to where we are going. The world in which humanities students are going to be living and working is no longer going to be dominated by the West in anything like the ways it has in the past. It is not going to be white, and it is not going to be monocultural.[25] The kind of education students will require to be successful, responsible citizens in a rapidly globalizing age will be fundamentally different from one designed for very different needs in the period 1850–1960. That form of the humanities, as we have seen, was nationalist. It was designed in large measure to establish and foster the moral, intellectual, cultural, and, in some cases, racial superiority of the West. Nineteenth-century humanism served to solidify the cultural power of a male educated class, to reign in and cultivate an increasingly urbanizing group of lower class workers and an emerging middle class, and often as a rationale for conquest, domination, and colonization abroad. And of course in the United States as Harpham (among others) has recently reminded us, the humanities developed during the era of the Cold War to help shore up America's ideological and political battle with Communism.[26] These worlds have evaporated. None of these goals serve the needs of students today. In a United States in which, by the middle of the twenty-first century whites will be a minority in an increasingly Hispanic nation, students studying the humanities will need to know at least as much about the history of the indigenous peoples of the Southwest and Mexico as they do about Greek and Roman culture. They should know as much about African and African Diasporic history, as well, and about the history and culture of our neighbors from the Caribbean, as they do about Renaissance humanism or the poetry of John Milton (which doesn't mean they should not study the poetry of John Milton). And of course, as China and India continue to emerge as dominant economic and cultural powers, they will need to know as much about the history and culture of these countries as they do about their own.

I have been arguing that the humanities in general—and literary studies in particular—will have to make the case for their value in the twenty-first century in terms of their practical value. What does the critique of humanism I've been reviewing have to do with *that* argument? A lot. For the kind of work I'm talking about is grounded in close reading, critical thinking, the questioning of fixed orthodoxies, and fostering the ability to develop spirited, informed, constructive arguments, just the set of skills employers are looking for. Developing the kind of critical perspective on humanism the humanities increasingly provide also insures that students will have a global historical perspective, a perspective invaluable in an age in which the rigidity of national borders is giving way to global economic and cultural relations. Humanism as a discourse, and the humanities as an institutional structure, as we have seen Harpham stress, are largely a feature of US educational institutions, and so it is incumbent upon US educators to help globalize our understanding of the human and the scope of a humanities curriculum. We need to build on the productive expansion of our understanding of the human—of the complex ways in which identity, agency, autonomy, and rights are constructed and circulated, how they expand and are restricted—produced in the last half century in the explosion of work done under the auspices of the theoretical and critical schools and movements I have been discussing. Collectively, this work represents an expansion and deepening of the very ideals of humanism it has explored. This way of conceiving the value of the humanities returns us to the vision we earlier saw outlined by Sheldon Hackney and Martha Nussbaum, an approach that attempts to meet the needs of students in a world where both economic and cultural globalization are accelerating, where populations are shifting and recombining, and where democratic citizenship is not simply a national but a global responsibility.

This does not mean simply dropping a traditional humanities curriculum or rejecting wholesale the premises of Western humanism and a Western conception of a humanities education. But it does mean submitting these traditions to historical and critical inquiry, and ultimately, broadening the scope of both scholarly approaches to the human, and the curriculum we employ to study them, so that they are truly and meaningfully more universal, respecting the diversity and complexity of human natures around the globe. Emphasizing a more global approach to the humanities can provide a context for engaging criticism of the limits of Western humanism and a traditional, Eurocentric humanities curriculum such as the ones I have been exploring in thoughtful, scholarly ways that meet our twenty-first-century needs. Talk about globalizing the humanities is potentially much more productive than talk about antihumanism or posthumanism, as I have already argued. A more global version of the humanities can provide a framework for studying human nature in all of its geographic, historical, and cultural varieties (literary, philosophical, religious, visual, artistic) in ways that do not subordinate non-Westerners and their cultural productions to secondary status. It can help illuminate the fact that we live in a world with multiple and diverse forms of humanistic expression reflecting a richly divergent range of religious beliefs and cultural practices. And finally, a version of the humanities conceived in more global terms has the potential to underscore the link between socioeconomic and material conditions, ideologies, public and private institutions, and the construction of individual identity and the forms of power and autonomy they both authorize and circumscribe. It has the potential to bring the theoretical, methodological, and historical insights about humanism and the human I have been discussing in this chapter to the very center of humanistic inquiry, enriching and complicating that inquiry by giving it a global scope, facilitating the study of human experience, and the variety of texts that have chronicled and grappled with it, in a way that reflects the diversity of the world we are living in.

Chapter 4

Getting to the Core of the Humanities, or Who's Afraid of Gloria Anzaldúa?

Virtually all of the issues central to debates about the nature and value of a humanities education have figured prominently in the history of the core curriculum in the United States. For this reason, I want to extend my exploration of the perennial nature of the so-called humanities crisis by looking at how debates regarding the practical value of a humanities education, and the role that theory, criticism, and professionalization ought to play in the design of both courses and programs, have also shaped the struggle to define what a core humanities education ought to be.

I want to begin with a story. In the early summer of 2010 faculty members in my department received an urgent email from our chairperson. As part of a recent initiative to revise the core curriculum in the College of Arts and Sciences we were being asked to develop a new set of core courses. Moreover, if we wanted to retain the current two-course requirement in literature (fulfilled jointly by a mix of courses in English, Classics, and Modern Languages and Literatures) we would have to come up with a new, two-tiered system, an initial foundational course required of all students, and a second set of courses at a more advanced level, from which students could choose one more course to complete their core literature requirement. Since we did not currently have such a foundational course, we would have to spend the summer developing one (along with the other departments), rearticulating the mission and goals of our core courses, and choosing a set of current or new courses that would fulfill the requirement for a second course.

An ad hoc group of faculty began to meet, and by late August they had hammered out the detailed outlines of a plan. The foundational or first-tier course would be called "Literature, Interpretation, and Value." It would introduce students to a range of literary forms (poetry, narrative fiction, drama, etc.), a critical vocabulary of terms and concepts often used in the analysis and interpretation of literature, and a framework for exploring the relationship between literature and culture. Faculty in the departments of English, Classical Studies, and Modern Languages and Literatures would teach this course. The foundational course would prepare students for a range of second-tier courses in which they studied literature in more focused and specialized kinds of ways, applying the critical vocabulary and methodologies—and exploring in more detail some of the issues—they covered in their foundational course. While I had some questions about the details of the foundational course, and about which courses ought to qualify for inclusion on the list of second-tier courses, I was basically in support of the proposal, which seemed like a reasonable compromise among competing views about what a core course should do. I assumed the core revision committee would accept it without much debate.

I was wrong. When the final product went to the committee it generated a number of concerns that revealed more clearly just what the committee was looking for and how it conflicted with our department's own vision of how core courses in our discipline should be shaped. It turned out that the committee wanted a foundational course mainly organized around the reading of canonical texts in the Western tradition. They were concerned that we did not stipulate that our foundational courses would have this orientation, and that we did not stipulate which specific texts students would be required to read. Indeed, the committee was so concerned about making sure our reading lists comprised canonical works that they urged us to come up with a single reading list or multi-department canon that students in all of the foundational courses would read. They also wanted us to keep the course content general in nature, to avoid focusing too much attention on critical approaches or intellectual subjects they believed were keyed to our own professional interests and areas of specialization. The committee's concerns echoed the deep anxiety about professionalization I discussed in chapter 2. In their view, core courses should not focus either on theories and methods specific to the disciplines, nor should they be about issues related to the faculty member's area of specialization. Rather, they should simply ensure that before they leave college students would have read the great works of the Western tradition in literature, philosophy, and history without the distractions that come with professional contextualization. The desire here was for a largely *unmediated* experience of classical texts and authors.

It turned out that the core revision committee's concerns, while fairly broad-based in philosophical terms, were set off by the inclusion of the name of a single author in the preamble to our description of the foundational course. That author was Gloria Anzaldúa. Here is the description in its entirety:

> The fundamental purpose of literature is to explore human experience. Whether it is Homer singing the wrath of Achilles, Shakespeare subjecting Lear to a wheel of fire, Baudelaire expressing spleen, or Gloria Anzaldúa exploring questions of identity in a transnational world, authors are inevitably engaged with human concerns. They lead us to ask fundamental questions: What matters in the world? How should we live our lives? What should we value? What kind of beings are we? No work of literature can fully answer these questions, but a probing novel, play, or poem can help us struggle with the problems and deepen our appreciation of the complex nature of human experience. The insights that literature can provide, though, are rarely transparent; we encounter them in works of art, and we can only access them by developing our interpretive skills. And so a foundational course in literature must also introduce each student to some of the basic terms of analysis and problems of interpretation. This course, then, will have a double purpose: it will ask students to engage some significant issue or issues relevant to our human experience, and it will help them develop the basic skills of interpretation needed to accomplish this task in a sophisticated manner.[1]

This struck me when I first read it as a fairly innocuous, boilerplate description of literature and its study effectively calibrated for a general audience. What was there, really, to disagree with here? Literature's purpose is to "explore human experience." Literature is "engaged with human concerns." Studying literature gets us to ask fundamental questions about our lives, our values, and what kind of people we are. And, although literature deals with a myriad of subjects, the study of literature should focus on the development of analytical and interpretive expertise because literature's insights are not "transparent," but rather, are produced by literary devices and embedded meanings. The opening sentence seemed to me the most innocuous of all. It was carefully constructed by a group of faculty to mirror both the diversity of texts and the linkages they share taught across the departments of Classics (Homer), Modern Language and Literatures (Baudelaire), and English (Shakespeare, Anzaldúa). The latter pairing, in particular, signals the diversity of texts long-taught in English courses, which range from canonical figures like Shakespeare to women and minority writers like Anzaldúa, who is a staple of American and multicultural literature courses all over the country.

Although I had heard the inclusion of Anzaldúa in this preamble had become a red flag for some core revision committee members, I was still taken aback when I ran into the chair of the committee on campus, a historian and a longtime acquaintance of mine, who wanted to know, "Who is Gloria Anzaldúa?" It was a sign of my own naïveté that I simply thought everyone knew who Gloria Anzaldúa was. Certainly everyone in my fields of specialization, American literary studies, border studies, and contemporary critical theory knew who she was. Indeed, a member of our department had just won the prestigious National Women's Studies Association Gloria Anzaldúa Book Prize.[2] Anzaldúa's major work, *Borderlands/La Frontera: The New Mestiza*, long ago became a classic text in American literature courses around the country. And even if my colleague had never heard of her, he could have looked her up on the Internet. There is an extensive, reliable Wikipedia article on Anzaldúa, and dozens of comprehensive websites about her work and its importance for literary studies, literary theory, and cultural studies.[3] But of course, the question my colleague was asking me wasn't really, "Who is Gloria Anzaldúa?" but "what is Gloria Anzaldúa doing in a list that includes Homer, Shakespeare, and Baudelaire?" The latter three, of course, were just the kinds of canonical, great writers central to the development of Western civilization the core revision committee wanted us to be including in our courses. But Gloria Anzaldúa was not. While most members of our department believed a foundational core course should include a diversity of texts and perspectives from the wider body of major writers we teach, reflecting changes over time in a fluid, expanding canon, many members of the core revision committee thought such a course should restrict itself to major figures whose writings were central to a humanistic tradition that certainly didn't include a lesbian Chicana feminist like Anzaldúa whom they had never heard of.

Almost all of the issues central to debates about the humanities I have been discussing in this book are telescoped into this episode. In particular we can observe the tension between the humanities' curatorial and critical functions Delbanco calls attention to: Should core literature courses be organized around the reading of canonical Western texts in order to insure a kind of cultural literacy, or should they emphasize practical, analytical, interpretive, and rhetorical skills to insure critical literacy—and include a range of canonical and non-canonical texts, both historical and contemporary, texts that embody a rich, even global diversity? This is in part because debates about whether or not colleges or universities should have core requirements (many, of course, do not), and if they do, what these programs and their particular courses should look like and what their educational outcomes ought to be, always tend to foreground the kinds of broad debates about the humanities I have been reviewing: What is the core mission of the humanities? Is it to expose students to a conventional "humanist" curriculum whose value is curatorial, focusing for the most part on the best that has been thought and said? Or, is its value *critical* both in the sense that it incorporates a thoughtful exploration of the invention of humanistic ideals and their subsequent critique by writers working from both within and outside that tradition, and in the sense that work in the humanities, as critics from Eagleton to Perloff have argued, shouldn't be concerned so much with which texts get taught but with what critical skills they help our students to learn? And what about literary studies in particular? Are they enriched when they are professionally rigorous and grounded in a set of methodologies and interpretive theories, or does this kind of professional expertise actually undermine the quality of literary studies, especially at more general levels? Should students simply study *literature itself*? Does the inclusion of a so-called professional apparatus distract from or enhance literary experience and our engagement with literature? Are the canon wars Perloff alludes to something our students should know about (should professors, as Graff insists, be teaching their *conflicts*), or can we regard them as a blip in the history of the humanities as we return to the teaching of canonical texts and rhetorical analysis?

One of the things the episode I have recounted foregrounds is the extent to which the curatorial function for humanities courses can turn into a name game and thus make courses be about authors rather than about issues and competing ideas. Our core revision committee's expectation that core literature courses should be based exclusively on canonical authors who deal with a core of so-called great ideas that have shaped Western civilization might seem like common sense, but it tends to subordinate ideas to authors in a way that more often than not ends up limiting the range of experiences and ideas covered in such courses. This is certainly the case with a writer like Anzaldúa, whose experiences growing up gay, Mestiza, and Chicana in the US/Mexico borderlands complicate a whole set of received humanist narratives about personal and national identity, introducing productively complicated questions about the role played by geography, ethnicity, history, and sexual orientation in the development of our identities and at the same time raising provocative questions about the construction of both "American" and "literature" as subject areas. Are these really subjects we should be protecting our students from in our core courses? None of this would threaten or preclude our students' engagement with Homer, Shakespeare, and Baudelaire, of course, but rather, would enhance and complicate it. The inclusion of Anzaldúa in a list that includes Homer, Shakespeare, and Baudelaire seems to threaten a number of traditional, cherished ideals about the humanities. One of them has to do with the idea that when it comes to literary studies students ought to be reading texts with the kind of aesthetic quality and intellectual value that have both stood the test of time and been central to the intellectual history of the West. One problem with the "test of time" idea, of course, is that it would tend to preclude modern or contemporary texts from core courses such as the foundational course I have been discussing, and indeed, in discussions with core committee members it did emerge there was a strong assumption that texts used in our core courses should all predate World War II, an assumption I found astonishing, since it would rule out not only major mainstream authors like Mailer, Roth, Morrison and Updike, but many African, Hispanic, Native, and Asian American writers who had produced crucially important texts in the last half of the twentieth century, exclusions that would make it impossible to give students anything like a clear picture of literary production and its study in the twentieth century.

One of the key things the core revision committee wanted to insure across the disciplines was a *shared* intellectual experience. The idea here is that because you restrict the reading material in *all* core courses to the great canonical works in Western literature, philosophy, art, and religion, students in a philosophy core course will be grappling with the same set of ideas from a philosophical perspective that students in a literature or religious studies or art history core course will be grappling with from their disciplinary perspectives because they will all be dealing with the same humanistic tradition and thus the same big ideas. The issues Anzaldúa's works engage would be just fine for a second-tier course, but not for a foundational course focused on the central texts and ideas of humanism. There are two problems with this point of view. The first is that it narrows and truncates the historical evolution of debates within the broad tradition of humanism about human nature, the construction of human identity, and the various forces at play in societies and cultures that both enable and circumscribe individual autonomy and agency. Leaving out texts by women and minority writers formerly excluded from study by humanists arbitrarily cuts off students' engagement with the history of humanism and its evolution in the last half of the twentieth century. The whole set of questions raised by contemporary writers, scholars, and theorists about the collective role played by gender, class, race, and sexual orientation in the construction of and debates about the humanist subject and its rights (a set of questions which, in the last chapter I argued are extraordinarily productive) simply gets left off the table, which means our inquiry into the humanist tradition itself gets arbitrarily truncated. The second problem is that simply mandating cultural, aesthetic, or philosophical homogeneity across courses (assuming that's a desirable thing in the first place, and I'm not convinced it is) does nothing to insure either that a particular humanistic point of view or set of issues is going to be covered in those courses, nor that a shared intellectual experience across course sections will occur. Nor would it insure those discussions would intersect with others going on in philosophy and history core courses (the level of intellectual policing that would have to take place to insure this last goal would be unacceptable to most faculty members).

Another problem with the author-centric model for core courses like those I have been discussing is that, ironically, in seeking to ground the courses in intellectual history they run the danger of making them *ahistorical*, stressing generalized kinds of links between texts in ways that can end up undermining their historical specificity. This is a danger in any kind of course that sees the most valuable texts in a tradition as being valuable because they transcend their own time and place, speak to some generalized notion of the "human condition," and so have a "universal" quality. To read and discuss *Macbeth* as a work of universal significance that transcends its historical time and place and speaks to some things that are essential about human experience is to talk about a very different *Macbeth* than the one we discuss if we situate the play in the historical contexts of its production and reception and ask questions about how it reflects—and reflects on—attitudes toward power, gender, sexuality, and identity central to a certain humanistic point of view operative (or emerging) at a particular time in history. Pick any Shakespeare play, any poem by Keats or Whitman, or novel by Austen, Dickens, or Hemingway and the same thing would be true. As I will argue at more length later in this chapter, rather than have core literature courses arbitrarily limited to a menu of great canonical works in the Western tradition in order to engineer a shared intellectual experience or enforce some traditional notion of cultural literacy, such courses should expose students to both the range and diversity of authors and texts studied within the disciplines, exploring the historical construction of canons along with a frank discussion of how they function to both authorize *and* circumscribe humanist discourse.

Even if it *were* true that requiring literature faculty to teach a fixed set of "great authors" would insure a shared intellectual experience focused on general humanistic issues, drawing up such a list would, for intellectual and historical reasons, be extremely problematical. Let's start with the question, "What writers *must* students be familiar with, and why?" Of course in my field, literary studies, everyone always starts with Shakespeare, and perhaps we needn't quibble with that. Shakespeare is so central to Western writing and is so often cited in other major and minor literary works both within and outside the Western tradition that some familiarity with Shakespeare seems essential for all students, certainly for English majors. Fine. But then, what other writers are essential in this kind of way? Perhaps two others: Chaucer (because his tales are some of the first foundational examples of formal story-telling in English) and Milton, because in *Paradise Lost* we get the whole apparatus of Western thinking about religion, liberty, and the supernatural running from Plato through Christianity converging in an extraordinarily influential poem. Beyond these three writers consensus would immediately begin to break down, however. The list of dramatists writing both before and after Shakespeare and on into the twentieth century, the poets of importance for one reason or another who wrote from the seventeenth century to the present, the vast and variegated tradition of prose fiction in English beginning with the rise of the novel in the seventeenth century and running into the so-called postmodern period would necessitate such a large and varied menu of writers as to be mind-boggling in scope and variety. One need only consult the astonishingly learned and solidly traditional critic, Harold Bloom (1994), to see that this would be the case (his list is enormous). The fact of the matter is that one could argue that *no* single writer other than Shakespeare stands out as absolutely essential based on any criteria. There may be consensus about Shakespeare, but after that, consensus—even among experts—breaks down. It is not surprising that debates about canons have superseded the actual importance of canons in literary studies and other disciplines in the humanities, for these debates focus our attention on the social and cultural role of literature and how definitions of what counts as literature and why it is important have changed over time. Indeed, it could certainly be argued that *the process of canon formation itself* is a more important, historically and intellectually compelling paradigm for organizing literary study, especially at the core level, than the great books model is. The great books model arbitrarily limits the range of texts students read and runs the risk of suggesting that we know what the really great books are because great books are, well, simply great. It is a model that risks obscuring, distorting, or hiding altogether the social, cultural, and political forces that shape such canons, and how those forces dramatize the role that ideologies and institutions play in deciding what counts as knowledge and why it is deemed valuable. "Great books" are not born they are made. Students deserve reading lists that reflect a diverse cross-section of books and authors that have been considered great, with some attention paid to *why* they were considered great, and by whom. They also deserve to read formerly marginalized or ignored texts that are now deemed important, with some attention paid to the reasons both for their marginalization and the renewed attention they have been receiving. Without such a mix of texts, and without this historical perspective on how canons come and go, we give students the decidedly mistaken impression that some authors and texts "just are" great, by some universal or transcendental criteria we have no need to question.

The author-centric, curatorial approach to core courses in literary studies is of course tied to the idea I discussed in chapter 2, that there is such a thing as "literature itself." This view holds that it is the professor's responsibility to let texts speak for themselves, unfiltered by professional specializations. This, it seems to me, is at the core of what Harpham has in mind when he stresses the importance of allowing students to have a "literary experience" by making sure they read "passively." Specialization from this point of view is akin to what Graff called context. Over here you have "literature itself," and over there you have different ways of contextualizing literature. To contextualize a literary work, so the argument goes, is to subordinate it to its historical or biographical origins or to submit it to the protocols of some critical methodology, aesthetic, formalist, psychoanalytic, historical, political, whatever. This is fine for professional critics or graduate-level education, but in the undergraduate classroom it gets in the way of students' engagement with the actual literary texts they are to read. But the problem with this argument, as we have already seen, is that this idea of literature itself freed from any contextualization is a chimera. *Reading is itself a contextualization*, a complex process of cognition, recognition, processing, and understanding symbols on a page, and it is a process we are taught to practice in ways that have an effect on what we read. We are all *taught* to read, which is to say we are taught to read in certain ways and with certain assumptions about what the process entails. And we inevitably bring to the process of reading our own experiences, training, beliefs, and ideas, all of which have in turn been produced within and mediated by the discourses, ideologies, and institutions that have shaped us as subjects in the first place. This means that the texts we read are in turn subject to our reading of them. There is no experience of reading that doesn't have its own context and doesn't constitute a context that shapes the text we read. "Literature itself" would be something like *Moby Dick* on a bookshelf, the actual physical object (although even this object might differ from one shelf to another depending upon which edition we owned[4]), but as soon as a reader takes the book off the shelf and starts reading it, even for a class that will be focused on literature itself without any contextualization, the book becomes contextualized through the readers engagement with it.[5] You simply cannot separate literature off from contextualization. You can speculate about intention, which is always a good place to *start* in discussing a literary text, but intention is itself a contextualization, is notoriously hard to pin down, and in any case is a place to *begin* the discussions of a text, not the place to end it.[6] It is a basic responsibility of anyone who teaches literature to get students to see that *how* we read determines *what* we read. If we foreground "literature itself" we create the illusion of texts as autonomous objects, shorn of the very reception history that made them important in the first place.

Another key issue implicit in debates about a core literature curriculum is the geographical, cultural, and intellectual range of the authors and texts it incorporates. My department, along with the other departments with which we share teaching responsibilities for core literature courses, was asked to create a foundational course that centered on great authors and texts central to the tradition of *Western* humanism, a typical focus of twentieth-century core curriculums and general distribution requirements. Yet, one of the most dramatic shifts in literary studies in recent years—and in the humanities in general—has been its embrace of a transnational, global context for the study of art, literature, philosophy, religion, and history. The shift in literary studies toward emphasizing the transnational and cross-cultural elements of literature across historical periods and at a quickly accelerating rate in our own times converges quite neatly with Nussbaum's insistence that the humanities have a primary role to play in helping students learn about people and cultures other than themselves in the interests of becoming productive global democratic citizens. The national paradigm for studying literature has for some time been giving way to a post or transnational focus animated by work in postcolonial and global theory, and by earlier work on multicultural and Diasporic literatures.[7] This work has called our attention to the extent to which early literature in English was often produced outside the context or even the existence of the modern nation-state, and to the extent to which texts studied in the narrow context of Western humanism are in fact embedded in transnational and cross-cultural forms of exchange and negotiation that are extraordinarily complex. Not only, in my view, should core literature courses focus on the process of canon formation, they ought to be paying more—not less—attention both to the diversity of texts in our literary traditions and to their intellectual engagement with other nations and cultures. The humanities will need to become increasingly global, and such an orientation ought to be included in core courses, not excluded from them.

One of the problems with Gloria Anzaldúa is that she does not fit very neatly into the conservative discourse of humanism and its evolution I discussed in the last chapter (and by using the term "conservative" I mean to underscore the protective, preserving sense of the word's meaning). Nor do her texts fit neatly into traditional concepts of literature itself. Indeed, they complicate our students' notion of "literature" in productive ways. Her work also calls attention to a range of experiences central to the history of humanism in the West but which are often excluded from that history when told through the lens of canonical works. Her *Borderlands/La Frontera* explores the experience of women under patriarchy in the context of colonization in a border zone between two nation-states, and in a way that also challenges the border between fiction and nonfiction. It simultaneously foregrounds the spiritual life and beliefs of a suppressed indigenous culture, emphasizes the difference that gender and sexual orientation make in the construction of identity and in the suppression of agency for people considered deviant by the dominant culture, and all in a way that features identity not as something pure but as mixed and contaminated in the sense we saw Appiah use the term. All of these elements in Anzaldúa's text productively complicate the neat picture of human nature, and theories about individuality, autonomy, and agency that have circulated within a traditional humanist discourse. Anzaldúa's voice represents the excluded voice that allows for the construction of the normative voice in traditional conceptions of the humanities in the first place, a voice grounded in the culture of dissent Nussbaum refers to. When such a voice is excluded the productive voice of dissent—productive not because it seeks to dismiss or excoriate humanism but rather demand from it the very recognition and rights it promises—is excluded as well. Anzaldúa's experiences capture a history central to Western civilization, not marginal to it.

As I note earlier, the kind of debate sparked by Anzaldúa's name almost always occurs when a college or university sets out to revise (or establish) a core curriculum. Should the requirements be general in nature across the disciplines (so-called distribution requirements) or should they be organized around a core of texts or subjects that facilitate shared explorations and transcend disciplinary boundaries? Should the core require students to study a classical and canonical tradition understood as central to the development of Western civilization, or should it require a diverse range of texts from both within and outside a Western tradition, exposing students to both Western and non-Western texts and the cultures from which they have emerged? Should core courses include modern and even contemporary readings, or should they be restricted to central works that have stood the test of time? To what extent should a core curriculum be about *historical* knowledge, and to what extent should it focus on contemporary social, cultural, and political problems and ways they might be solved? What role should secondary materials (both historical and critical) play in the study of primary texts? Should students read only primary texts, or should they be required as well to read critical and historical materials about the texts they study that reveal different ways those texts have been read, and which document the historical context in which they have emerged as important texts? Should these courses focus on a historically significant body of *knowledge*, or on a set of analytical, reading, rhetorical, and interpretive *skills* that are used across the disciplines in the humanities and are connected to how professional work in each one is conducted? And finally, should colleges and universities even *have* core curriculums, or are students better served by a so-called open curriculum, one in which students take the responsibility for designing their own course of study?[8] All of these questions, in one form or another, have been at the center of debates about core curriculums for well over a hundred years—and therefore at the center of debates about the nature and value of the humanities themselves.

Indeed, the history of arguments about a core education in the humanities shows that faculty and administrators debate the same issues over and over again, staging a kind of repetitive drama performed whenever they start worrying about the humanities and their place in higher education. We can see this by taking a look at the historical development of one of the country's most prominent core curriculums, the one at Columbia University, which over the course of the century has been used as a model at many colleges and universities.[9] Columbia's current core curriculum has its roots in the parallel development in the early decades of the twentieth century of required sequences in contemporary civilization (a kind of social studies sequence taught by faculty from the history, economics, government, philosophy, and sociology departments) and literature and the humanities (with combined readings in literature and philosophy). The first thing to note about these early general education requirements is that they did not develop simply in the context of narrow debates about the pursuit of knowledge but as a response to social and political change and upheaval, a fact that refutes the idea that the humanities have only recently become politicized. Indeed, they were specifically developed to help students deal with political and social upheaval. As we shall see in more detail below, while the move to develop a set of general education requirements for Columbia was connected to the university's diminution of Greek and Latin, (the university added a modern language requirement in 1880 and, subsequently, dropped requirements in Greek in 1897, and Latin in 1916), it actually crystallized in the years leading up to World War I and in its aftermath, years in which immigration brought new waves of students into the university and in which issues related to war and peace began to reshape the undergraduate curriculum. Just as more recent debates about a core education in the humanities were animated collectively by responses to the Civil Rights movement, the anti-Vietnam war movement, the Immigration and Nationality Act of 1965, and the Women's movement, among others, so too were original calls for a core curriculum a response to social and political forms of change. It is disingenuous to assert that "radicals" in higher education have politicized core requirements and humanities programs because they are always to some degree engaged with concrete social, cultural, and political change. Core requirements seek to manage and direct those changes, not to avoid or transcend them.

Current debates about the professionalization of higher education and the effect that debate is having on how we think about the practical value of a humanities education are also reflected in the historical development of Columbia's core curriculum. Indeed, early arguments at Columbia about the value of a general liberal arts education developed in response to the professionalization of higher education and the practical needs of students during the years just prior to and after World War I. The years preceding the war saw an increasing emphasis on specialization and professionalization, for example.[10] In 1905, Columbia's president inaugurated the "Columbia Plan," which allowed students to pursue work at professional schools after just two years of undergraduate study, a plan that was hotly debated. While "advocates of liberal education saw [the Columbia Plan] as a major step in the wrong direction, some saw this as a visionary accommodation of the needs of students, especially the sons of immigrants, for a more efficient path to professional careers."[11] Here, in essence, we can observe the beginning of the debate I have been tracking between those who see the humanities in ideal terms as fostering general cultural literacy, and those who view higher education as largely vocational training. The Columbia Plan helped shape the curriculum for the university's first general education requirements, inaugurated in the period 1917–1919, which was largely a response to the First World War. During the war Columbia, along with many other universities, implemented a Student Army Training Corps and, along with it, an "Issues of the War" course. This course "rested on the fundamental principle that in the long run man's accomplishment can rise no higher than his ideals, and that an understanding of the worth of the cause for which one is fighting is a powerful weapon in the hands of an intelligent man." It provided practical training in military law, topography, and map-making, but it also mandated distribution requirements in French and German, mathematics, and the study of political issues related to the war.[12] With the end of the war, faculty at Columbia voted in 1919 to replace both the "Issues of the War" course and the required Philosophy A and History A courses with a yearlong Introduction to Contemporary Civilization (CC) course. Why? "With the end of the war," wrote John J. Coss in a 1919 article titled "The New Freshman Course in Columbia College," "the faculty sensed the need for considering the issues of peace and felt that the students should be stimulated to reflection on present-day problems very early in their study" (247–248).[13] This was not a great books course, nor was it designed to introduce students to the history of Western civilization. Its aim was practical, to consider "the problems of the present" and "the issues of our time" (248), to introduce students "to the insistent problems of to-day through acquainting them with the materials of their situation: nature's resources and human nature and its recent history" (248–249). The particular focus of the second semester was on "the recent history of the great nations," a history that is "reviewed in order that the social and political forces operating may be understood."

The early history of Columbia's general education requirements, the precursor to its core curriculum, makes clear that it was based less on a desire to insure students read great books than as a pointed response to the practical, professional needs of students, and as an effort to shape national character and focus on pressing social and political issues. Broadly interdisciplinary and drawing its faculty from history, philosophy, government, economics, and sociology, the Introduction to Contemporary Civilization course was conceived as a kind of modern anatomy of human nature and character. It surveyed types and kinds of human behavior, discussed the roles of instinct and socialization in the development of human character, and explored "man's" need for privacy and solitude. Its discussion of the development of the self focused on individual differences based on race and sex, an inquiry into language and communication, religious experience, art and aesthetic experience, as well as the role of science and the scientific method in understanding human behavior.[14] In 1928 the Contemporary Civilization course became part of a two-course sequence with the addition of CC-B, "Introduction to Contemporary Problems in the United States," which again emphasized the thoroughly practical "question of making a living in the United States." It was not until after the end of the *Second* World War that the Contemporary Civilization A course shifted from its original focus on character toward a historical focus with primary readings in classical works of Western civilization. That year (1946) Columbia issued a new edition of its textbook for the course, an anthology of readings that cut down significantly on introductory essays in order to feature more primary readings. It is only at this point that the course shifted from its earlier focus on human nature and character to a survey of great texts in the Western tradition, with readings that began by exploring classical influences on medieval culture and ran through the Enlightenment (beginning with Plato, Aristotle, and Cicero, and ending with Rousseau, James Madison, and de Condorcet). The reader for Contemporary Civilization B contained selections running from 1861–1954. Described broadly as a reader in "social studies," it contained an ambitious collection of readings in sociology, philosophy, anthropology, and the political and economic sciences running from Dewey and Freud through Sartre.

The core curriculum in the humanities developed separately from, but in tandem with, the Contemporary Civilization sequence. The humanities sequence had its roots in Professor John Erskine's honors literature course, developed in 1920, and in his 1932 "Colloquium on Important Books" (the reading list for which ran only into the nineteenth century).[15] The watershed year for a humanities component in what would become Columbia's core curriculum was 1937 when, under Professor Irwin Edman's direction, Columbia formally inaugurated its humanities sequence as a counterpart to the Contemporary Civilization sequence. This course marked a departure from the practical, vocational orientation of the Columbia Plan and the Introduction to Contemporary Civilization course, for it was explicitly rooted in a great books ideal. Humanities A covered literature and philosophy, while Humanities B focused on music and the visual arts. Humanities A surveyed "classic texts of Western literature and philosophy, spanning from antiquity through the end of the eighteenth century." The required readings for this course, according to a contemporary description, were nothing if not ambitious: "twenty-eight or thirty authors are read in each of the two years...one author in each week."[16] Readings for the Humanities A sequence were chosen from among the *Iliad*; the *Odyssey*; plays by Aeschylus, Sophocles, and Euripides; Plato's *Republic* and the *Symposium*; Vergil's *Aenid*; Dante's *Inferno* and *Vita Nuova*; Rabelais, selections from Cervantes, Hobbes's *Leviathan*; Milton's *Paradise Lost*; plays by Moliere, Goethe's *Faust*; Adam Smith's *Wealth of Nations*; Gibbon's *Decline and Fall*; and novels by Balzac, Stendhal, Dickens, Dostoevsky, and Tolstoy (49). This course was conceived along the curatorial lines we saw Delbanco advocate, and its genesis in Arnold's valuation of the classics is made clear by James Gutmann, a philosophy professor who taught the course when it was founded. While "there is no expectation, no pretense, of doing justice to any of these authors in a week's reading and study," such a course "would do justice to our own sense of educational values by concentrating attention on 'the best that has been thought and said'—some of it, at least, certainly not all" (49). The ideal of canonical coverage clearly trumped the new critical ideal of close reading. It also left no room for historical context or scholarship. "Most of the so-called classics," Gutmann insists, were surely not written for the research of the specialist but for the delight of the cultivated layman without benefit of glossary or lexicon" (50). The ideal for this course, then, was that students would come fresh to great books, and read them very quickly in an unmediated way, directed by faculty often working outside of their fields of specialization. Gutmann rehearses here what we have already seen will become a dominant and recurrent claim in debates about literary studies, the idea that students ought to focus on literature itself without being distracted by historical or critical contextualization, without the so-called professional apparatus that produces disciplinary knowledge.

By 1937 the claim had already come to structure debates about not only literary studies but also the humanities in general.

Lit Hum A put in place all the components of a great books core course, the kind that was emulated in one way or another all over the country from the University of Chicago to St. Johns College. It focuses on canonical primary texts and eschews historical contextualization and all the apparatuses of professional study associated with the disciplines—indeed, it is based on separating disciplinary approaches from simple reading and discussion in just the way the core revision committee at my university wanted us to do. It also follows both the historical coverage model and the pursuit of "literature itself" Graff discusses, emphasizing an engagement with timeless truths and universal meanings at the expense of historical contextualization and formal training in analytical, rhetorical, and interpretive skills. It is, in effect, the baseline from which conservative critics have more recently attacked theory and professionalization and called for a return in the humanities to canonical texts and humanist ideals.

Columbia's format, always somewhat controversial for its looseness, ran into trouble in the early 1960s, and the debate it aroused at that time is worth our pausing over, since it emphasizes the long history and cyclical nature of the arguments about professionalization I have been discussing. In 1962 a committee chaired by history professor Fritz Stern found that the "aims" of the course were not "easily defined" and that the course needed to provide more "context" for students as they read the required texts. This last suggestion proved controversial with both faculty and students, who, in a survey, expressed "no interest in having background readings or critical essays added to their reading list." The case for including critical and interpretive essays in the course was made most forcefully by the eminent literary critic and Columbia professor of English, Lionel Trilling. He insisted at the time "great books do not exist in isolation, but stand in a milieu of the responses that have been given them over the ages."[17] Trilling's intervention on behalf of scholarship and criticism repays review, for it gets at the heart of one of the enduring assertions I have been tracking in this book, the idea that professionalism, with its emphasis on scholarly research, criticism, historical contextualization, methodologies, and theories, gets in the way of students' engagement with the texts they are assigned to read. As we have seen, this argument is not simply used in regard to core courses but has become important in debates about the contemporary fate of literary studies in general. Indeed, all the debates I earlier reviewed about the extent to which theory and criticism distance us from "literature itself" largely rehearse the one the faculty at Columbia wrestled with.

Trilling begins by praising the "very simple" idea behind Lit Hum A, "the belief that no one could be thought educated who was ignorant of the chief works of the intellectual and artistic tradition of his own civilization" (29). The simplicity of this idea, he points out, is "matched by the simplicity of its method...the student was to read the books...but there were to be no 'background' lectures or readings, no 'guides,' either in textbooks or outline forms, no 'secondary material' of any kind" (29).[18] However, Trilling identified two general problems with this method. For one thing, the course had a very long and arduous reading list. How could students comprehend so many books read so quickly, Trilling wondered, books it had taken scholars years to learn (30)? A second problem had to do not with the stamina of students but the qualifications of professors. Trilling pointed out that professors teaching the humanities courses are not specialists in most of the texts they teach in the Lit Hum A course. Given the wide historical range of readings, professors would necessarily have specialized expertise in just a fraction of the texts they were teaching. However, as troubling as he found these two conditions, he was even more disturbed by the exclusion of secondary readings from the course. Indeed, he goes so far as to claim that the lack of critical and historical contextualization for the texts taught in this course produces an *unnatural* situation. "The exclusion of all works of scholarship and criticism, so far from keeping the situation natural, actually seemed to have the contrary effect" (30).

Trilling's invocation of the word "natural" is worth pausing over since it is connected to the distinction I discussed earlier between "literature itself" and literature studied in context, a distinction we have seen is almost always invoked in arguments about the importance of allowing students to have an *unmediated* experience of the texts they read. "Natural" in this context refers to the idea that there can be something like an organic, unmediated, precritical experience of a text, an experience that is nearly instinctual or innate, spontaneous and unaffected. But, as we have already seen, *all* reading is always mediated reading. We cannot help but bring to our experience of literature *prior* experiences of reading, prior forms of contextualizing, and our own trained and untrained assumptions and beliefs. From this point of view—and it seems to me this is what Trilling is getting at—the fantasy or nostalgia for an unmediated, personal, spontaneous experience with a text is a desire for something that is actually unnatural. Our natural engagement with texts is an engagement that is always contextualized and mediated in all kinds of ways. This is why Trilling can argue that sequestering off primary texts from historical contexts and scholarly/critical debate is "unnatural." Texts may be artificially *read* in a vacuum, but they do not naturally *exist* in a vacuum. They are living documents belonging to—indeed, the product of—long historical conversations. To bracket off the conversations is, paradoxically, to de-historicize the texts taught in historical survey courses. The impulse to exclude secondary scholarly and critical readings from a course is, Trilling insists, "the impulse to deny, at least in some measure, the historicity of the books we read" (31). The problem with trying to preserve a fantasy of purity in our engagement with texts is that it aims for a kind of innocence that borders for Trilling on "passivity": "What we mean by a fresh innocence is often a bland passivity, and if it is, then how fortunate the fall from that Eden" that comes with reading scholarship and criticism (31). Recent calls for a return to close reading (which I will take up in more detail in the chapter 5), and for a return to "literature itself," all tend to be based on what Trilling rightly calls this desire for something unnatural: the text itself, pure and unmediated.

The mistake here is to think of scholarship and criticism narrowly in terms of sheerly professional practices and then to banish them from a core education because they're exclusively professional. They are not. They are *core practices* central to knowledge production and ought to be central to undergraduate, as well as graduate education. It is important, as well, to recognize that reading texts for their so-called universal or timeless significance runs the risk of dehistoricizing them. Artificially bracketing off the historicity of the books we read is always the danger in any course in which the readings are chosen because they are thought to have withstood the test of time. Trilling points out that any literature course, indeed, any humanities course, has to balance two competing propositions about human nature:

> In the study of any literature of the past there are two propositions that must be given equal weight. One is that human nature is always the same. The other is that human nature changes, sometimes radically, with each historical epoch. The great charm—and one chief educative value—of reading works of the past lies in perceiving the truth of the two contradictory propositions and in seeing the sameness in the difference and the difference in the sameness. (31)

The "human nature is always the same" position is metaphysical and idealist, committed to the humanist ideal that there are fixed, timeless, innate qualities that define us as human. The "human nature changes" position is obviously a historicist one, committed to the idea that what we call human nature is not fixed but fluid, what we now would call socially and historically constructed, a set of characteristics that change over time. The idea of a canon, especially one based on the belief there are a set of great books in the Western tradition that have stood the test of time, that they contain universal truths that transcend their author's time and place, is of course rooted in the first approach to human nature. So it is hardly surprising that, as Trilling puts it, "in the interest of asserting the 'eternality' of certain 'values,' we inclined to reduce the actuality of history" (31). Excluding "all scholarly or critical considerations of our books" precludes the ability to explore the "historicity of what we were dealing with" (31). Such exclusions are unnatural because they attempt to engineer some kind of illusory "purity" in a reader's relationship to texts. By "excluding all scholarship and criticism from our courses" we "pretend that our great books existed in circumstances which were quite contrary to the fact. The great books do not have their being...in splendid classic isolation or only in a kind of royal relation to each other. They exist in the lively *milieu* that is created by the responses that have long been given to them...Some part of their reality consists in the way they have figured in the life of the world, certainly in the intellectual life of the world, a large part of which is contained by what has been said about them" (31).

The case Trilling is making here for the place of scholarship and criticism in Columbia's humanities core also works as a more general argument against those who would impose restrictions on theory, criticism, disciplinary methodologies, and research as elements of an undergraduate humanities education in general. Trilling intervenes before the fact in current complaints that professionalism has ruined literary studies and that we need to return to unmediated, de-professionalized, precritical, ahistorical forms of engagement with literature itself, forms of engagement that are not theorized. He not only makes a case here for the important role of scholarship and criticism but a case as well for what Graff would later call teaching the conflicts, for the kind of course Trilling is advocating is one in which the professor and his or her students are positioned to analyze the conflict between seeing human nature as fixed and seeing it as socially constructed, and the conflict between the imperative to study texts out of historical and critical context and studying them within that context. As Trilling saw, the ability to teach students about such fundamental conflicts and work through what is at stake in them is short-circuited, even prevented, by excluding historical and critical readings from humanities courses.

At nearly the same time as Trilling and the Stern commission questioned the shape of the Humanities A course a report was issued calling for the suspension of the Contemporary Civilization sequence. Here, again, the issues were specialization, professionalization, and the tension between disciplinary and general education requirements. Written by David Truman, appointed by Columbia's president to review the sequence, the report focused on critical staffing problems but also found that with "increased specialization in the social sciences...student interest" had turned to "studying in specific departments." While the courses were not suspended, they became electives in 1961. *The New York Times* actually treated the proposed suspension as a watershed moment in the history of general education requirements.[19] Their article on the proposal pointed out that Columbia had "pioneered in the general education field." "Since the early Nineteen Twenties," the article began, "general education in the college has been considered the all-American road to the all-around man. Different colleges have mapped out that road in different fashion, but all had in common the aim to pull together the scattered areas of knowledge and to try to make Western civilization emerge as a comprehensible idea." The general education movement, the article pointed out, "was a true revolution. It was the reaction to the earlier extreme elective system, itself associated originally with Harvard, descended from the German universities and then considered a triumph of academic freedom." According to the *Times*, any change that would focus on contemporary issues and problems "runs aground on the lack of contemporary unity" about what the key contemporary problems *are*. Where the CC-A courses "deal with the classical unity of the Western tradition," the attempt to incorporate the "truly contemporary" challenges that unity. And "laissez faire led to an excessive specialization. The general or liberal education movement was an attempt to pick up the pieces and recreate the Renaissance Man during the undergraduate years."

This article captures the deep structure of debates about core requirements as they have reverberated into the present: general education provides a way to unify the undergraduate educational experience, whether around war issues, peace issues, the nature of human character and behavior, or around great books. However, emphasis on disciplinary knowledge fractures that unity with its emphasis on specialization and professionalization. The *Times* article frankly positions the general education model at Columbia as a kind of rear guard action to keep humanism alive in an age of increasing professionalization by attempting to recreate "Renaissance man." Specialization, professionalization, and a focus on the contemporary are perceived as disrupting the kind of cultural unity a great books course can ostensibly provide. The "unity" lent to the CC-A by the classics, the *Times* article insists, was systematically undermined by the inclusion of the "truly contemporary," a problem exacerbated by a lack of consensus among the disciplines about which contemporary problems are worth studying in the first place. Moreover, according to the article, the disciplines are "increasingly divided from one another by the jargon, training, and thought of their specialized disciplines."[20] It is striking how consistent the educational issues here are, whether we are looking at 1919, 1961, or 2011. Higher education has to continually mediate between professionalization, vocational training, and practical value, on the one hand, and the more abstract ideals of a humanistic education, on the other, ideals that eschew professionalization and anything that smacks of vocational utility. As the disciplines become increasingly important over the course of the century, characterized as they are by specific theoretical, methodological, and analytical protocols, they come to represent a threat to the ideal of a general education, one that has to continually balance what Delbanco identified as the curatorial and critical functions of higher education. The more the curatorial function is emphasized, the less rigor humanities core courses seem to have, and the more they take time away from specialized training. And, conversely, the more time is devoted to specialized training and contemporary issues, the less time is available for general education, with its ostensible focus on cultural literacy and timeless ideals. The more time students are required to spend with classics, deemed valuable because they transcend their historical time and place, the less time they have for contemporary texts and issues—and vice versa.

The problem of the contemporary for the Columbia core came to the fore in the mid-1960s in terms of the persistent question of what to do with the twentieth century. This was a central issue raised by the eminent sociologist, Daniel Bell, in a report commissioned by Columbia's president in 1966 titled "The Reforming of General Education: The Columbia College Experience in its National Setting." Bell's report ironically brings us full circle back to the founding of the Introduction to Civilization course with its focus on the present and on exploring and dealing with contemporary problems specific to the immediate years after World War I. Bell underscores how dramatically the Contemporary Civilization courses has drifted *away* from this engagement with the present, for his report argues that the "present" confronts students with "new and distinctive" challenges that bring "the old practices of general education at Columbia [and by implication at a host of other colleges and universities that had followed Columbia] into question." Professionalization, as it was way back in 1905, is the culprit once again, for one of the key changes Bell cites has to do with the number of students at Columbia who now move on to graduate school. Where in the 1930s only a small number of Columbia undergraduate students proceeded to graduate school, "the reverse is true today." Bell reports that the graduate school "has...encouraged the trend toward intensive specialization in the undergraduate colleges. It has drained away teachers from the colleges and reinforced a status distinction between those who teach in the graduate school and those who teach only in the college."[21] But there was another problem as well, one that has to do with the Western civilization focus of general education requirements at a time in which what we now call globalization was beginning to accelerate. America's new position as a world power, Bell observed, "has made us sharply aware of non-Western societies and cultures. The emergence of half a hundred new states has enlarged our area of political and intellectual inquiry and created a vast new 'laboratory' for the comparative study of nation-building, economic and political development, rapid social and psychological change, and the like." The accelerating centrality of science and technology in higher education had converged with the pressing needs of the cold war to cement "the relationship between the government and the intellectuals," a relationship that "is now clearly permanent." In addition, increasing specialization has led to the development of "sub-specializations and fields" that have "multiplied the number of subjects a university is now called upon to teach" (he cites, among other things, game theory, cybernetics, and information theory). Where formerly the "chief function" of the university was "that of conserving and transmitting the intellectual traditions and cultural values of society," now, with the rise of new "intellectual technologies...the university serves more as the center for research and innovation. Though the university once reflected the status system of the society it now determines status." While in earlier decades of the twentieth century the university seemed to serve its students, "more so than ever before in American life, the university has become a public service institution," used by "government, industry, and the local communities."[22]

All of these changes, of course, represent what has turned out to be the inexorable corporatization of higher education, changes that put the squeeze on the humanities. Indeed, Bell's report was criticized in some quarters for seeming to value the sciences over the humanities. Most of the developments Bell touches on *are* related to science and technology, which is where the forms of professionalization he cites, are taking place. However, Bell's report does touch on the humanities, and in a way that takes Trilling's side when it comes to the question of the intellectual rigor of the Lit Hum course and its exclusion of secondary critical readings. Bell writes in his report that the Lit Hum course undeniably presents students with "a set of great works," but he wonders, "read for what purpose?" He cites the previous review done by the Stern committee, which stated, "it may be considered significant that we found it difficult to define the philosophical or pedagogic ends of the course." In Bell's view, the problem has do with the course's exclusive focus on the student's "own immediate response, emotionally and intellectually," to the assigned works. What they miss, and what would give the course the pedagogic focus Stern's review found lacking, is giving something like equal weight to how "the same work has evoked successively different styles of self-consciousness," making students "aware...of the *scholarly context* in which it arose, not only of his own sensibility" but the sensibility of other key figures who have read and commented on the work in question (emphasis mine). This is precisely what Trilling said was missing in the Lit Hum course, how "literature is embedded in history," how the "meaning of the work itself changes when we view it in relation to other works and to the social situation in which it first appeared."[23] Bell agrees tacitly with Trilling that this is the way to introduce what is missing into both the Humanities and Contemporary Civilization courses: "intellectual sophistication."[24]

Importantly, Bell's report ties this kind of sophistication to disciplinary knowledge and the methods that facilitate its production, a form of rigor that we have observed has always seemed to be at odds with the cross-disciplinary, synthetic, "great ideas" orientation of a core curriculum, and anathema to traditional critics who see professional methodologies, protocols of research, and theories as a threat to a general humanities education. Bell would like to find a way to reconcile these traditional aims with the growing emphasis on specialized disciplinary knowledge grounded in professional training. "Mastering a discipline," Bell insists, is "the heart of a college education today" and that means learning a "method of analysis and a logical framework of concepts at high levels of generality, and, indeed, of abstraction." The emphasis here on analytical methods, general concepts, and abstract thinking recalls Perloff's argument that a core education at the end of the twentieth century ought to have as much to do with fostering practical analytical skills as making sure students have broad knowledge of classical and canonical texts. Like Trilling's, Bell's conception of a revised core would emphasize the social, cultural, and institutional contexts for the production of knowledge rather than the knowledge itself arbitrarily cut loose from that context, one that would demonstrate how a discipline "acquires, utilizes, and revises its basic concepts," and how those concepts are in turn applied to "different subject matters" within and outside its field.

Nearly all of the questions raised by my department's inclusion of Gloria Anzaldúa's name in the preamble to our foundational core course proposal register in Bell's report. Most of them are telescoped into the question of what to do with the twentieth century, for it is the inclusion of the contemporary that disrupts what both the Bell and Truman reports see as the kind of unity the Contemporary Civilization courses created, and, by extension, the Lit Hum course as well, based as it was on the unity of a timeless tradition of great books.[25] For a focus on the twentieth century requires not only attention to the contemporary moment, but a focus on non-Western cultures and histories as well, all of which portends the inevitable complicating or even dismantling of the very Eurocentricity that gave these courses their coherence in the first place. When my university's core revision committee balked at the inclusion of Anzaldúa's name in the preamble to our course description, they were balking at including just the kinds of changes Bell enumerates: the incorporation of the twentieth century, a broadening of the geographic and cultural scope of our reading lists, and the way in which attention to the contemporary problems Anzaldúa's text deals with complicates the classical unity of a great books core course. Likewise, when they insisted our foundational course should focus solely on great works and eschew the methodologies and issues related to faculty areas of specialization, it evinced the same kind of wariness about professionalization that has made the humanities a paradox for nearly a century—an academic area in which too much academic rigor undermines traditional humanistic ideals, and too little makes its academic value suspect.

Bell's recommendations received a mixed reception and had little impact on the direction of core education at Columbia. In response to persistent complaints that core requirements had proliferated and become a burden for students, there was a proposal in 1968 to make the core elective, but the faculty voted it down. In 1988 the program's designation as a "general education requirement" was formally changed to a "core curriculum," and a standing committee on the core was established to oversee it. In an ongoing effort to give core education a more transnational orientation, a requirement was added in 1990 that students take courses in cultures not covered in the Cultures and Civilization course and Lit Hum (the requirement was called "The Extended Core"), and later revisions turned this into a "Major Cultures" requirement (Asian, African, Latin American, Native American). In terms of revising and updating the core at Columbia, that is about it.

Indeed, looking at the 2011 core curriculum at Columbia it is remarkable how much the great books orientation associated with the original Lit Hum course has endured.[26] According to the current Columbia website, the core is still based on a set of common courses required of all undergraduates irrespective of their major. The emphasis is on "communal learning—with all students encountering the same texts and issues at the same time." Courses continue to focus on a set of general questions that have their roots in earlier iterations of the core but which also respond to controversy and calls for change: "What does it mean, and what has it meant to be an individual? What does it mean, and what has it meant to be part of a community? How is human experience relayed and how is meaning made in music and art? What do we think is, and what have we thought to be worth knowing? By what rules should we be governed? The habits of mind developed in the Core cultivate a critical and creative intellectual capacity that students employ long after college, in the pursuit and the fulfillment of meaningful lives." Along with the long-standing, traditional emphasis on what it means to be a human individual, what is worth knowing, what rules and habits should govern our behavior, what makes for a meaningful life, there is an emphasis as well on *how* information is produced and transmitted, and how societies determine what is worth knowing, a cluster of questions that clearly seek to address the criticisms Trilling and Bell put forward in the 1960s.

However, when one looks at the current syllabus for the Literature and Humanities core courses it is striking how resistant to change they seem to be. They are both overwhelmingly organized around classical and canonical texts by male writers read without the kind of critical, historical, or disciplinary contextualization Trilling and Bell called for. And while we have noted there were recurrent complaints as early as the 1960s that the core did not have enough of a transnational context, it remains almost exclusively Western. Finally, although we have seen that the core's lack of engagement with modern and contemporary history and culture has been an ongoing controversy, the Lit

Hum course in particular contains only one (one!) twentieth-century writer, Virginia Woolf. Let's take a closer look at the reading lists for both the Lit Hum and Contemporary Civilization courses. The fall Contemporary Civilization reading list is almost uniformly classical and canonical, and might (with the exception of *The Meaning of the Holy Qur'an*) have been drawn up in 1919, the year of the course's founding. Students begin with Plato's *Republic*, move on through Aristotle to the *Holy Bible* and then Augustine, Machiavelli, Descartes, Hobbes, and Locke. The spring reading list picks up with Rousseau, Adam Smith, Hume, Kant, and Burke, and moves on to Wollstonecraft, Tocqueville, Hegel, Mill, Marx, Darwin, Nietzsche, Du Bois, Freud, and Woolf (*Three Guineas*). The Lit Hum course is now organized as a course on "Masterpieces of Western Literature and Philosophy." The fall reading list begins with the *Iliad*, the *Odyssey*, Aeschylus, Sophocles, Thucydides, Aristophanes, and Plato, and concludes with books from the *Holy Bible* (Genesis, Job, Luke, and John). The spring course begins with the *Aenid*, Ovid's *Metamorphoses*, and then moves on to Augustine, Dante, Boccaccio, Montaigne, Shakespeare, and Cervantes. Later comes Austen (*Pride and Prejudice*), Dostoevsky (*Crime and Punishment*) and, once again, Woolf, the only twentieth-century writer deemed appropriate for *either one* of the Contemporary Civilizations or Lit Hum course (*To the Lighthouse*).[27]

A few things are worth noting here. First of all, these are about as close to "great books" courses as one could get without enrolling at St. Johns. These are what I earlier called "author-centric" courses organized around the necessarily quick reading of great books in the Western tradition (without secondary historical or critical readings), with a heavy emphasis on the classics. What is particularly striking, as I noted above, is the absence of depth and breadth in the modern and contemporary periods. *In the four courses combined two writers, Virginia Woolf and Sigmund Freud, represent the whole of the twentieth century.* That's it, Woolf and Freud. There seems to be an odd definition of "contemporary" informing the Contemporary Civilization courses, with nothing worth reading after Freud. Nothing is required from the fields of anthropology or sociology, no exploration of phenomenology, existentialism, or structuralism. Nothing related to the modern Women's movement or the Civil Rights movement. And all of the efforts to give this course more geographical and cultural breadth seem to have been for naught. Students in the Contemporary Civilization course are required to read a commentary on the Qur'an, but that is it. There is nothing requiring them to engage with the histories and cultures of the two emerging economic powers of the twenty-first century, China and India. No Confucius, no *Ramayana*, no *Mahabharata*, and no Gandhi. And nothing related to Africa at all, from the slave trade to Nelson Mandela.

The same things are true of the Lit Hum course, as well (now called "Masterpieces of Western Literature and Philosophy"). Students do not get beyond the classics until they are a third of the way through the second semester, and then there are only five writers who come after Shakespeare: Cervantes, Goethe, Austen, Dostoevsky, and Woolf. The novel exploded in the nineteenth century yet only Austen and Dostoevsky represent it. There are, in this core course offered at one of America's premier universities, no American writers at all. No Emerson, no Hawthorne, no Whitman, no Dickinson, no Twain. And of course there are no twentieth-century American writers on the list because, with the exception of Woolf (carried over from the CC course) there are no twentieth-century writers *at all* on the list. No modernism, no Eliot, Pound, Williams, Stevens, Faulkner, Auden, Hemingway, Fitzgerald, and of course, no postmodernism. And while arguably the most significant development in literary culture of the second half of the twentieth century was the explosion of literature by African, Asian, Hispanic, and Native American writers, none are included in the syllabus. When it comes to geographical scope, the Lit Hum course has the limited scope as the Contemporary Civilization course, sticking to a Western tradition: no literature from or engaged with Africa, India, Asia, or countries in the Americas outside the United States.

The paradox here is that these courses are designed to prepare students for citizenship in the twenty-first century, yet they contain no texts that deal with the history, or the social, cultural, and political problems of their own time or even the time of their parents, or, in many cases, their *grandparents*. The rationale for these reading lists, of course, is that students should be exposed to the best that has been thought and said by the great writers of the Western tradition because what they have to say speaks across the ages to the problems of our own time. But why not read authors who actually *do* speak directly to the issues of our own time? These courses smack too much of trying to play an academic game: let's see what we can learn about our own time by *not* reading texts from our own time but seeing how we can extrapolate from ancient texts lessons for our own time instead. The desire to make sure students read a selection of great works actually trumps the desire to shape a curriculum around texts from a range of periods, cultures, and writers that engage in a historical *and* contemporary way the issues students have to face.

The near absence of twentieth-century readings, and their lack of geographical and cultural scope, guarantees the absence of a context for dealing with the challenges of living in an increasingly multicultural nation, and a rapidly globalizing world. The emphasis here is on requiring students to gain a necessarily superficial acquaintance with classical and canonical texts from Western civilization at the expense of engaging with texts from the twentieth and twenty-first centuries that are specifically engaged with the geographical, cultural, social, and political realities of the world in which they actually live, which explore a range of important, even revolutionary aesthetic styles, and which have challenged humanism to expand and rethink many of its ideals. What is even worse, the general description of the Contemporary Civilizations course, which says it is aimed at introducing students to "a range of issues concerning the kinds of communities—political, social, moral, and religious—that human beings construct for themselves and the values that inform and define such communities," runs the risk of conflating specifically Western issues, communities, and human beings with some universal representation of the human. Ironically, what is missing is the kind of focus we have seen was at the center of the *original* Introduction to Contemporary Civilization course offered in 1919, a course that, as Cross put it at the time, was based on the belief "students should be stimulated to reflection on present-day problems very early in their study," a course that dealt explicitly, rather than obliquely through a historical lens, with "the problems of the present" and "the issues of our time."[28] One has to look no further for a pedagogical approach to the humanities that foregrounds its practical value, based on its relationship to an inquiry into actual human concerns in our own time.

How do you add all of this to core courses like the ones at Columbia and still find time for students to read the classics? You don't. It seems to me that if, as I have been arguing, the humanities need to do a better job stressing the practical utility of the educational experience they provide then it ought to be along the lines of Columbia's 1919 vision, not its twenty-first century vision. Whether we are talking about a core curriculum, or about general education requirements, any set of humanities requirements ought to demonstrate concrete learning outcomes that support the needs of students living in a dramatically multicultural United States and a rapidly globalizing world. The key question ought to be: What can an education in the humanities in particular offer these students that they cannot get in the natural and social sciences? It seems to me that this question can be answered in a number of concrete ways. First of all, the humanities can offer students engagement with a diverse range of *aesthetic* materials, works of art that can surprise and move them through lyrical language, drama, and the experience of sheerly formal beauty played out across a variety of times and cultures. Students cannot nurture these crucial—and uniquely human—capabilities in any other set of disciplines. The quality of the mind's engagement with art, philosophy, and religion is fundamentally unlike the quality of the mind's engagement with the materials students encounter in the natural and social sciences, as exciting and even moving as their engagement with those materials may be. The humanities can shift their attention from quantification, measurement, calculation, and formulas to affect, interpretation, ethical and moral thinking, dramatic representation, and the kinds of emotional and intellectual experiences they shape. It is important, in this context, to underscore the extent to which the literary and visual arts in particular engage the emotions as well as the minds of readers and viewers, but it is even more important to stress the *intersection* of the emotional and the intellectual that characterizes our engagement with art, philosophy, and religion, for it is this intersection that is so pronounced and therefore peculiar to the disciplines that comprise the humanities. The personal, social, cultural, and political issues creative writers grapple with are of course fundamental to our interest in reading literature or engaging the visual arts in the first place, but we can engage all of these issues in the social science classroom. What is unique about literature—and by extension, each of the creative arts—is that it treats social and cultural issues in a *literary* way, which is to say, refracted through all of the linguistic, dramatic, and narrative devices at the disposal of poets, dramatists, and novelists. If we simply focus on the issues, the subject matter, then we run the danger of reducing literature to something like sociology or politics. There's nothing wrong with either, but in doing so we lose the uniqueness of the literary. However, if we focus only on the aesthetic dimension of literature or visual art—its formal, linguistic, and aesthetic qualities—without studying the work of art's engagement with issues of historical import at the time of its writing and of interest to us in our own, then we are also missing what is unique about these works, their treatment of personal, social, cultural, and political issues in a specifically artistic way.

Because subject matter and aesthetic form are complexly linked in this way we must pay balanced attention to both, which means that students in core courses need to learn a critical vocabulary and become adept at applying analytical and interpretive methodologies in their analyses of how texts operate in a particularly literary way to engage us intellectually and emotionally (the same holds in pretty much the same way or the fine arts and even philosophy and history). The kinds of courses I have been discussing associated with the Columbia core, which require superficial quick reading and therefore sacrifice close attention to textual detail and historical context, simply cannot accomplish this. This is why Trilling and Bell were correct in calling for a more rigorous historical and critical perspective in the courses they wrote about. Students need to pay attention to the sheerly literary qualities of the texts they read, but they should not be required to read them shorn of their historical or critical context. Indeed, they should be required to understand the difference between reading a text out of context and studying it *with* knowledge of historical context and some familiarity with critical debates in mind, not because they need to be professionalized but because they need to learn how to read in an active and engaged way. More than that, they need to learn how to *study,* not just be made to read, the texts they are assigned. For the same reasons, students should be required to learn different ways of interpreting the texts they study. They should be able to not only analyze the linguistic and formal properties of a text but to interpret its meaning in a variety of ways, not just in terms of their own personal responses but in ways that are related to social, cultural, and political approaches. Only in this way will they see that reading is always an *interpretive* process, that any kind of text from any period can be analyzed, for example, in terms of its representation of the relationship between gender and power, how class operates to legitimize some ideologies and stigmatize others, or to facilitate the agency of some and circumscribe the agency of others, how romantic or social relations are determined by cultural norms, or what role the writer's biography might play in shaping our sense of the meaning of a text.

It is striking how this century-long debate between reading texts without reference to historical and critical context, and reading them framed by such contexts, continues to shape arguments about a humanities education. As we shall see in the next chapter, these two positions have deeply influenced current arguments about the direction my own field, literary studies, ought to take in the twenty-first century. In reviewing this debate in my next chapter, I want to take a closer look at the claims made for redirecting the study of literature to its aesthetic and formal properties rooted in practices of "close reading" that ostensibly protect texts from the distortions introduced by historical, cultural, and ideological forms of criticism. I will be arguing that while paying attention to the aesthetic and formal properties of literary texts is crucial, and that close and careful reading is essential to any critical practice, the idea that doing so will give students access to literature itself and foster precritical reading is misguided. Indeed, I will be demonstrating that the best new work on aesthetic and formalist approaches to textual analysis, and to close reading, actually serves to underscore literature's inextricable connection to broader social, cultural, and political forces. Often aimed at saving literature from cultural and historical studies, the new aesthetics and a renewed attention to close reading actually serve to reinforce the relationship between literary and cultural studies.

Chapter 5

Aesthetics, Close Reading, Theory, and the Future of Literary Studies

We have seen throughout this book that a kind of "back to basics" mentality tends to set in whenever the humanities seem to be in crisis. Whether we have been looking at general debates about the value of the humanities, arguments about revising core curricula, or narrower debates about how disciplines such as literary studies ought to respond to theoretical and methodological innovation, we have repeatedly encountered the idea that the humanities are in crisis because they have strayed from their traditional, basic mission. And it is almost always professionalization, with its theories, methods, and esoteric areas of specialization that is the culprit. I want to look more closely in this chapter at how a rhetoric of return has structured recent debates about the future of literary studies. What we will see is a kind of mirror image of the larger humanities crisis we have been tracing. In literary studies, the "back to basics" argument goes something like this: Literary studies went off the rails when it stopped caring about literature and became preoccupied instead with a variety of ways to contextualize it. The obfuscating jargon of theory has replaced an appreciation of the beauty of literary language, and the tendency to read literary texts as containing bad ideologies that have to be ritually corrected in front of students has turned the literature classroom into a space for political proselytizing. The antidote is a return to fundamentals: close reading and the analysis and appreciation of literature's aesthetic and formal qualities. Such a return promises to restore literature itself to the center of literary studies, and it will have the salutary effect as well of depoliticizing the field.

Let's take a closer look at this argument in order to see what is wrong with it. The argument in favor of a narrowly aesthetic approach to literary study, of course, is that literature is first-and-foremost an artistic object with particular formal qualities. Thus, the study of literature should focus on these elements and not get distracted by the imposition of interpretive frameworks that too often distort the literary text itself in the interests of using it to grind an ideological axe in favor of feminism, multiculturalism, social justice, or to fight racism or the remnants of colonialism. This argument is neatly encapsulated in the title of Stanley Fish's provocative book, *Save the World on Your Own Time* (2008), which argues professors have but two jobs: to impart knowledge to students in the area of their academic expertise, and to teach them a set of analytical skills. Not only should professors avoid overtly politicizing the classroom, they should even avoid trying to make students into good citizens, moral actors, or enlist them in the fight against racism or sexism. For Fish, the job of the literature professor is essentially to teach literature itself. And what better way to return literary study to literature itself, and to protect it from becoming a pretext for saving the world, than by focusing on its sheerly aesthetic and formal structures? Such an approach would focus literary study on the formal object of the artistic text itself. At the same time, it would seem to inoculate both classroom teaching and literary criticism from politicization, for what could possibly be political about the form of a sonnet or the application of objective standards of beauty or the identification of the sublime in a romantic poem? And while such forms of criticism do not do away completely with professionalization, they dramatically restrict the professional theories and methods critics in and out of the classroom would use. Such a move would also have the salutary effect of enforcing disciplinary boundaries, for a study of literature organized around its aesthetic qualities and forms should prevent the discipline from becoming the locus for generalized and highly theorized forms of social, cultural, and political analysis.

This kind of return to aesthetic and formal approaches to the study of literature has almost always been presented as a correction to the politicizing of literary studies. Linked to an emphasis on forms of reading that avoid producing symptomatic interpretations of literary texts (interpretations that assume novels and poems have a hidden political unconscious or ideology it is the job of the critic to reveal), these approaches are meant to blunt the collective effects of theory, cultural studies, and all forms of historicism, both new and old.[1] Cultural studies, we shall see, is a particularly popular culprit, and not just in literary studies but in history, sociology, and the fine arts as well. According to its critics, cultural studies, by subordinating literature (or art) to the larger category of culture, and by opening literary studies to a broad examination of other cultural media—film, television, advertising, fashion, digital media, etc.—has had the paradoxical effect of marginalizing literature as the key object of knowledge in literary studies. At the same time, the recent focus on studying the historical, cultural, and political contexts of literary texts has produced overtly politicized interpretations that have distracted attention from literature itself as embodied in its aesthetic, formal, and linguistic characteristics. The argument here is that because critics have become preoccupied with the historical contextualization of literary texts, and the relative role they play among a wide range of cultural media, cultural studies have effectively taken over and marginalized literary studies. In so doing, a cultural or historical approach robs literature of the very universality and timelessness traditional humanists associate with the texts they teach. If the best literature transcends its time and place to speak across the ages to the universality of human experience, then it would seem counterproductive to insist on studying literature in the context of the time and place of its production. With culture and history replacing literature as the key objects of knowledge in literary studies, the renewed emphasis on the aesthetic and formal qualities of literary texts aims to resituate literature itself at the center of literary studies, reaffirming the very qualities that help it transcend its historical and cultural boundaries, and providing renewed coherence for a field that many argue has become fragmented.

This prescription for how to liberate literary studies from cultural studies and forms of symptomatic reading might make superficial sense to those who find it appealing, but it doesn't work. As we shall see in what follows, the contemporary shift to an aesthetic or formalist paradigm for literary studies, allied with close reading, almost always fails to provide a narrowly *literary* coherence for literary studies. Indeed, as we shall see in a moment, there is a deep irony running through much of this new work. While it calls for a renewed focus on the aesthetic, much of it actually ends up underscoring the arbitrary nature of limiting categories such as the aesthetic and form to literature itself. For it turns out that these categories, far from returning literary studies to literature, actually take critics outside literature to a range of other discourses that are illuminated by these categories and practices, resituating the study of the aesthetic within a larger, interdisciplinary humanities framework. The same happens with renewed attention to close reading. Why? Because while you can limit yourself, if you like, to a narrow study of the aesthetic and formal qualities of literary works, you cannot study things such as the aesthetic, narrative, form, or reading per se without looking at how they function not only in—and with respect to—other media, but in everyday experience as well. Aesthetics, formalism, and close reading, far from being a path back to literature itself, lead inevitably to resituating literature in the larger matrix of cultural and social processes.

We can observe how this happens by comparing an early call for literary studies to eschew theory and political correctness and return to aesthetics, George Levine's Introduction to the 1994 anthology he edited, *Aesthetics and Ideology*, with the work of two critics of the aesthetic who came after him, Isobel Armstrong and Sianne Ngai. Levine insists aesthetic criticism is a path back to literature itself, one that will restore the dignity of literature and protect it from the kind of ideological criticism he associates with cultural studies. Armstrong and Ngai, however, extending the logic of Levine's argument just a few years later (Armstrong in her 2000 book, *The Radical Aesthetic*, and Ngai in her 2007 book, *Ugly Feelings*), find that a return to aesthetic criticism actually requires a wholesale rethinking of aesthetic theory, one that takes them back through literature to the role of the aesthetic in everyday life. Levine's plea for renewed attention to aesthetics reflects a kind of standard line about the need for a corrective to the politicization of literary studies widely criticized by conservative critics in the late 1980s and early 1990s. His argument is rooted in the familiar concern that "theory" has led to the displacing of literature by "ideology" (1), since ideological criticism shifts attention from the artistic elements of the text itself and how it operates to "questions about the systems that contain them, about material conditions," about "mediation, discourse" (2). This has lead, in his view, to a "resistance to the idea of literary value" and of "literary greatness" altogether (2). Theory's determination that "all things are political" means that "literary study is primarily political," leading to a situation in which "the study of literature is not an adequately serious or important vocation" (2).

Anyone who has read this far in my book will find this an altogether familiar—even formulaic—critique of contemporary literary study, and indeed, of the humanities in general. According to Levine, there is literature itself over here, and the world of history and politics over there, and we confuse the two at our peril. Literary texts are works of art containing a certain set of identifiable aesthetic, formal, linguistic, and structural properties. These properties ought to constitute the proper domain of literary studies. A truly rigorous approach to literary study, therefore, can only proceed if we pay scrupulous attention to these properties and do not go outside of the text in ways that subordinate it to historical, social, cultural, or ideological subjects.[2] One thing that particularly worries Levine about ideological analyses of literary works is that they don't pay due *deference* to their greatness *as* literary works, concerned as they are with demonstrating how literary works embody and circulate dominant or repressive ideologies. The problem with literary studies in the 1990s, according to Levine, is largely a problem of prestige. Literature has not only lost its place as the center of literary studies. It has lost its aura of greatness. "What I am attempting," he writes, "is movement toward a climate of opinion that will not identify deference to the text and admiration of it with political complicity, will not assume that the text is a kind of enemy to be arrested, will not inevitably associate the 'literary' with a reactionary right, or dismiss the aesthetic as a strategy of mystification of the status quo" (3). Levine insists that a return to the aesthetic is the best way to recapture this lost prestige. Literary works should not, he insists, be judged good or evil depending upon which ideological positions they seem to support but ought to be appreciated for their artistic merit, something that in his most extreme moments Levine claims ought to put them outside or above criticism.

One of the key problems for Levine is that in his view ideological criticism privileges the critic over the literary text he or she is analyzing. "In discovering the complicity of texts with an ideology they never formally articulate," Levine writes, "critics tend to assume that they are smarter and more honest than the writers, who either didn't know what they were doing or, worse, thought they could get away with their devious moves" (3). In Levine's view, this form of criticism distracts the critic from his or her primary responsibility: to pay deference to the text and to demonstrate why it is great. Never mind that *The Merchant of Venice* may traffic in forms of anti-Semitism or that Hawthorne's "The Birth-Mark" seems to miss the extent to which its sympathetic treatment of masculine striving for scientific power is achieved at the cost of a complex kind of misogyny. Our primary responsibility as readers, teachers, or critics is to pay deference to, and admire their sheerly aesthetic quality, not to think critically about the ideologies they may contain. This way of thinking about the critic or teacher's responsibility takes for granted a whole set of clichés about literary study that we have already seen simply do not stand up to scrutiny. It tends to take an either/or approach, setting the aesthetic qualities of literary texts over-against their social, cultural, and historical contexts when in fact aesthetic quality itself is determined by those contexts. It also seeks to privilege a veneration of the ostensibly universal, timeless qualities of literary works over an exploration of the social ideologies they embody. Criticism ends up being a threat to the prestige of the literary work and thus undermines the deference and admiration we ought to feel toward it. Although Levine would cringe at the comparison, it is broadly consistent not only with the positions taken by Roger Kimball, Lynne Cheney, and William Bennett during the culture wars, it also reflects the distinction we saw Andrew Delbanco make between curation and criticism, in which the critic's responsibility to preserve and display literary art trumped criticism of that art. More often than not, as we have seen, such calls tend to demonize so-called professional approaches to literary criticism for making literary studies overly technical, alienating us from the emotional pleasures of literary experience.

This leads to what I believe is a particularly misguided claim, that theory and professionalization end up alienating both faculty and students from the pleasures associated with reading literature:

> Most of the readers of this book probably starting early in their lives, will have had extraordinary moments reading a novel or a poem, listening to music, looking at a painting, gazing out at a landscape—moments when they have felt overwhelmed, perhaps on the verge of tears, the whole body thrillingly tensed. Such moments have led many to careers in the arts or in criticism, in which the almost mindless physicality of that engagement with what might be called the beautiful or the sublime has been displaced by professional strategies of unsentimental analysis, demystification and historical contextualization, and the discovery that the very "experience" was probably invented in the eighteenth century with the development of the idea of the aesthetic. (4)

Here the aesthetic is contrasted with the ideological in a scenario in which the truly literary is associated with a kind of preprofessional, purely sensual, and largely emotional response to literature. From this point of view professional approaches to criticism actually undermine what should essentially be an aesthetic experience, primary and mystical because it is rooted in the "mindless physicality" of our engagement with the two most prominent categories in the history of aesthetic theory: the beautiful and the sublime. The problem with professional forms of criticism, according to Levine, is that they always threaten to undermine or ignore this kind of primal connection. "The value" of such aesthetic experience is "dismissed or minimized or sufficiently historicized that it has lost, for those whose careers have been shaped by it, precisely the power it had to initiate careers" (4). This is a stunningly presumptuous claim. Levine seems incapable of conceiving that trained critics can still be capable of experiencing pleasure when they read, or that the pleasure one experiences in reading texts can actually be intensified by the forms of critical analysis he associates with professionalized kinds of criticism. But they can. As I argued earlier, the theoretical and critical sophistication of our engagement with literature need not disrupt but can actually enhance our emotional, intellectual, and aesthetic experience of literary texts.

Another problem Levine has with so-called ideological criticism is that it isn't clear what authority literary texts—and literary critics—have to say anything meaningful about social, cultural, and political matters in the first place. He is uneasy with "using literature primarily as a means to broad cultural conclusions" because "using literary texts to write history and to tease out of literature sociological evidence" about a culture's attitude toward some belief or behavior (Levine is writing here about Eve Kosofsky Sedgwick's work on attitudes toward homosexuality) is, in his view, very problematical (5). Why? Because we have to consider "the question of the status of literature itself" as evidence for or against broad generalizations about human behavior at any given time or place (5). Chaucer, Milton, Shakespeare, Austen, Baudelaire, Woolf, Baldwin, and Louise Erdrich all have literary authority because they are creative writers who know something about literariness and the uses of the aesthetic to construct plots and organize drama, to move us through their use of language. But what authority do their texts have when it comes to making historical, political, cultural, or sociological observations, observations critics might draw on, for example, to construct the image of an age? What authority does a literary writer have on any topic except literature itself? Keats was not a psychologist, nor was George Eliot a sociologist, and if we want to know something about nature it would perhaps make more sense to turn to a botanist than to Emerson. The same goes for the critic: "If literary criticism really is social criticism, then it needs to confront the question of what sort of authority it can have" (5). In Sedgwick's case, which for Levine is paradigmatic, "the problem is that in using literary texts to write history and to tease out of literature sociological evidence about the culture's attitudes and actions towards homosexuals and women, it is very difficult...to take the 'evidence' as authoritative....If literary criticism really is social criticism, then it needs to confront the question of what sort of authority it can have" (5).

This question of authority, of course, is a double one, for it involves not only the literary work but the critic as well. It is important to understand that these two forms of authority are ultimately interdependent. The authority literary works have is derived from the authority given them by scholarship and criticism. They are not inherently authoritative. Authority is both a power and a right, but it is also a form of agency delegated from one person or institution to another. We can think of literary texts as having a kind of inherent authority, but that is a rather abstract and odd notion of authority, one that perhaps even mystifies authority. Of course authority can come from a collective belief that some person or text just *has* authority. Sacred texts are the best example of this kind of authority. Those who believe that the bible is actually the word of God might insist it has a kind of inherent power that wasn't granted by any outside agency, but that view is itself derived from a collective belief in the bible as the word of God (or of the Torah or the Koran) that invests it with authority in the first place. If no one believed it contained the word of God it would not have this authority. In this sense the believer stands in for the critic, investing the text with its importance and status, and therefore, with its authority. By analogy, Shakespeare's plays do not have any kind of inherent authority. Their authority is derived from their critical reception (and by critical reception here I mean to include the vast array of theatergoers and reviewers, as well as formal critics, who have invested "Shakespeare" with the authority he has). More often than not, authority is not some inherent thing. It is invested in a work through institutionalized practices.

For this reason it doesn't make any sense to argue literary works don't have any authority to speak about social, cultural, or social problems. Levine seems to take the view that Sedgwick is making arguments based on texts that have no authority to make pronouncements about the subjects she is writing about in the first place. However, if—as I have been arguing—all literary texts derive their authority from a reader's understanding that they are saying X and that what they are sayings about X has evidentiary validity, then there is no difference between the kind of authority she believes the texts she's writing about have and authority per se. In fact, there is no such thing as authority per se, save for the authority invested in a certain office or position. Objects such as poems or books do not have inherent authority. Their authority is always derived from some other agent or power, and since our arguments about authority and validity are rhetorical, it is always the power of the critic that invests a literary text with authority (of course this is precisely the process we saw Trilling insist students ought to have some exposure to).

Interestingly, Levine's argument hinges on a certain notion of expertise in reading, a form of expertise connected—even limited to—the realm of the aesthetic on behalf of which he is advocating. For Levine, "there is a tension," between Sedgwick's instinct "to read literature imaginatively, and her decision to use her texts to make the cultural argument" she is making about homosexuality (5–6). As a literary critic Sedgwick (or any other critic, for that matter) has the professional authority and expertise to read imaginatively and thus to make authoritative comments on the aesthetic operations in the texts she discusses, but she presumably has no formal training as a sociologist and therefore is not authorized to make cultural arguments. But there is a problem with this formulation. It assumes too narrow a definition of the imagination, one that precludes the obvious argument that Sedgwick's original and provocative observations about attitudes toward homosexuality in the literary texts she discusses are in fact quite imaginative. To "read literature imaginatively" ought not to be limited to one's attention to the play of aesthetic elements in a text, to register beauty or the sublime and point out where it exists. To read imaginatively is also to see dramatized in literary texts attitudes and forms of behavior toward things in the world that may not be obvious to the general reader and are worth pointing out, more than pointing out, worth drawing together into reasoned, evidence-based arguments about what is being represented in a text (intentionally or otherwise) and how it is related to historically specific social, cultural, and ideological formations that had relevance when the text was being written and in our own time. It will not do, then, to limit the critic's authority to imaginative reading, for imaginative reading involves the production of cultural, social, and even political arguments.[3]

Certainly we should not reduce literary texts to political tracts about this or that issue or ideological conflict without paying close attention to how a particular text uses the specific resources of literary writing, for that would miss paying attention to how literary texts operate as literary texts to deal with issues that could also be treated by a historian, philosopher, or social scientist.[4] Critics such as Levine want literary studies to focus more on literature as its subject and less on the subjects that literature treats. However, too often this position operates with too fine a distinction between subjects in literature and the subject of literature. The subjects in literature may be psychological, cultural, historical, sociological, or anthropological, but for him the subject of literature is literature itself, that familiar but elusive category I explored earlier. Regrounding the study of literature in the aesthetic is an attempt to return literature to the center of literary studies, which seems logical and appropriate enough, but only if in doing so we understand that the aesthetic and the imaginative are intricately connected to the social, cultural, and political subject matter of texts, that they are in the service of the expression of ideas about society, culture, and politics. And when we acknowledge this, the whole polemical force of the distinction between aesthetics and ideology employed in debates about what's wrong with literary studies tends to break down. The only tenable position to take on this whole question, of course, is to insist that historical, cultural, social, political, or ideological analyses of literary texts pay attention to how writers use the aesthetic, formal, and technical devices of literary writing to treat the subjects they treat. It make no sense to study how literature treats social phenomena without doing so, but it also makes no sense to focus on the aesthetic qualities of literary texts in themselves, as if they weren't put in service to say something about the world outside of the text.

Levine quite correctly notes that these disputes are far from trivial, for they are ultimately connected to how we define the nature and value of academic disciplines and so are connected to the perennial "battle over the humanities" I have been discussing in this book (8). So when he insists that if teachers of literature are not able to "define what it is they are doing to an unsympathetic taxpaying world" they may have to "concede that literature is no longer a subject or a discipline," he is probably correct (8). However, the idea that teachers of literature cannot have a discipline without it being organized solely around literature is based on an overly narrow view of the coherence of disciplines such as English and comparative literature. The problem with this idea is that the vast majority of literature teachers do not actually teach in literature departments. They teach in English or foreign language departments. Their professional association, the MLA, is not the Modern Literature Association; it is the Modern *Language* Association. It is worth recalling that English started out as philology, the study of language. It was only later in the twentieth century that English came to focus so narrowly on literature. But English and foreign language departments have always been about much more than literature. They are also about teaching language, grammar, writing, rhetoric, and literary and critical theory.[5] Seen in this context, Levine's complaint that in Greenblatt's or Sedgwick's exploration of the "poetics of culture" (7, the phrase is Greenblatt's) the "distinctiveness" of literature "has no privileged place" does not have quite the force he wants it to have. The privileged place of literature, defined as a canonical work in the British and American belles letters tradition whose aesthetic qualities set it apart from more pedestrian writings, only dominated the teaching of English for a relatively brief period, beginning with the decline of rhetoric and philology in the first couple of decades of the twentieth century and receding with the growing dominance of rhetoric and composition, literary and critical theory, and then the rise of cultural studies in the 1980s.[6] Literature was at the undisputed center of English for only 50 years, from roughly 1920 to 1970, a period now matched by the 50 years since the rise of theory, cultural studies, multiculturalism, and postcolonialism, and composition. Literature has almost always been viewed within a cultural system of other discourses, from philology, rhetoric and linguistics to philosophy, political theory, and historicism. There has actually never been a time when aesthetics as such dominated the study or teaching of literature.

The main problem with an aesthetic-based position develops when it wants literature to be exempt from anything other than aesthetic criticism, to treat literature as a kind of free and disinterested space. The return to aesthetics is based on reinvesting the aesthetic with just the kind of essentialist and universalizing qualities Kant formulated for it in the first place and which contemporary theorists have been at pains to debunk. Levine too often seems to claim the aesthetic as a free and autonomous place safe from political critique, making it a frankly utopian space. Doesn't literature, he pleads, "have any standing that might, even for a moment, exempt it from the practical and political critiques to which all other artifacts of culture are apparently subject" even though it might at times be aligned with "politically or socially objectionable ends"—aren't there "any grounds for giving it the privilege disallowed to other enemies of the good, the true, and the just?" (11). In the end Levine's plea is that we see literature as a privileged, safe, reserved space, a space that paradoxically "encourages what is disallowed" (16) yet is protected from criticism and exists to be studied "in its own right" (16). It is a place "where the very real connections with the political and the ideological are at least partly short circuited," a "realm where something like disinterest and impersonality are possible" (17).

One problem with exempting literature from political and cultural forms of criticism, with thinking of literature as a disinterested place apart from social conflict, is that it reaffirms the old divide between high and popular culture, and threatens to ground literary study in an elite, even undemocratic notion of both the aesthetic and the literary.

It also runs the risk of seeming to reclaim a class-bound, rigidly high culture conception of aesthetic experience itself that has been used historically to distinguish between the cultivated and the uncultivated. Contemporary literary and critical theory, no matter what its particular orientation (deconstructive, feminist, postcolonial, new historical, etc.) has been at pains to open up the study of literature and literary experience to a broad range of authors and readers, many of whom were excluded from study under the dominance of aesthetic-based forms of criticism. If contemporary theory veered away from the aesthetic (and this is not as clear-cut as it might seem),[7] it was in an attempt to explore the literary in the very contexts of the critical categories of history and culture that were marginalized by traditional aesthetic criticism. A truly revitalized approach to the aesthetic criticism of literature would have to find a way both to get beyond this narrow conception of literature and the literary, and to reconceive the aesthetic, and aesthetic experience, in a more broad-based way.

The problem with calls such as Levine's for renewed attention to the category of the aesthetic is not his desire to call attention to the role the aesthetic plays in literature (who would protest that?), but his failure to rethink the category of the aesthetic from a contemporary perspective. Locked into a static, eighteenth-century version of the aesthetic derived from German idealism, connected as it has always been to the highly cultivated experience of beauty and the sublime in reading the great texts of canonical literature, he is working with a woefully out of date conception of the aesthetic and of aesthetic experience. The only reason the aesthetic can protect literature from being contaminated by historical, social, and political contextualizations is because traditional aesthetic theory largely seals off aesthetic experience from the realms of the political and the social. The experience of aesthetic beauty from this traditional perspective is thought of as spontaneous, private, totally affective, and universal yet at the same time a product of cultivation. It isn't the aesthetic per se, but an anachronistic approach to it, that is the problem. A narrow focus on aesthetic qualities and aesthetic experience runs the risk (or has the virtue of) insulating the literary from historical, cultural, and ideological criticism. A better approach is not to banish the aesthetic from criticism, but to find a way to think about it in new ways that underscore the link between aesthetic qualities, aesthetic experience, society, culture, everyday experience, and power. It turns out, however, that such an approach does not provide a rationale for returning literary studies to literature itself. Instead it tends to take a historical and cultural approach to aesthetics that underscores the futility of trying to isolate "literature" itself from its social, historical, and political contexts.

The most interesting new work in this field has developed among critics who have recognized both the need to reconceptualize aesthetic criticism and to connect analyses of our aesthetic experience in literature to a broader cultural inquiry into the role of aesthetic experience in everyday life. Both Isobel Armstrong and Sianne Ngai, for example, have recognized that any serious study of both the aesthetic qualities *of* literature, and aesthetic experience *in* it, requires that we reconceptualize our inherited notion of the aesthetic. They recognize that in a twenty-first-century humanities the category of the aesthetic needs updating. Armstrong, for example, in *The Radical Aesthetic*, insists that reclaiming the aesthetic as a category for criticism must involve a reconceptualization of aesthetic experience itself. Like Levine, she endorses the return to a serious engagement with aesthetic theory and criticism, but unlike him, she insists on the importance of developing what she calls a "democratic aesthetic" (2), one that is not subordinated to older, Enlightenment forms of aesthetic theory developed by philosophers like Kant and Schiller, and one that does not limit aesthetic experience to art and literature. Ngai, in effect, is employing the kind of critical humanism I discussed in chapter 3 in order to rethink the aesthetic as a critical category.

While traditionalist calls for a return to aesthetics want to use the aesthetic to get back to literature, Armstrong recognizes that serious work on the aesthetic inevitably takes one out of literature as well and into other cultural discourses and mediums. Her democratic notion of the aesthetic is built on both "broadening the scope of what we think of as art," and focusing on the role of the aesthetic in everyday life, linked as she insists it is to "playing and dreaming, thinking and feeling" (2). Unlike Levine, she doesn't see the urgency in using the aesthetic as a way to recover literature's prestige. She does, however, agree with Levine that the humanities need to find a way to counter "the turn to an anti-aesthetic in theoretical writing over the past twenty years" (1) fostered by deconstructive, Marxist, cultural materialist, feminist, and post-structuralist critics, who often (but not always) viewed aesthetic theory and aesthetic experience as complicit with a range of dominant humanist ideologies (1–2). This diagnosis has a lot in common with Levine, but Armstrong is not interested in returning to a classic conception of aesthetics. She wants to "challenge the anti-aesthetic" dominant in contemporary theory not by returning to a focus on literary art as the utopian space for a Kantian, disinterested free play but by "remaking its theoretical base and changing the terms of the argument," to "give a new content to the concept of the aesthetic... broadening the scope of what we think of as art" and aesthetic experience (2).[8] "The politics of the anti-aesthetic," in her view, "rely on deconstructive gestures of exposure that fail to address the democratic and radical potential of aesthetic discourse" (2).

There are two positions in play here. Critics on the Left have often dismissed the aesthetic as a discredited critical category complicit with forms of ideological and cultural domination, while traditional critics have used the aesthetic as a rallying cry to return literary studies to a narrow artistic analysis of canonical texts. Armstrong, in effect, wants to inhabit the excluded middle by formulating an approach to aesthetic forms and aesthetic experience that neither sees the aesthetic as, ipso facto associated with ideological domination, or as something associated solely with the sublime and the beautiful and intrinsic to the products of high culture. She wants instead to connect aesthetic experience to everyday life, arguing, "the components of aesthetic life are those that are already embedded in the processes and practices of consciousness—playing and dreaming, thinking and feeling" (2). In her view, "language-making and symbol-making, thought, and the life of affect," the "creative and cognitive life," are central to what we think of as aesthetic experience (2). This more capacious approach to the category of the aesthetic, and to aesthetic experience, does not subordinate the aesthetic to literature or art but, rather, focuses our attention on the ubiquity of aesthetic experience in everyday life. Armstrong avoids relying on the simple-minded, either/or binary that puts the study of literature on one side of the table and the study of culture on the other, demonizing cultural studies, historical criticism, and "theory" for having distracted our attention from literature itself. Instead, work such as hers reaffirms the importance of critical attention to the aesthetic, but insists that we cannot study the aesthetic without paying attention to how it operates both within and outside of literature and art. A "democratic aesthetic" is thus democratic in two ways: it opens up literary studies to the analysis of a wide variety of canonical and noncanonical, Western and multicultural texts and to the operations of the aesthetic in other media, and it seeks to reformulate aesthetic experience as a broadly cultural and social form of experience. Rather than view the aesthetic as something exclusive and cultivated, she argues it is a paradoxically pedestrian experience we all have, but in a variety of ways.

Following up on this more expansive approach to the aesthetic, Sianne Ngai extends the logic of Armstrong's argument but pushes it even further. She begins by pointing out that while "the recent return to aesthetics in literary studies has been embraced by some of its advocates as a polemical riposte" to forms of criticism that do "artworks the disservice of reducing them to encryptions of history or ideology" (948), many of those critics fail to point out that the aesthetic is itself a historical and an ideological category. "Our aesthetic experience," she points out, "is always mediated by a finite if constantly rotating repertoire of aesthetic categories" that are "by definition conceptual as well as affective and tied to historically specific forms of communication and collective life" (948). Thus, studying the aesthetic does not absolve anyone from paying attention to the disruptive influences of theory and historicism but, instead, requires humanists to think theoretically and historically about the category of the aesthetic, to ask "what kind of object is it, and what methodological difficulties and satisfactions does its analysis pose?" (948). Ngai insists, quite correctly in my view, that a focus on the aesthetic does not give us some privileged, pre-theoretical access to essential, universal artistic elements that produce forms of aesthetic experience that magically link viewers and readers across time in the same kinds of transcendent experiences. Instead, aesthetic experience is often historically contingent and culturally specific. It is even connected to economic changes that dramatically effect what is considered "aesthetic" and who can have aesthetic experiences in the first place. Aesthetic qualities and categories are not in this sense innate to literature or art, nor do they transcend history in a way that necessarily gives us access to timeless, universal forms of beauty.

Renewed attention to the aesthetic cannot, then, be part of a posttheoretical return to literature itself but rather ought to be part of a larger interdisciplinary effort across the humanities to study the artistic, philosophical, historical, and even religious role of the aesthetic—both in canonical texts and everyday experience. Such an enterprise remains within the humanist tradition I discussed in chapter 3, yet in a way that challenges some of its entrenched orthodoxies. The category of the aesthetic does not solve problems blamed on theory, political correctness, or overly professionalized critical practices. Rather, it becomes the locus for new theorizing and critical thinking about art and its social and cultural functions. Like Armstrong's, Ngai's approach to the aesthetic is not based on reclaiming it as a refuge from political and cultural criticism, but rather, on linking aesthetic criticism to materialist and historicist forms of criticism. This link is based upon the "close relation between the form of the artwork and the form of the commodity," for in her view shifting aesthetic categories actually "index economic processes," processes that "inform the production, dissemination, and reception of literature and art" (949). Following this logic, to study the aesthetic quality of literary texts is not simply to appreciate how they facilitate our affective responses to them, but also to track changing definitions of the aesthetic and thus, shifting categories that are central not only to affective experience but also to the commodification of literary texts. Ngai's historical and materialist approach to the aesthetic is exemplified by the distinction she makes between major and "minor" aesthetic categories (950), and her emphases on the proliferation of new aesthetic categories in the modern and postmodern periods, categories that are broadly cultural, linked to economic change, and challenge the narrow dominance of traditional categories such as beauty and the sublime. She does not dismiss the importance of what she calls "canonical aesthetic theory," but points out how ill-suited it is to "grasping how the concept of 'aesthetic' has been transformed by the performance-driven, information-saturated and networked, hypercommodified world of late capitalism" (948).

This new kind of approach to aesthetic criticism frees it from narrowly tracking how major categories such as the sublime and the beautiful operate in canonical literature and high art, allowing us to focus attention as well on what Ngai calls minor, seemingly trivial contemporary aesthetic categories such as "the zany, interesting, and cute" (948). "Minor aesthetic categories," she points out, "crop up everywhere, testifying in their ubiquity to how aesthetic experience, radically generalized in an age of design and advertising, becomes less rarefied but also less intense" (951). What better way, she asks, "to get traction on art's diminishing role as the privileged locus for modern aesthetic experience than an aesthetic category of and about inconsequentiality?" (951). In her view the more attention we pay to minor aesthetic categories, and to aesthetic experience in everyday life, the better able we'll be to "figure out what the discourse of aesthetics might mean or become in the wake of aesthetic idealization" (951).

I began this chapter by pointing out that the nature and scope of literary studies is always changing, so much so that calls for a return to traditional forms of coherence, a regular feature of debates about how to respond to those changes, are empty. There never has been any such thing. Indeed, this is a pattern repeated in virtually all of the disciplines associated with the humanities, since the same critical and theoretical movements have dramatically affected them all. Critics who blame theory, ideological criticism, and professionalization for what's wrong with the humanities find the idea of centering literary studies on the aesthetic qualities of literature particularly appealing because they believe it will reconnect students to literature itself, unspoiled by historical contextualization and specialized professional discourses. The problem with this view, as I have been arguing throughout this book, is that there is no such thing as literature itself, and that historical and critical thinking, professional methods of inquiry, and training in how to think theoretically about art, philosophy, history and their relation to culture, equips students with important skills they can draw on when they graduate, no matter what career they choose. The best candidate for most jobs will not be the young man or woman who, as a student, was simply required to read a set of classical texts in literature, philosophy, history, and religion. The best candidate for most jobs will be the young man or woman who was required to think conceptually, critically, analytically, and theoretically not only about the texts they were required to read but also about the historical construction of their value and the competing critical methodologies that have been used to interpret them.

A humanities education that takes an aesthetic education seriously in the kinds of ways I have been discussing has the potential to make the whole question of aesthetic experience interesting and engaging to twenty-first-century students by linking it to their own cultural and social experiences. And because it is organized around a historical and theoretical understanding of the category of the aesthetic it has a practical value, for it helps train students to think critically about how objects of knowledge are conceptualized in the first place. Whereas Levine's proposals for centering the study of literature on aesthetic qualities and experiences is, in the end, a classically conservative one, aimed largely at fostering a wholly interior reading experience that does not seem to make much effort to connect the study of literature to contemporary life, the kind of approach Armstrong and Ngai and trying to conceptualize has the opposite effect. It promises both to encourage students to become aware of the literary devices and social structures that help produce aesthetic experience, and it encourages them to see such experiences as central to their social and cultural lives. The emphasis here shifts from valorizing the reading of canonical texts that just *are* great to training students in a kind of reading practice that actually analyzes how aesthetic experience—in both high art and popular culture—actually works.

This kind of focus on reading practices is part of a larger movement in literary studies—and in the humanities in general—to foreground the practical value of training in close reading. Like the best new work on aesthetics, the renewed interest in close reading is partly animated by the illusory idea that such reading will somehow avoid subordinating literature to premanufactured critical categories and theories (an argument I've been arguing ends up being counterproductive), but the most important work by critics in this area also recognizes that close reading has a broadly cultural and social value. In the final analysis, teaching students close reading practices does not help return literary studies to literature itself, but instead, teaches students a practical skill they can apply to the reading of any text, whether it is literary, journalistic, or produced in the workplace.

Historically, of course, close reading was associated with the American New Criticism, dominant in literary studies from the mid-1930s well into the 1960s. As Graff points out, the New Criticism became a "principle of order" for the modern English department (145). It is striking the extent to which the circumstances of its founding mirror those of our own time when critics have looked to close reading to solve disciplinary conflict in literary studies. While New Critical forms of close reading were always associated with calls for a return to the literary in reaction to the rise of theory and the politicization of literary studies during the 1980s and 1990s, and were therefore seen as important to restoring disciplinary coherence, in the 1930s New Critical close reading was also thought to provide a principle of order that would resolve the incoherence brought on by the conflict between "moralistic Humanists, Marxist propagandists, and historical reductionists" (Graff, 145). And where the New Criticism was seen as perfectly calibrated to add rigor to English at a time when there was strong "external pressure" both to provide needed "professional respectability" and to show that literature was "an autonomous mode of discourse with its own special 'mode of existence,' distinct from that of philosophy, politics, and history" (145), so too is close reading often seen in our own time as a way to separate literature from a generalized form of cultural studies or sociological criticism and restore the centrality of literature to its study. We seem to have come full circle. Then as now, close reading promised to separate literary study from politics and historical contextualization and to recenter its practice on literary questions. Just as in the 1930s, when the culturally conservative New Critics envisioned close reading as a form of resistance to liberal ideologies associated with modernity, so too during (and well after) the culture wars close reading became an instrument with which traditionalists attempted to counter the forces of liberalism in higher education, particularly in the humanities.

It is important to note the historically close relationship between aesthetic criticism and the form of close reading associated with the New Criticism, since, of course, the New Critics essentially treated literary works as self-contained aesthetic objects. Avoiding biographical, cultural, and historical contextualizations, close readings focused solely on the language, form, and literary devices inherent to the work itself as a kind of self-contained, autonomous, unified artistic production. The quality and effectiveness of a poem or short story, in fact, was measured in terms of its internal aesthetic coherence, so that close reading functioned as a kind of guardrail against the kind of subordinating of texts to critical contextualization more traditional critics have found so disturbing. Yoked together, close reading and aesthetic criticism from the 1930s through the late 1960s worked to keep the study of literature focused on the linguistic and formal structures of literary texts, all the while resisting the temptation to read them as reflections of—and reflections on—social, cultural, and political issues operating outside them.

Like aesthetic criticism, close reading has played a prominent role in debates about the focus and coherence of literary studies in the first decade of the twenty-first century. Many critics find the idea of reorganizing literary studies around close reading seductive. However, there are a couple of things that distinguish this new interest in close reading from both the New Critics and those in the 1980s and 1990s who saw it as a simple way to resist theory and return literature to the center of literary studies. While many recent advocates of close reading do in fact see it as a way to resist the subordination of literature itself to cultural and historical theories, they come to close reading through the experience of theory and so both suggest ways in which the New Critical approach to close reading needs complicating, and, perhaps more importantly, they have stressed the fact that close reading is a practical skill that transcends the reading of literary texts. Because what we usually think of as literary readings can produce extraordinarily productive analyses of any kind of text, advocates of close reading have in recent years argued for its broad practical utility in the humanities curriculum.

It is important to note that prominent recent advocates of close reading, such as Jonathan Culler, Marjorie Garber, and Jane Gallop, are all steeped in post-structuralist theory and have spent much of their careers writing about it. For them, close reading has less to do with the New Criticism and more to do with protocols of reading associated with structuralism and deconstruction. Culler (2010), for example, has recently pointed out that there are "different traditions of close reading." There is, of course, "Anglo-American New Criticism," but there is also the "French tradition of explication de text, as well as more recent versions of deconstructive, rhetorical, and psychoanalytic reading" (20). Thus, close reading is not a narrow orthodoxy, and it can hardly be invoked as an antidote to French or Structuralist theory, since those theories are themselves theories of close reading. Close reading, as Culler rightly insists, is something we have to learn, something we're *trained* to do. For this reason, it is not "something more basic, more fundamental, than theories of literature or critical methodologies." There is, he insists, no *mere* reading. Close reading is a theory of reading, so it cannot be described as giving us precritical access to literature itself.

Notwithstanding Culler's insistence that there is no such thing as mere reading, the idea that close reading can be precritical and pretheoretical, that it can take place prior to any kind of contextualization whatsoever, is still a seductive one—even for critics steeped in post-structuralist theory. For example, as we saw earlier, in her 2010 book, *A Manifesto For Literary Studies*, Marjorie Garber both insists on the largely salutary impact of continental theory on literary studies and complains that the field is in trouble because it has drifted away from literature by subordinating its study to cultural and materialist reading practices, practices that can be corrected by a return to close or slow-motion reading.[9] As we saw earlier, like many other critics I have discussed in this book, Garber is concerned that historicist and culturalist critical practices have displaced literature and literariness in literary studies, and she believes that a return to reading itself can rectify this situation. The problem with cultural and historical contextualization, according to Garber, is that it undermines the special status of literary texts *as* literature. Under the aegis of materialist and historicist criticism, she writes, "'the literary' had changed, and changed substantially," losing its privileged status as art and taking its place as simply "one realm among many"(9). This line of analysis leads Garber to what are by now a familiar set of conclusions: Because contemporary theory and cultural studies read literature in a dramatically different context than had the new critics, who treated literary texts narrowly as aesthetic objects, bracketing off the social and historical contexts of their production, the business of literary studies began to look increasingly strange both to outsiders and traditional insiders. In this narrative, theory and cultural studies become responsible for the estrangement of literary studies. "The place of literary studies in the pantheon of the humanities," Garber writes, "came under both tacit and explicit critique" because "literary study was in the process of disowning itself" (11). The problems Garber highlights here—literature's displacement by theory, and by cultural and historical forms of contextualization, the replacement of an ideal relationship to the literary by a materialist one, and, perhaps worst of all, the loss of literature's prestige—echo precisely those Levine lamented 16 years earlier.

Ultimately, however, this stress on close reading, which is meant to return literary studies to literature, is predicated on the value asking literary questions has for reading other kinds of texts and dealing with larger social and cultural problems that lay outside literature itself. On the one hand, Garber laments, "some literary historians and historicist critics are in danger of forgetting, or devaluing, the history of their own craft and practice, which is based not only on the contextual understanding of literary works but also on the words on the page" (12). This focus on craft should stress how literary study "*differs from* other disciplines...rather than the way in which it *resembles* them" (12). How? By "asking literary questions: questions about the *way* something means, rather than *what* it means, or even *why*" (12). Close reading that asks literary questions is reading that focuses on "style, form, genre, and verbal interplays, as well as on social and political context...intrinsic structural elements like grammar, rhetoric, and syntax; tropes and figures; assonance and echo" (12). Much of this language is completely compatible with New Critical close reading, but with a large caveat. On the other hand, however, Garber does not rule out considerations of social and political context, and, perhaps more importantly, she points out that close reading is a skill "literary scholars can offer to the readers of all texts," not just literary ones (12). Although she is clearly sympathetic to the idea literary studies have lost their coherence in drifting away from literature to theory, culture, and history, and though she often presents close reading as a corrective that will get scholars and students back to literature itself, she ultimately sees close reading less as a literary skill than as a *humanities skill*, and a broadly social and cultural one, as "the best way for literary scholars to reinstate the study of literature, language, and culture as a key player among the academic humanities," and "to engage in big public questions of intellectual importance" (13).

Advocates who believe close reading offers a way to avoid problems associated with historical and cultural contextualization, and who view it as a tool for returning literary studies to literature itself, thus run into the same paradox advocates of a return to aesthetics run into: Just as any narrow focus on the aesthetic qualities of a literary work leads inevitably to a focus on the social and cultural function of aesthetics and aesthetic experience, a focus on close reading, aimed, at returning literary studies to literature itself, ends up focusing on a skill whose import lies in its broad applicability *beyond* literature. Close reading, like aesthetic criticism, designed, as an antidote to cultural studies, becomes itself a tool for cultural studies. Jane Gallop turns this paradox into a virtue and puts it at the very center of her argument for the centrality of close reading in literary studies. Rather than use close reading as a pretext for returning literary studies to literature itself, Gallop insists that its value lies in its applicability outside literature studies as a broadly social, cultural, and even political skill. Gallop argues not only that the profession of literary studies has its historical origins in close reading but that it has always been "the most valuable thing English ever had to offer," the thing that "transformed us from cultured gentleman into a profession" ("Close Reading in 2009," 15). According to "standard histories of English," she points out, "we became a discipline...when we stopped being amateur historians and became instead painstaking close readers" (15). Like Garber, her point is not that "close reading is necessarily the best way to read literature but" that it is "a widely applicable skill, of real value to students as well as to scholars in other disciplines" (15).[10] From their point of view the main value of close reading is not that it returns literary study to literature itself, but that it is broadly applicable outside of literary studies. The point both Garber and Gallop make regarding the broad applicability of close reading as a skill is worth underscoring if we want to connect the new interest in close reading to larger debates about the value of literary studies in particular and the humanities in general. While, as we have seen, some critics advocate close reading as a way to counter historical and ideological interpretations with attention to literature itself, thus putting literature back at the center of literary studies, Gallop puts the emphasis less on literature than on the skill of close reading, arguing for the value of literary studies from a practical, utilitarian perspective rather than an idealist one. While in "the New Critical framework, the value of studying literature lay in literature's intrinsic value, which justified the method of close reading," Gallop suggests "the very opposite: it is the value of close reading that justifies the study of literature" (16). From this point of view, the value of literary study has less to do with the value of literature itself than with a skill learned by studying it.

Gallop's position here is shored up by her point that most "literature" professors teach in language departments, not literature departments. Her conception of close reading puts the ultimate emphasis on skills with language rather than skills with literature, emphasizing that the form of close reading she teaches her students is broadly applicable to the reading of any kind of text. While close reading may have its origins as a literary skill, it is broadly applicable because, like writing, it is a language skill.[11] Gallop points out, for example, that as a theorist she does not (for the most part) teach literature but "non-fiction prose," taking the skill of close reading and applying it "to a wider range of texts," in the process "generalizing literary reading so that it becomes not the way to read a particular kind of text but a particular way to read all texts" (16). While we have seen that close reading can be invoked as a way to counter the drift of literary into cultural studies, Gallop emphasizes the value of close reading for work in cultural studies, and as a general approach to our engagement with textuality across the discourses of the humanities—and the social sciences, as well. This inevitable transition from a focus on literature itself to a wider set of cultural discourses, to textuality in general, is, as we have seen, associated as well with new work on aesthetics and form. Thus the new close reading, like the new aesthetics, has a logic built into it that leads to the very decentering of literature many of its early advocates hoped it might help correct. Gallop's emphasis on a practical skill counters the romantic, idealistic notion that the value of literary studies in particular—and the humanities in general—is grounded in cultural tradition or aesthetic greatness, in the canon and great books, in literary history or in knowing the best that's been thought and written.[12] Instead, Gallop makes a utilitarian, practical claim about the value and import of literary studies grounded in the skills it teaches.

It is important to note, as well, that Gallop does not associate close reading with a naïve, unmediated engagement with literature itself ("mere reading"), but with a professional approach to reading. It would be a mistake then, to lump her emphasis (or Garber's) on the importance of close reading in with those critics who see reading the text itself without the interference of secondary materials or critical contexts as either a critique of, or a corrective for, the professionalization of literary studies. On the contrary, close reading here emerges as a central—if not the central—professional methodology of literary studies. And, as I have been stressing, it is this methodology and not literature itself that Gallop sees as central to the whole disciplinary practice of English.[13] As we saw Culler point out, it is not as if "close reading" is something unique to formalists, or to those concerned with "literature itself." Close reading is utilized by critics from all schools and movements and is commonly practiced among so-called theorists and political critics, cultural studies critics, and new historicists. It would be hard to think of critics who read more closely than J. Hillis Miller, Roland Barthes, Frederic Jameson, or Stephen Greenblatt, for example, not to mention Edward Said, Gayatri Spivak, Henry Louis Gates, and of course, Gallop herself. More often than not, close reading is in the eye of the beholder. Accusations that a critic has strayed from close reading often have to do less with the absence of their close attention to detail than with how those details are being interpreted.

One problem with the concept of close reading is that it is often invoked in a vague, monolithic way, and is associated with attention to the text itself, with its genesis in the practical criticism of I. A. Richards, codified by the New Critics, and then generalized into a phrase no one seems to be able to define very clearly. As Gallop puts it, "Close reading, like motherhood and apple pie, is something we are all in favor of, even if what we do when we think we are doing close reading is very different" (20). For this reason, any serious return to a focus on reading in literary studies (and in the humanities in general) has to broaden attention away from a narrow notion of close reading (that too often can make a fetish of the text itself) to focus instead on *practices of reading.* To explore practices of reading is to acknowledge there is no single way of reading in literary studies. It emphasizes instead that humanists have at their disposal a range of styles and types of reading geared to produce different results for different purposes. Such an approach to reading also stresses that reading is not innate; it is a practice, and therefore has a professional dimension. And of course this means it is something we have to continually practice. A focus on practices of reading also allows us to consider how reading strategies evolve over time, not only in relation to critical methodologies but also in relation to evolving technologies. We need to take a historical, not a fixed, idealist approach to reading. What we will find if we do is that practices of reading in our own time have proliferated in a dizzying but productive way. Advocates of close reading, for example, have had to make room for literal reading, surface reading, symptomatic reader, hyper reading, machine reading, and distance reading, among others.[14] All of these different approaches to reading help to both deepen and complicate the orientation of literary studies around reading, emphasizing the extent to which literary studies—and the humanities in general—has increasingly balanced an idealized approach to curating great literary texts with an emphasis on practical skills applicable across a broad range of disciplines and cultural practices associated with the humanities. As Gallop reminds us, while reading may be linked inexorably to the field of literary studies, it is a broadly useful skill that transcends it.

This kind of broad-based and pragmatic approach to reading practices is best exemplified by the work of Katherine Hayles. Hayles is less interested in making claims for one particular approach to reading than in encouraging scholars and students in the humanities to focus on the value inherent in the variety of ways we read. Unlike many of the critics I have discussed in this chapter, Hayles does not approach the question of reading in the narrow context of disciplinary debates about the practice (and politics) of literary criticism, demonizing critical approaches she doesn't like and calling for a return to tradition. Instead, she comes at the whole question of reading in a much less polemical and more pragmatic way, calling not for a return to twentieth- or even nineteenth-century conceptions of reading, but forms of reading that engage the needs and realities of twenty-first-century humanities students. She starts with a fact that everyone is aware of: the reading of print books is on the decline as "young people, in particular, are doing more screen reading of digital materials than ever before" (62). Rather than lament this situation, however, Hayles recognizes the importance of both print and digital reading, and she insists we need to explore the strengths of each, and, more importantly, how they can work together to enhance print and digital literacies. In making distinctions between close reading, hypertext and machine reading, Hayles is interested in the question of "how to convert the increased digital reading into increased reading ability," but especially in "how to make effective bridges between digital reading and the literacy traditionally associated with print" (62).

Like Gallop, Hayles sees close reading as the "sacred icon of literary studies," a practice that constitutes "the essence" of its "disciplinary identity" (63).[15] However, the problem with close reading is that it is a print-based form of reading. Making a distinction between print and digital literacies, Hayles insists that the "chapter of close reading" associated with print culture is "drawing to an end" with the emergence of digital reading and the different forms of attention it invites (65). She argues that in this context the humanities cannot "remain focused exclusively on print close reading," that both a narrowly literary and a broader humanities education today requires a "shift to a broader sense of reading strategies and their interrelation" (65). This involves making some distinctions, not only between print and hypertext reading, but the forms of attention we pay to each and how they can mutually benefit one another. Key among them is the distinction between what she calls "deep attention," associated with close reading and useful for the analysis of "challenging literary works," and "hyperattention," which is "useful for its flexibility in switching between different information streams, its quick grasp of the gist of material, and its ability to move rapidly among and between different kinds of texts" (72). Rather than call for separating out hyperattention from deep attention in order to reiterate the exclusive importance of deep attention for reading in the humanities, Hayles wants to "ensure that deep attention and close reading continue to be vital components of our reading culture," especially as they "interact synergistically with the kind of Web and hyperreading in which our young people are increasingly immersed" (72).

These forms of reading, in turn, ought to in her view be integrated with the kind of machine reading being explored by Franco Moretti.[16] We might, she points out, restrict the notion of reading to something humans do, but she insists that such processes as word-frequency counts, programs that "find and compare phrases, identify topic clusters, and are capable of learning" ought to be thought of as forms of reading as well and added to an expanded notion of practices of reading (74). Her goal is to encourage an exploration of the "interrelations between the components of an expanded repertoire of reading strategies that includes close, hyper, and machine reading," exploring not only the differences but the "overlaps" between these practices (74). "Close and hyperreading," she insists, "operate synergistically when hyperreading is used to identify passages or to home in on a few texts of interest, whereupon close reading takes over" (74). Hyperreading—including skimming and scanning—can overlap with machine reading in identifying patterns in literary texts readers might not otherwise notice, which in turn can help give direction and focus to the kind of close reading we usually associate with careful literary analysis. Hayles envisions a reciprocal relationship between these modes of reading, assuming readers will be adept enough to switch between them. "Relatively context-poor," she points out, "machine reading is enriched by context-rich close reading when close reading provides guidance for the construction of algorithms" (75). One example Hayles cites is the classroom work of Alan Liu at the University of California, Santa Barbara. In a graduate course he calls "Literature +" Liu "asks students 'to choose a literary work and treat it according to one or more of the research paradigms prevalent in other fields of study,' including visualization, storyboarding, simulation, and game design," a project that attempts to link literary close reading to "methodologies in other fields, including the sciences and engineering" (75). Hayles stresses how Liu's approach links "traditional literary reading skills with digital encoding and analysis," strengthening his students' "ability to understand complex literature at the same time it encourages students to think reflectively on digital capabilities" so that "digital and print literacies mutually reinforce and extend each other" (76).

Like the best work I've discussed in this chapter, Hayles's approach to reading does not return us to literature itself but rather connects literature to a wider set of discourses that potentially cut across not only the humanities but the social and natural sciences as well. It is tempting to define the coherence of literary studies in terms of either some canonical concept of "literature" or the literary practice of close reading, but Hayles sees in the work she reviews a "transformed disciplinary coherence" in which "literary studies teaches literacies across a range of media forms, including print and digital," focusing on "interpretation and analysis of patterns, meaning, and context through close, hyper- and machine reading practices" (78). For anyone with a traditional sense of what literary studies is or ought to be, of course, this is a radical proposal. In her revised approach to disciplinary coherence, literary studies are organized around practices and proficiencies rather than literature itself, the narrow, essentially nineteenth-century idea that students ought to know a particular body of works associated with a Western cultural tradition. The focus here is not on literature narrowly defined and separated off from the social, cultural, and historical, but on media literacy—and its analysis—broadly defined. Interpretation and analysis remain central, but they are foregrounded specifically in terms of a constellation of twenty-first-century reading practices.

Hayles's vision of a new disciplinary coherence for what we call literary studies has a lot to recommend it, especially given that the current crisis in the humanities centers to a significant degree on questions about the practical utility of a humanities education, and on the relevance of the academic humanities to the culture outside academia. She puts the emphasis on useful, up-to-date, training in twenty-first-century skills, the broadening of the study of literary forms to include media forms, and the linking of print and digital cultures.[17] It is not hard to see how the coherence of this disciplinary practice would be enticing for a generation of students who have grown up in a digital culture and are interested in studying it in a literary framework that focuses on the historical transition from print to digital texts and methods for their production and analysis. As I will be arguing in my conclusion, there is no reason why this kind of approach to a humanities education cannot, in a pluralistic and democratic vision of the humanities, exist alongside the humanities' traditional commitment to teaching core texts and ideas central to humanism. If the humanities are to be central to a twenty-first-century education they will have to move away from a narrow, one-size-fits-all approach, embracing the variety of subjects and skills I have been reviewing throughout this book, and even more importantly, engaging the humanities in a public way with the world beyond the ivory tower.

Conclusion: The Humanities and the Public Sphere in the Age of the Internet

Throughout this book I have been arguing that if the humanities are in a state of crisis the way out is forward, not backward. The last thing that will save the humanities is a return to some traditional core humanities practice. Why? Because there has never *been* a traditional core humanities practice. For the humanities to remain vital in the twenty-first century they need to do what they have always done best: change. The question now is not *should* the humanities change, but *how* should they change? Returning to some traditional notion of the humanities will not do the trick, because such a return would require reverting to a narrow, outdated, and arbitrarily truncated version of humanism, as well as to an outmoded set of methodologies with which to study things such as literature, history, philosophy, and theology. Nor will it do to blame professionalization for the challenges now faced by disciplines like my own or by the humanities in general. Indeed, the humanities need more professionalization, not less. The argument that humanities professors ought to leave their specializations outside the door of their undergraduate classrooms—along with the theories and methodologies that inform their scholarly practice—is antithetical to the whole aim of *higher* education. Indeed, as I have been arguing throughout this book, specialization and the increased theoretical and methodological rigor of college and university classes is precisely what put the *higher* in higher education in the first place. That is the case in the natural and social sciences, and it ought to be the case in the humanities as well. Like the sciences, the humanities must continue to find a balance between a general and a specialized education for its students. To argue that the humanities ought to eschew specialization and professional rigor and stick to making sure students simply read great books and talk about the meaning of life threatens to impoverish the humanities for both students and faculty. We don't need a two-tiered system in which specialization and methodological rigor are a hallmark of the natural and social sciences while the humanities provide a kind of service function, a space where students can simply talk loosely about big ideas and great books.

For the disciplines of the humanities to remain central to higher education they need to sustain the kind of theoretical and methodological rigor they have developed over the last four decades, not turn away from those theories and methods. Bu they must also find better, more effective ways to explain to the general public what they are and why they matter. This means pushing back against critics who argue professionalization is a problem in the humanities, insisting on the link between professing and professionalization in the undergraduate as well as the graduate classroom. To profess, of course, is to make a set of claims, claims not only about the importance and value of *what* you are saying, but to make claims as well about the *skills* you use in the production and the critique of knowledge. As we have seen, the skills humanists utilize in their professional scholarship directly intersect with the skills they teach their students. The practical expertise I've argued students gain in the humanities, the ones that are of keen interest to employers in both the for-profit and not-for-profit sectors of our economy, are directly related to the professional expertise research scholars hone as they work to produce specialized knowledge. This is certainly the case, as we have seen, in literary studies. Calls for a return to literature itself, linked as they often are to fears that professionalization, theory, and criticism have spoiled literary studies too often ignore the fact that when we teach students "literature" we are teaching them to think theoretically and write critically, which means they need *more,* not less theory, *more,* not less training in critical approaches to contextualizing and writing about literature.

In addition to defending professionalization and theory, I have also been arguing that attention to political issues in the humanities—what critics dismiss as "political correctness"—is something that should be defended, not lamented. We saw earlier that the idea that there is something wrong with thinking about humanism in terms of power and politics is profoundly unhistorical, since humanism has always been about politics and power. From this point of view, paying attention to the social, historical, and political context of literary texts, works of art, or philosophical debates, exploring how they are engaged with questions regarding power and social justice, how they reflect—and reflect on—a complicated set of ideologies, ought to be seen as thoroughly orthodox. The odd thing is to try to remove literature, art, philosophy, or history from their critical, social, political, and even ideological embeddedness, to treat them as abstract, ahistorical objects containing a timeless set of universal meanings. For as we have seen, the so-called political turn in the humanities actually marks the *return* to a set of questions about power and agency that were central to the tradition of humanism all along. In literary studies, of course, it was largely the intervention of the New Criticism, which attempted to bracket off the social, historical, and political in a largely ideological reaction of modernization, that disrupted this focus. Theory and historical, cultural, and political forms of scholarship have actually served to put traditional questions about power and agency and social justice back on the front burner where they belong.

For all of these reasons, the humanities in the twenty-first century ought, more than ever, to rely on—and teach—professional approaches to critical thinking grounded in disciplinary and interdisciplinary theories and methodologies, and to stay focused on connecting the texts, authors, and ideas it teaches to broad questions about power, agency, and social justice, and to do it all in a *global* context. This does not mean the humanities have to abandon the curatorial responsibility they have. There is no reason why a more diverse set of readings in the disciplines of the humanities has to relegate canonical texts (and works of art) to the historical trash heap. On the contrary, one of the best things about the introduction of formerly marginalized writers, artists, and their works into the humanities curriculum is that they create just the kind of dialogue humanists need to facilitate real critical thinking. Having students read *both* Ernest Hemingway and Zora Neale Hurston insures critical thinking about what American literature is, who writes it, and why those questions matter. This kind of juxtaposition confronts students with radically different versions of American identity and experience, foregrounding how gender, race, and class operate in literature, literary studies, and the larger social world. We shouldn't be embarrassed by those topics, or to see them as "politicizing" something that isn't in fact already political. And there is no reason in the world why these topics have to cancel out attention to the aesthetic quality of literary works, and to the forms of aesthetic experience they facilitate.

Toward an Engaged and Public Humanities

Throughout this book I have highlighted what I think is a debilitating standoff among humanists and their supporters, a standoff that complicates our ability to make a case for the value of the humanities in general, and for literary studies in particular. How do we set about creating a balance between the various positions I've been discussing? First of all, by moving beyond the counterproductive claims and counter claims of traditional and progressive humanists that have helped structure the humanities crisis from the very beginning. As we have seen, the debate here is all too familiar. From the traditionalist's point of view the humanities are supposed to carve out a space for students to escape the world of the utilitarian and the practical, where they can be free to read the great canonical texts in literature, philosophy, history, religion, and the classics for their own sake. Hopefully they will also learn to read carefully and write well, but the main imperative is to have students read the great texts—and familiarize themselves with the great ideas—of a canonical tradition of writers, thinkers, and artists. Liberal or progressive humanists, on the other hand, insist the humanities ought to be a place where these same canonical texts can be subject to constructive critique. From this perspective, the value of the humanities has less to do with fostering cultural literacy defined in terms of knowing a great tradition of Western texts, and more to do with fostering a skeptical, critical, and even oppositional relationship to the ideologies many of them embody. Here too, learning how to read carefully and write well is important, but reading in cultures of dissent is paramount. Both these positions tend to put the teaching of useful skills in a relatively negative light. The traditionalist's insistence that the value of studying great humanistic texts shouldn't be measured in terms of practical, utilitarian skills that will credentialize students for a vocation gets turned by revisionist or progressive humanists into outright, monolithic resistance to the utilitarianism of an increasingly corporate culture. One model sees the humanities as a rarefied refuge from the world of practical concerns and vocational goals, while the other sees the humanities as openly hostile to the utilitarian values of the world of business, a place in which to develop concrete opposition to those values. The longer both sides continue to reject the idea the humanities have anything in the way of practical, transferable skills to offer the world outside academia, the easier it is for conservative critics and politicians who want to defund higher education to justify their efforts by arguing the humanities have nothing useful to offer at all.

The divide between traditionalists and progressives has for too long blocked constructive change, and such change won't get real traction until it's overcome. As long as humanists remain caught in this twentieth-century divide they are going to have a tough time creating a consensus about how to reconfigure the humanities as a valuable twenty-first-century enterprise. To create such a consensus humanists need to acknowledge that the humanities have to be plural, inclusive, integrative, and open-ended; able to embrace a range of different approaches to knowledge, analysis, and critique; be tolerant of opposing views; and committed to multiple, and at times conflicting goals. There is no reason why an emphasis on the vocational opportunities study in the humanities affords has to push aside the valuable work of both traditionalists and revisionists. Indeed, humanists ought to emphasize both how these competing models usefully and productively contest one another, and explore ways in which they can be integrated so as to insure that students develop the specific proficiencies they need for whatever vocational choice they make. We ought to see calls for a stronger stress on writing, analytical, and critical skills as connected to—not a break from—the dramatic increase in theoretical and methodological sophistication we have witnessed in the humanities over the last four decades. Emphasizing the transferable skills a humanities education affords, and tackling the tough structural problems facing higher education today, should not be construed as a call to turn away from those developments. On the contrary, we ought to reject the idea that what gets dismissed as "theory," "political correctness," and "multiculturalism" has ruined the humanities, for as we have seen that is simply a false claim.

So, a key requirement moving forward ought to be that humanists let go of this shopworn, culture-war-era posturing once and for all. One can observe an unfortunate, corrosive stridency on both sides of the divide, on the part of an overtly politicized humanities that sometimes has come off as overly dogmatic, even hectoring about the correctness of its politics, and on the part of traditionalists who have reacted with caricature and high-minded hand-wringing about what they claim is nothing less than the demise of Western culture. But the fact of the matter is that the humanities today are immensely more engaged, vital, and meaningful than they have ever been. Humanists have not abandoned their commitment to traditional texts and forms of knowledge, yet they have dramatically increased the theoretical and critical sophistication of their work, expanded the range of texts, problems, and issues they study with their students, and created a humanities not simply in pursuit of knowledge for its own sake but knowledge that can help make the world more just, more respectful of—and responsive to—differences that were hardly acknowledged before the so-called theory revolution.

The recent turn to concrete discussions by organizations such as the Modern Language Association and the American Historical Society about the jobs crisis in the humanities, in which too many PhDs compete for too few jobs, emphasizing the particular proficiencies humanities students develop, reforming graduate studies, tackling the problems of student debt, and attending to the woefully deteriorating conditions of academic labor, suggests humanists are moving beyond the old political debates I've been discussing.[1] To be truly productive, these changes must lead to a more democratic, tolerant version of the humanities. A truly plural, integrated humanities has to embrace a responsibility to preserve and explore key texts in the Western tradition, and a commitment to think critically about ways to improve, resist, or change dominant and oppressive economic, political, social, and cultural constructs, while at the same time tackling structural problems in the humanities. There is no reason why the humanities cannot accommodate the work of traditionalists and revisionists while also helping students capitalize on the skills the humanities foster as they seek employment in the corporate or not-for-profit worlds. These three pursuits need to be seen as integrated, not separate.

While both sides have blamed the other for the crisis in the humanities, I have been arguing that this crisis was largely a product of that blame game and the paralysis it produced. One of the reasons why the humanities have begun to focus on these structural problems is that financial pressures, the dysfunction of graduate education, the jobs crisis, the corporatization of the university, and the increasing popularity of a largely nonideological digital humanities have displaced, and even marginalized, the paralyzing ideological debates I've been discussing. The humanities will never again be the bastion of a narrow, monocultural elite. Nor can the humanities simply set itself up monolithically as the opposition party, the seat of resistance to all things corporate, scientific, and technological. Focusing on the structural problems I've been discussing gives humanists an opportunity to work together across their intellectual differences, which in the final analysis transcend both positions. The challenging question is how humanists can tackle these problems in a way that does not marginalize or distract them from a historical responsibility to conduct research in specialized areas, produce knowledge, increase theoretical and critical sophistication, and honor the plural, democratic character of the humanities. This kind of pluralistic approach can go a long way toward insuring that a renewed focus on skills will not produce students who simply want to be well-behaved cogs in the corporate wheel. Valuing the humanities means valuing its inherent pluralism, finding ways to accommodate and to feature its various enterprises and commitments. People do not simply study the humanities. People use the humanities. They can be used not only to enjoy and learn from traditional texts and works of art for their own sake, but also to think critically about how those same texts and works of art have been either complicit with or resisted injustice. But out of this use should come the development of reading, writing, analytical, critical, and interpretive abilities that, while central to academic work, are also applicable outside it in a multiplicity of workplaces in our society.

In spite of the standoff between the positions I have been discussing, there are a number of encouraging developments in the humanities that suggest this logjam might be beginning to break up. These developments are focused on both articulating and implementing a more public, engaged role for the humanities in American society, which include finding ways to place humanities students, those with the BA, but also the MA and the PhD, in nonteaching jobs within academia, and jobs outside academia as well. These developments are not aimed at replacing classroom learning, nor are they meant to undermine the pursuit of knowledge for its own sake, or the discussion of general ideas that might seem to have little in the way of practical application. They are meant to both supplement and enrich classroom work, to help add a new, more socially engaged dimension to study in the humanities. And they involve producing institutional structures that link students and their teachers to the public sphere, creating alliances that flow two ways, from the university into the community, and from the community back to the university.

These developments are taking place under the umbrella of what has come to be termed the public humanities. Academic programs in the public humanities train humanities students at the postgraduate level for work outside academia—in museums, historical associations and preservation leagues, cultural heritage groups, federal and state humanities councils, arts and performance groups, oral history projects, and a variety of other not-for-profit or for-profit cultural organizations. Some of these programs offer certificates in the public humanities to graduate students already enrolled in PhD programs in traditional humanities departments. Public Humanities at Yale, for example, offers a Masters of Arts degree in Public Humanities to students already enrolled in Yale's PhD Program in American studies.[2] This program supplements their conventional academic training with preparation "for public intellectual work such as museum and gallery installation, documentary film and photography, and oral/community history," preparation aimed at "building bridges" between its PhD students and "a wide range of local and regional intuitions and their respective publics." A similar program at Brown University's John Nicholas Brown Center for Public Humanities and Cultural Heritage offers an MA in public humanities.[3] The program, according to its website, which can be completed en route to a traditional PhD or as a terminal program, "offers a dynamic interdisciplinary opportunity for students interested in careers in museums, historical societies, cultural planning agencies, heritage tourism, historic preservation, and community arts programs." The University of Washington also offers a Certificate in Public Scholarship to both graduate students and faculty from around the university. The program hopes to foster "public scholarship that engages in cultural practice and inquiry," generating "campus-community partnerships across all sectors of higher education" engaged with "digital and multimedia publication, exhibitions, performance, and other innovative modes of disseminating scholarship."

These new humanities programs have developed out of recognition that humanities students have transferable skills that can be utilized in a variety of ways in jobs across the spectrum of arts and humanities programs and institutions outside academia. They recognize that humanities students are uniquely positioned to draw on their specialized knowledge of history, literature, philosophy, and the arts, *and* on their particular skills in writing for both old and new media to help forge a bridge between scholarship and society. All the skills I have been discussing in this book—close reading, the ability to summarize, analyze, and interpret texts and data, to think critically and construct persuasive narratives—can be applied in a wide range of vocations, but they are particularly crucial for jobs in the public humanities. With the academic job market shrinking for students who seek teaching positions (especially at research intensive universities) the public humanities offer a range of alternative career options that deserve to be worked into the fabric of postgraduate programs, which ought to be training graduate students for *both* academic and nonacademic jobs. Professional groups in the humanities are beginning to recognize this fact, and they are paying increasing attention to what is now called "Alt-ac," alternative careers to those in academia.[4]

In addition to these innovative degree-granting programs in the public humanities are a new, expanding range of exciting interdisciplinary practices involving the intersection of the humanities, medicine, and science. One example that has fascinating implications for the future of literary studies is the field of narrative medicine. According to one of its key founders, Dr. Rita Charon, narrative medicine is based on the idea that "the effective practice of medicine requires narrative competence, that is, the ability to acknowledge, absorb, interpret, and act on the stories and plights of others." (2006, 15). Charon, who earned a PhD in English from Columbia in 1999 (on top of a 1978 MD from Harvard Medical School), helped pioneer the idea that "adopting methods such as close reading of literature and reflective writing allows narrative medicine to examine and illuminate 4 of medicine's central narrative situations: physician and patient, physician and self, physician and colleagues, and physicians and society." By incorporating the idea of "narrative competence" from literary studies, Charon insists physicians can bridge the divide that separates "physicians from patients, themselves, colleagues, and society." While narrative medicine connects to the humanities by acknowledging that the practice of medicine is in part the practice of an art, that it has a broadly humane dimension that ought not to get lost in the technical and scientific side of its practice, it is defined very specifically in terms of a practical skill.[5] Narrative *competency* adds to the other practical competencies of the physician. The ability to carefully read, analyze and think critically about the range of narratives about illnesses (from patients, their families, nurses, other doctors, etc.) they encounter, and to develop their own narratives about illness—indeed, to read illnesses *as* narratives, becomes part of the skill-set of physicians and thus dramatizes the extent to which the literary skills of close reading and analysis are transferable to a wide range of practices and vocations. Indeed, degree programs in narrative medicine, such as those in the public humanities, are now available at a variety of medical schools including Columbia University and the University of Florida.[6]

Another emerging area of academic work that links the humanities and sciences is field philosophy. Field philosophy, according to Robert Frodeman, is based on a distinction "between lab science and field science" (Frodeman, 2010). "'Getting out in the field' means leaving the book-lined study to work with scientists, engineers and decision makers on specific social challenges," so that instead of trying to understand in the abstract "traditional philosophic problems like the old chestnut of 'free will,'" or "seeking to identify general philosophic principles," field philosophers "begin with the problems of non-philosophers, drawing out specific, underappreciated, philosophic dimensions of societal problems." Philosophers have of course for years worked with ethics boards at hospitals, Frodeman points out, but newer work in field philosophy involves "embedding" philosophers in fields including environmental science and nanotechnology (examples he cites include the US Geological Survey, the food industry, the National Science Foundation, and the Great Lakes Fishery Commission). Philosophers embedded in these fields can advise on the ethical, epistemological, ontological, or even metaphysical aspects of scientific work in labs and in the field, but they can also help contribute to the development of narratives that explain the relationship between various disciplines, including chemistry, geology, anthropology, public policy, and economics. Here field philosophy, of course, intersects with narrative medicine, for as Frodeman points out, "such narratives can provide us with something that is sorely lacking today: a sense of the whole."

Crucially, field philosophy is not top-down but bottom-up. It does not begin in theory but "with the needs of stakeholders...drawing out philosophical insights after the work is completed." This means adapting philosophizing to the practical demands and real time of workers in a field, which in turn means adapting the traditional protocols of scientific research and publishing to philosophical work. Field philosophers, Frodeman explains, have to balance the traditional demands for rigor in academic publishing with the real-time demands in the field for concise, accessible, and useful narratives. It does not "reject traditional standards of philosophic excellence," but it does seek to "master the political arts of working on an interdisciplinary team," balancing the "field rigor of writing grants and framing insights for scientists and engineers" with the expectations of traditional philosophical research practices. Frodeman and his colleagues see their work in the general context of the "industry of knowledge production" rather than in the narrow context of academic philosophizing for the sheer sake of philosophizing. And they see the value of this work in terms of its *accountability*. Both philosophers and scientists, now more than ever, are being pressed to demonstrate the social relevancy of their work, to "justify our existence," as Frodeman puts it, in terms of the "direct impacts" of their work on society.

Narrative medicine and field philosophy are both excellent examples of what is often called the *engaged* humanities. The term "engaged humanities" refers to humanities work that is involved with broad public and community needs, work, as Gregory Jay puts it in "The Engaged Humanities: Principles and Practices for Public Scholarship and Teaching," that is based "on the organized implementation of project-based engaged learning and scholarship" that intersects with the "continued advancement of digital and new media learning and scholarship" (51). Much of this work, as Jay points out, involves "collaborative cultural development work with a social justice orientation" (54). One of his examples is the "Imagining America

Curriculum Project," which documents examples of such work. Much of it involves the kind of hands-on fieldwork Frodeman endorses for philosophers, projects that "go beyond public performance to public engagement." They "advance community cultural development, enrich democratic dialogue, create exciting aesthetic advances, and fashion meaningful collaborations among diverse partners" in the academic, cultural, and corporate sectors of the public sphere (54). Building on the traditional practice of service learning, an engaged humanities attempts to be much more collaborative, adopting the kind of "bottom-up" model characteristic of field philosophy. Jay cites a range of dramatic new initiatives at the University of Texas; the University of Washington, Stanford; and his own Cultures and Communities Program at the University of Wisconsin-Milwaukee.[7]

All of the programs I've been discussing embody forms of engagement and outreach that connect a humanities education—and the competencies it teaches—to the public sphere and a host of vocations that sorely needs them. There are two challenges in sustaining and expanding endeavors such as these. One is the challenge of mainstreaming humanities competencies, finding a way to emphasize the value of the skills taught in humanities courses, moving beyond the kind of embarrassment felt by too many people about the instrumental value of a humanities education (without reducing the value of the humanities to purely instrumental measures). The other challenge is to build career planning for undergraduate humanities students into the undergraduate humanities experience. One place where this is being done is at Brigham Young University's (BYU) Humanities+ program. This program, designed for humanities undergraduates at BYU, is aimed at taking advantage of "the evidence for the marketability of humanities skills" by developing institutional resources for preparing, advising, and strategizing with students about their career goals.[8] Recognizing that the humanities offer "excellent preparation not only for teaching but for other professional schools" including law, medicine, library science, and business administration, the Humanities+ program is also designed to help students prepare and plan for employment at government agencies, NGOs, and other places where their "foreign-language and intercultural expertise, their leadership abilities, communication skills...and intellectual flexibility and creativity" can be put to use. Faculty in the program work closely with students to help them think early and creatively about a career that will utilize their capabilities, and the program's website has a rich offering of careers strategies, which in turn is supported by a detailed blog with news and articles about careers in the humanities. These engaged, public, field-oriented approaches to a humanities education promise to help revitalize the humanities, making a humanities education relevant for twenty-first-century students who need exposure to both the subjects and competencies it is uniquely positioned to offer. They should not be seen as marginalizing or replacing the humanities' traditional classroom focus on the study and discussion of key literary, philosophical, and historical texts—and works of art—central to both a Western and global intellectual tradition, but as a component that expands the relevance and application of such study.

The Digital Humanities

Finally, one of the most significant new developments in the humanities, indeed, one that promises perhaps more than any other to remake them, is the emergence of the Digital Humanities, a field that is becoming particularly fertile in literary studies programs around the country.[9] As I briefly noted in my Introduction, the Digital Humanities are increasingly bridging the traditional divide between the humanities and science, introducing into the humanities training in a broad range of computer skills directly applicable across a variety of vocations in both the for-profit and not-for-profit sectors of the economy. At their core, the digital humanities explore new technologies for embodying, transmitting, and studying texts and works of art traditionally central to a humanities education. But they are also engaged with the digital production of *new* humanities texts and tools for study—creative texts and educational tools that are "born digital"—and this promises an even more dramatic revolution in the humanities in general, and the study of literary texts in particular. Every facet of a humanities education, from the texts students study to the classrooms they meet in and the research tools they utilize, are being dramatically transformed by the digitalization of knowledge. These developments, in turn, offer new professional opportunities to humanities students, from writing computer programs to text encoding and text editing, electronic publishing, interface design, and archive construction.

Where did the idea of the Digital Humanities come from? The concept of a digital humanities grew out of the older, less formal field of humanities computing, the use of computers for research, data collection, writing, and publishing in the humanities. To a significant degree, the digital humanities are about the organization of knowledge and the adapting of computational skills to the management of humanities materials. In this sense, they provide a new infrastructure of services for humanities scholars. Seen from this angle, it is not hard to imagine how the digital humanities may offer a way not so much to solve but even to transcend many of the vexing questions about humanities study I have been tracing in this book.[10] Why? Because, at least on the surface, the digital humanities seem largely to operate outside debates about great books and the canon, about critical theory and the politicization of the humanities. Since the digital humanities do not constitute a critical approach to humanistic study such as formalist, psychoanalytic, feminist, postcolonial, or queer forms of criticism, they do not seem to be weighted-down by the kinds of arguments about theory and ideology I have been discussing in this book.[11] Indeed, the digital humanities seem to promise that the whole debate about the politicizing of humanities study can be put on the back burner—or will disappear altogether. In the age of a truly digital humanities, students will learn how to write code for digitized humanities resources, not how to overthrow patriarchy.

However, this thoroughly instrumentalist vision of the digital humanities is increasingly being contested and debated by digital humanities scholars themselves. Indeed, the division between scholars who want to define the digital humanities narrowly in terms of using technology to write code and build things, and those who insist on a big tent that includes critical and cultural theory deployed to think critically about digital culture and instrumentality itself, replicates the larger debates within the humanities I have been discussing throughout this book.[12] Beyond the general tension we can observe here between defining the humanities in terms of particular subjects and specific objects of knowledge (canonical texts, authors, works of art, etc.) students ought to know, and defining the humanities in terms of practical skills it teaches, we can also observe the specific tension between the curatorial and critical functions of the humanities I discussed earlier. If the digital humanities are about technologies and methods of organizing knowledge, then they are facilitating the humanities' curatorial function. If, however, they are about fostering critical thinking about technology and instrumentality, then they are facilitating the critical function of the humanities. Another way to look at this division is in terms of whether or not the digital humanities perform a service function for other disciplines or is itself a subject area or discipline with a critical function of its own. How the relationships between these different ways of thinking about the digital humanities get worked out will, to a significant degree, determine the impact this digital turn will have on the humanities in general, and on cultural and literary studies in particular.

The technical, methodological, computational, knowledge-organization vision of the digital humanities has its roots, of course, in the science of computing. From this perspective the main value of digital technology for the humanities, as Johanna Drucker has pointed out, "resides in the creation, migration, or preservation of cultural materials" (85). The emphasis here was initially on tasks such as "creating metadata, doing markup, and making classification schemes or information architectures," and "the terms of production were, necessarily, set by technological restraints," and of course with such work "quantitative, engineering, and computational sensibilities prevail" (85). This meant that the largely *interpretive* orientation of humanities work was replaced by the *positivist* orientation of computation. The result is that the

> protocols for information visualization, data mining, geospatial representation, and other research instruments have been absorbed from disciplines whose epistemological foundations and fundamental values are at odds with, or even hostile to, the humanities. Positivistic, strictly quantitative, mechanistic, reductive and literal, these visualization and processing techniques preclude humanistic methods from their operations because of the very assumptions on which they are designed: that objects of knowledge can be understood as self-identical, self-evident, ahistorical, and autonomous. (85–86)

For all of these reasons, in the late 1990s, according to Drucker, "getting the work done" in the digital humanities meant "humanists came into" the "conversations as relativists and left as positivists out of pragmatic recognition that certain tenets of critical theory could not be sustained in that environment" (88). There were debates about theory and its role in the digital humanities, to be sure, but mostly "scholars shrugged and went back to coding" (88), for "to play in the digital sandbox one had to follow the rules of computation" (88).

The problem, of course, is that in the late 1990s the humanities had just finished systematically critiquing all of the assumptions about reality, knowledge, and truth associated with the very positivism that seemed to form the foundation of the digital humanities and its practices. Seen through "a humanistic critical frame," Drucker points out, all of the precepts of positivism associated with computation, data mining, and the forms of knowledge they produce ought to look suspect (86). The very "platforms and protocols" associated with a digital humanities defined in terms of computation and building were "created by disciplines whose methodological premises are often at odds with—even hostile to—humanistic values and thought" (86). For this reason Drucker insists that "the ideology" of something as innocent as "information visualization" may be "anathema to humanistic thought," even "antipathetic to its aims and values" (86). She worries that "the persuasive and seductive rhetorical force of visualization performs such a powerful reification of information that graphics such as Google Maps are taken to be simply a presentation of 'what is,' as if all critical thought had been precipitously and completely jettisoned" (86). In this scenario, theory's insistence on the contingent, historical construction of knowledge seems to go right out the window.[13]

Anyone who has read this far will see that we are right back where we started. The digital humanities, thought by many to be the next big thing, an enterprise perhaps poised to even save the humanities, embodies the central contradiction that has dogged the humanities all along. The digital humanities seem to be replaying all over again the larger "theory crisis" that plagued the humanities in general from the late-1970s through the mid-1990s. For, as Drucker reminds us, "the intellectual traditions of aesthetics, hermeneutics, and interpretative practices (critical editing, textual studies, historical research) are core to the humanities" (86), but even these practices became subject to a "systematic critique" from "poststructuralism, postcolonialism, and deconstruction," which have "altered our understanding of notions of meaning, truth, authorship, identity, subjectivity, power relations, bodies, minds, nations, intelligence, nature and almost any other ontological category of cultural thought" (87). For the digital humanities, this raises two problems. The first is that an overly technological and positivist practice threatens to displace at least three decades of theoretical and critical work in the humanities, something that is awfully displeasing to many mainstream humanists trained in critical and cultural theory and with only a vague understanding of what the digital humanities entail. The second problem is that the digital humanities threaten to further nudge the humanities toward a largely service function.

A number of scholars want to tackle this problem by finding a way to reconfigure the digital humanities as a specifically *humanities* practice, one that values theory and produces cultural criticism. Drucker herself, for example, looks forward to a "new phase in DH" that would "synthesize method and theory," and she calls "for more work that will "theorize humanities approaches to digital scholarship" (87). The phrasing here is intriguing. While the phrase "digital humanities" puts the emphasis on digitalizing humanities materials and on the uses of digital materials for humanities study, the phrase "humanities approaches to digital scholarship" puts the emphasis on a specifically *humanities* approach to digital scholarship. Her argument, in effect, is that the digital humanities, narrowly construed, threaten in their instrumentalism to take the "humanities" out of the digital humanities. The word *humanities* in digital humanities seems to simply stand for the disciplinary fields in which computational work is being done, rather than for a set of theoretical and methodological practices associated explicitly with humanities thinking. This is an important distinction. In the scenario she envisions, things such as "interpretation," "ambiguity," "contradiction," the social constructedness of objects of knowledge, the "relation of 'object' to 'context,'" all values in the humanities, are threatened with marginalization by a narrowly computational turn (88). Her argument, finally, is that "the theoretical underpinnings of humanistic interpretation are fundamentally at odds with the empirical approaches on which certain conventions of temporal and spatial modeling are based" (90). Such sheerly instrumentalist approaches run the risk of emphasizing positivist, computational, empirical, service-oriented work at the expense of marginalizing the traditionally less empirical, more interpretive, and critical work the humanities have always been known for.[14]

Concerns such as Drucker's are part of a larger set of questions currently being asked about the scope and orientation of work in the digital humanities, the answers to which will help decide how big a tent they constitute, and thus determine how well they can accommodate not only new and exciting technological practices but how those practices can be scaled to the humanities' more traditional interpretive and critical practices. To a significant degree these questions come out of the very theoretical, cultural, and political work the digital humanities seem poised to marginalize. For example, many digital humanities critics, as Matthew Gold has noted in his introduction to *Debates in Digital Humanities*,[15] worry about "a lack of attention to issues of race, class, gender, and sexuality . . an absence of political commitment," and "an inadequate level of diversity among its practitioners" (xi).[16] Beyond these questions are even broader ones about the relationship between the digital humanities and new media studies, a field that traditionally has been associated with cultural critique but which many digital humanities scholars want to distinguish from digital humanities work.[17] Gold insists that the digital humanities need to ask where "new media studies leave off and digital humanities begin" (xi)? It also, in his view, needs to work out its relationship to literary and cultural theory, and to figure out what kind of relationship it has to political power, if any. In a similar vein, Gary Hall asks in the provocatively titled, "There Are No Digital Humanities," to what extent "the take up of practical techniques and approaches from computing science" is simply "providing some areas of the humanities with a means of defending (and refreshing) themselves in an era of global economic crisis and severe cuts to higher education, through the transformation of their knowledge and learning into quantities of information— deliverables?" He worries that narrowly computational digital humanities will simply feed a "movement away from what remains resistant to a general culture of measurement and calculation and toward a concern to legitimate power and control by optimizing the system's efficiency."

The questions Hall poses push the digital humanities toward thinking critically about their own orientation and practices, and thus associates them with the kind of cultural criticism Alan Liu insists the digital humanities have to take up in an essay that asks, "Where is the Cultural Criticism in the Digital Humanities?" (2012). Liu shares two linked concerns with Drucker and Hall. The first is his worry that the digital humanities remain too heavily weighted toward the instrumental and computational, toward code writing and building; and the second is that while they might save the humanities, they might simply save them as a service enterprise. In Liu's view this orientation toward service and instrumentalism feed one another. "Within the digital humanities, to start with, we observe that service and instrumentalism are part of a tangle of related concepts—including functionalism, toolbased, and (as I earlier deployed the term) practice—about which the field is deeply insecure" (498). Liu points out a paradox in all this, for some digital humanists worry "their field is too instrumental" (498), dominated as it is by "industrialization, purely technical concerns, implementation, standards," and so on (498), while others worry it is not instrumental enough, especially when compared to fields such as engineering, where "prestige" comes from innovation and building things (499). On the extreme end of this position, Liu cites Stephen Ramsay's paper at the 2011 Modern Language Association ("Who's In and Who's Out"), which included the following remarks about what it takes to be a digital humanist: "Do you have to know how to code?...I say 'yes.'...Digital Humanities is about building things.... If you are not making anything, you are not...a digital humanist" (499).

Ramsay's is an extreme position, of course, but it helps to make clear where the lines are being drawn. The main concern here, as Liu puts it, is that the instrumentalist, service function of the digital humanities is poised to overwhelm its critical function, and more importantly, its ability to perform cultural criticism. "I believe that the service function of the digital humanities," he writes, "as literal as running the actual servers, if need be—can convert into leadership if such service can be extended beyond facilitating research in the academy . . to assisting in advocacy outside the academy in the humanities' present hour of social, economic, and political need" (495). Here Liu touches on exactly the debate about the humanities I've been discussing throughout this book: "On the one hand, the humanities...struggle against the perception that they are primarily instrumental because their assigned role is to provide students with a skill set needed for future life and work" (500), a vision of the humanities weighted far too heavily for most on the practical skills and service side. "On the other hand, the humanities suffer even more from seeming to be noninstrumental to the point of uselessness" (500). Liu sees in this the same "catch-22" I identified in the opening chapter of this book, for the more noninstrumental the humanities look, in Liu's view, "the more cut off they seem from practical use" (500). The way to thread the needle, he insists, is to make sure that the digital humanities become a space for cultural criticism as well as instrumentality. "The contribution that the digital humanities can make to cultural criticism at the present time is to use the tools, paradigms, and concepts of digital technologies to help rethink the idea of instrumentality," to "think critically about metadata," and to "enter into fuller dialogue with the adjacent fields of media studies and media archaeology so as to extend reflection on core instrumental technologies in cultural and historical directions" (500). Doing so would mean that "standard issues in the digital humanities...could be enlarged with sociocultural meaning" (500). Configured this way, the digital humanities both grapple with technological infrastructures and use critical and cultural theory to deal in new ways with pressing social issues inside and outside of the academy.[18]

Liu insists that "to be an equal partner—rather than, again, just a servant—at the table, digital humanists will need to find ways to show that thinking critically about metadata, for instance, scales into thinking critically about the power, finance, and other governance protocols of the world." The digital humanities may be "poised to make the jump from a niche field to a field-of-fields," he observes, "but joining the mainstream," for Liu, means that the digital humanities must "show that it can also take a leadership role" for "the cause of the humanities" in an age when they "are being systematically or catastrophically defunded by nations, states, and universities." There are two related issues being raised here when it comes to the place of cultural criticism in the digital humanities. One has to do with what role, if any, cultural criticism plays *inside* the work of digital humanities scholars. To what extent, for example, do they draw on the whole panoply of close reading, textual and visual analysis, and aesthetic and ideological criticism, in a specifically social and cultural *critique* of digital culture? This kind of interpretive work, of course, would link the digital humanities to the engagement of the humanities per se with critical thinking about cultural and social issues. The second issue has to do with the role the digital humanities can play in advocating for the critical value of the humanities in the culture at large, something the 4Humanities site is dedicated to. This kind of work promises to engage the digital humanities in *defending* the humanities, something it seems to me it is particularly well-situated to do since it has a commitment to twenty-first-century technologies and their real-world practical application, *and* a commitment to sustaining and preserving for future generations the documents and works of art central to the tradition of humanism.

Can all of these various responsibilities be reconciled in a single digital humanities practice? Perhaps. Chris Forster (2010), for example, has put together a very reasonable and forward-looking proposal regarding what the digital humanities ought to cover, one that seeks to reconcile some of the differences I've been discussing. Forster breaks the digital humanities down into four related areas: (1) Direct, Practical, Uses of Computational Methods for Research, (2) Media Studies folks studying "New" Media, (3) Using Technology in the Classroom, and (4) The way new technology is reshaping research and the profession. The first involves "statistically grounded," "computer-enabled" research products, "data-mining," and so on, the kind of work most dramatically distinguished from a "'theoretically' grounded humanities" with an interest in "ideology" critique. The second, however, does involve the use of critical theory in the "political critique" of digital media, so here the kind of thing Liu worries over promises to get concentrated, sustained attention. The third and fourth, obviously, have to do with the role technology plays relative to pedagogy and the spaces (literal and virtual) in which teachers teach and students learn, and the new, increasingly open-access ways in which scholars publish their research. In many ways the digital humanities represent a paradigm shift, one that is beginning to dramatically affect the material and institutional ways in which people in the humanities perform their work in every sector—teaching, research, and even service. In this sense it is not hard to see how the technical infrastructure of everything from the production, collection, display, and study of data of all kinds to the literal and virtual configuration of learning environments is going to change dramatically. It is a little more difficult to see, however, how the balance between curation and criticism in a newly digitalized humanities will shake out. Specialists in the field, as I write, are currently debating this balance, and they are doing so with the sense of urgency dramatized in Liu's concern about the need for digital humanists to find their voice when it comes to defending and valuing the humanities. It may be that the digital humanities can save the humanities, but it remains a little unclear what it will save them for—and even where it will save them *to*.

All of the movements I have been discussing—the public humanities, the engaged humanities, and the digital humanities—seek to reconcile the tension between seeing the humanities as a place set apart for reflection and critique, and as a place in which students learn practical skills transferable to, and applicable in, the world of work in the public sphere. The emphasis is clearly on adapting academic competencies to the world outside academia, putting the expertise students develop in the humanities to work solving real social, cultural, economic, environmental, and even political problems. And, as we have seen, it is a two-way street. An engaged, public humanities tends to take a bottom-up approach in which problems outside of academia drive approaches to solving problems inside of academia. And of course the digital humanities are integral to all of the projects I have been discussing, since work in the engaged, public humanities is increasingly technological and digitalized, so that the skills digital humanities students learn are going to be particularly crucial to the work they do in jobs in the larger public sphere of the humanities.

The Humanities Classroom

All of the forces I have been discussing in this book—shrinking budgets, the digitalization of knowledge, the new stress on teaching practical skills, and an emphasis on engaged learning—have produced dramatic new institutional initiatives that threaten to transform the traditional humanities classroom. Distance learning, virtual classrooms, massive open online courses (or MOOCs), and the increasing presence of for-profit higher education, all seem to threaten the very existence of the brick-and-mortar classroom. But the demise of the traditional classroom for humanities learning would be a shame, for the conventional classroom does things none of these other classrooms can do, and when right-sized it allows for the teaching of the range of capabilities I have been discussing in this book in a way that other formats cannot. I want to close by insisting that while online educational formats certainly have their place in the future of higher education, they are not particularly well-equipped to do what the humanities do best, and that is to put students and their teachers in face-to-face dialogue with one another in structured but ultimately spontaneous discussions that are not always focused on solving specific problems, but rather deal conceptually and critically with abstract ideas, exploring a range of diverse interpretations where the stress is often on ambiguity, contingency, and the development of what the poet John Keats called "negative capability," the capacity to live with uncertainty. In a world increasingly dominated by technology, and an educational ethic committed to an engaged, public humanities grappling with real social problems, it is imperative that we make room for the kind of free-form exchange humanities classes have always been known for, and for the kind of substantive feedback on critical writing that is key to developing the skills humanities students learn. This kind of feedback simply cannot be done via distance learning or in a MOOC, and, as *Academically Adrift* reminds us, student writing is the most important factor in higher education learning.

One of the biggest challenges facing the humanities today is how to manage the industrialization of higher education. Colleges and universities today are increasingly turning to the massive, assembly line processing of students in order to maximize resources and revenue flows, a trend that is particularly unsuitable for an education in the humanities. This is especially the case when it comes to for-profit higher education, but it can be observed as well in the move of traditional universities into the world of online education. What started out innocently enough as distance learning—students taking courses online for credit through their local college or university—has morphed into the huge—and highly controversial—business of online, for-profit higher education. Most of the evidence to date suggests these institutions are more about profit than education.[19] According to a 2012 article in *The New York Times*, three-quarters of the students enrolled in for-profit colleges and universities are studying in institutions owned by large publicly traded companies and private equity firms.[20] And the profits they make come directly out of the pockets of US taxpayers. Over 80 percent of the tuition and fees paid to nonprofits by students comes from federal aid in the form of Pell Grants and Stafford loans. These institutions are long on recruiters but short on faculty. Educational oversight is lax, and the dropout rate extraordinarily high when compared to traditional brick-and-mortar colleges and universities. A two-year US Senate study chaired by Senator Tom

Harkin, the Iowa Democrat, recently issued a scathing criticism of both the business practices and poor learning outcomes of for-profit institutions of higher education such as Kaplan University and the University of Phoenix.[21] As Harkin notes, the report contains "overwhelming documentation of exorbitant tuition, aggressive recruiting practices, abysmal student outcomes, taxpayer dollars spent on marketing and pocketed as profit, and regulatory evasion and manipulation" (quoted in Lewin, "Senate Committee Report").

It was perhaps in part due to the scandal surrounding for-profit online institutions that the roll out in 2012 of Massive Open Online Courses (MOOCs) became *the* story in higher education. Under the MOOC model, classrooms themselves, along with the traditional forms of interaction between students and their professors that take place there, largely disappear.[22] MOOC consortiums such as Udacity, edX, and Coursera emerged with great fanfare in early 2012, and on November 12 of that year *The New York Times* declared it "the year of the MOOC." For developers and their supporters, MOOCs seemed like a perfect solution to the bleak economic plight of higher education, a low-cost way to produce and disseminate high quality courses taught by faculty in a range of disciplines at elite institutions to disadvantaged students around the world.[23] Freed from having to pay tuition at brick-and-mortar institutions, students can enroll at little or no cost in courses they may take in their own homes whenever they want to take them. Videotaped lectures and other course material can be streamed to thousands of students taking the same course everywhere. Free initially, these courses would eventually be monetized, forming a new revenue stream for brick-and-mortar institutions, which could eventually begin to grant degrees, based on the completion of required MOOC courses. The university would become, in effect, one big iTunes store. Students win, universities win, the economic crisis of higher education gets solved, and a nineteenth-century model of education gets transformed into a twenty-first-century engine of innovation and efficiency.

However, two years after the roll out of MOOCs their initial promise seems largely to have evaporated. What happened? First of all, educators themselves became highly skeptical of both the educational quality and the financial viability of MOOCs. Universities are of course in the business of education, but it seemed to many that in the case of MOOCs education was being trumped by business. Faculty skepticism about MOOCs crystallized in May 2013 when the philosophy department at San Jose State University refused to use a course developed by edX and taught by the eminent Harvard philosopher, Michael Sandel. The department published an open letter to Sandel explaining their position on May 2, 2013, in *The Chronicle of Higher Education.* It begins by pointing out that the course does not solve a single "pedagogical problem" in the philosophy department, since they have no "shortage of faculty capable of teaching" the material Professor Sandel's course would cover. They go on to point out that at a time when the lecture format is under fire on a number of fronts as an outmoded and ineffective system for educating students, it is ironic that edX proposed replacing live courses with recorded lectures. "After all the rhetoric questioning the effectiveness of the antiquated method of lecturing and note taking," they observed, "it is telling to discover that the core of edX's JusticeX [the title of Sandel's course] is a series of video-taped lectures that include excerpts of Harvard students making comments and taking notes." Instead, San Jose State's philosophy department believes that "having a scholar teach and engage his or her own students in person is far superior to having those students watch a video of another scholar engaging his or her students." They also expressed concern about the packaged homogeneity of philosophy courses using edX's model. "The thought of the exact same social justice course," they wrote, "being taught in various philosophy departments across the country is downright scary—something out of a dystopian novel.... Diversity in schools of thought and plurality of points of view are at the heart of liberal education."

San Jose State's philosophy faculty were also deeply concerned that MOOCs were part of an economic movement to "replace professors, dismantle departments, and provide a diminished education for students in public universities." They worry that "should one-size-fits-all vendor-designed courses become the norm...two classes of universities will be created: one, well-funded colleges and universities in which privileged students get their own real professor; the other, financially stressed private and public universities in which students watch a bunch of video-taped lectures." This concern led another prominent advocate of MOOCs to abandon his own course. Princeton sociologist Mitchell Duneier stopped teaching his introductory sociology course on Coursera after the company asked his permission to license his course so other colleges and universities could use its contents in a blended format of online and face-to-face instruction. The rationale was that this would save institutions a lot of money, but he declined. Why? "I've said no, because I think that it's an excuse for state legislatures to cut funding to state universities," Mr. Duneier says. "And I guess that I'm really uncomfortable being part of a movement that's going to get its revenue in that way. And I also have serious doubts about whether or not using a course like mine in that way would be pedagogically effective."

On the heels of faculty skepticism such as this came studies raising serious questions about just how beneficial MOOCs are for the students who enroll in them. Among students who enrolled in for credit courses through Udacity at San Jose State in the spring of 2013, for example, the pass rates were much lower than for conventional courses.[24] In February 2013, *The Chronicle of Higher Education* reported technical and logistical failures at Georgia Tech so serious that they required the suspension of some MOOCs there.[25] Perhaps most significantly, the "Alliance for Higher Education & Democracy at Penn GSE" analyzed the movement of a million users through 16 Coursera courses offered by the University of Pennsylvania from June 2012 to June 2013 and it found that "massive open online courses (MOOCs) have relatively few active users, that user 'engagement' falls off dramatically—especially after the first 1–2 weeks of a course—and that few users persist to the course end." Furthermore, "course completion rates are very low, averaging 4% across all courses and ranging from 2% to 14% depending on the course and measurement of completion." Worse still for a platform touted as having the potential to democratize higher education, the study found that the majority of users were well-off white men with a college degree. Penn GSE reported that "the 'educational disparity is particularly stark' in Brazil, Russia, India, China and South Africa, where almost 80% of MOOC students came from the wealthiest 6% of the population. Across the board, Penn's MOOC students had already far exceeded the educational standards found among the general population in their countries."[26] According to the study's author, Ezekiel J. Emanuel, "far from realizing the high ideals of their advocates, MOOCs seem to be reinforcing the advantages of the 'haves' rather than educating the 'have-nots.'"[27]

As if all these negative reports were not enough, 2013 ended with the CEO of Udacity, Sebastian Thrun, a MOOC pioneer, declaring that the MOOC experiment had largely turned out to be a failure. Thrun, analyzing the kind of data I've just been reviewing, realized the huge gap between the hype about MOOCs and their reality. As he told Max Chafkin of *Tech Forecast*, "We were on the front pages of newspapers and magazines, and at the same time, I was realizing, we don't educate people as others wished, or as I wished. We have a lousy product."[28] Thrun for now seems to have given up altogether on developing MOOCs as a replacement for the classroom and is instead focusing his attention on transforming Udacity into a tool for corporate training.

Given what looks at this writing to be the collapse of the MOOC experiment, at least in its current iteration, it is hard to see how MOOCs are going to save higher education, especially when it comes to humanities courses, where teaching both knowledge and skills requires face-to-face discussion and the time-consuming reading and grading of student essays by professors or teaching assistants, complete with opportunities for revision. The possibilities and pitfalls of the MOOC model are nicely summed up in a recent exchange between Cathy Davidson and Ian Bogost. Davidson is wary of MOOCs but she points to the inability of the conventional brick-and-mortar institution to handle contemporary educational demands. "Let's start with the numbers," she writes:

> *4.1:* That's the grade point average of a high school student entering the University of California, Irvine this year. *450,000:* students on the waiting list for community colleges in California alone. *74%:* the percentage of students from the richest quartile of households enrolled at the top 150 colleges in the US—even though high-income students make up only a third of high-achieving high school graduates. While the G.I. Bill and the Great Society were founded on the principle of higher education as the ladder to the middle class, in 2013 state schools are so starved of funds, and private ones so expensive, that higher education is becoming the province of the high achieving and the wealthy global 1%.[29]

"It is in this context," she explains, "that I find MOOCs a useful goal toward educational experimentation that may lead to methods for educating more students and in ways more responsive to the connected world they inhabit everywhere except in school." However, she concludes "given the history of for-profits in the education arena, professors at brick-and-mortar institutions have reason to worry that MOOCs are being hyped by venture capitalists who have no real interest in learning. I share that fear. However, our justifiable worry about the future of the professoriate doesn't help those students being excluded from higher education today."

Bogost takes a much more skeptical approach than Davidson, even questioning whether MOOCs ought to be thought of as *courses* at all. He writes, "Even if MOOCs do sometimes function as courses (or as textbooks), a minority of their effects arises from their status as educational experiences. Other, less obvious aspects of MOOCs exert far more influence on contemporary life." You can think of MOOCs as courses if you like, according to Bogost, but doing so runs the risk of missing the other forms they actually take. These include MOOCs as a type of "marketing," MOOCs as "a financial policy for higher education," MOOCs as "an academic labor policy," MOOCs as "speculative financial instruments,"[30] MOOCs as "an expression of Silicon Valley values," and MOOCs as "kind of entertainment media." From this point of view MOOCs can be linked to what Naomi Klein has called "disaster capitalism." First you systematically defund higher education, then you call the lack of funds a crisis, then you farm out education to third-party Internet platforms. As a labor policy, Bogost worries that MOOCs simply feed the casualization of academic labor, adding a new layer to the army of adjuncts and part-timers who are taking over the education of our children from full-time tenured and tenure-track professors. In this sense they are a part of the rampant corporatization of higher education I have referred to throughout this book. While it seems to me that Davidson is right that we face a crisis in terms of figuring out how to manage the education of our children, I think Bogost makes a convincing case that MOOCs are a poor substitute for committing more funds to real education, face-to-face, in brick-and-mortar classrooms. Worse still, they threaten to contribute to the very industrializing and technologizing of our culture the humanities traditionally—and usefully—help keep in check.

So while the Internet may see like a dramatic, exciting new delivery system for higher education, the two dominant models at this point look awfully problematic. For-profits have been roundly condemned for putting profit ahead of education, soaking students of their taxpayer loans, and providing a poor educational product in institutions with high dropout rates. MOOCs, on the other hand, are giving away the same courses that students on campus pay thousands of dollars to take, offer no credit, and no degrees, and their track record to date is not very impressive.[31] It's hard to see how MOOCs can provide a model for stabilizing the faltering budgets of established colleges and universities, and harder still to see how they can have anything but a negative effect on the humanities, since MOOCs are ill-suited for the educational needs of humanities students. The strength of enterprises such as Coursera—"our technology enables the best professors to teach tens or hundreds of thousands of students"—is also its weakness, for there is no way for one professor to teach a hundred thousand students enrolled online in her Introduction to Philosophy or Romantic Poetry course to develop and then fine-tune their analytical, interpretive, critical, argumentative, and writing skills. MOOCs can do a respectable job delivering subject matter to thousands of students, but they cannot pay much attention at all to honing the practical skills humanities students learn and that I have been arguing is a central value in their education. Indeed, the mass-produced, industrialized form of education MOOCs represent seems designed to short-circuit the teaching of such skills, reducing a humanities education to the delivery and memorization of content. They cannot replicate the kind of spontaneous, face-to-face exploratory exchanges and debates professors can facilitate in a classroom setting where 15–30 students are together and engaged with one another, nor can they allow faculty to read student writing and provide the kind of feedback they need to hone their analytical, interpretive, argumentative, and writing skills. At the very moment when communication and interpersonal skills are in demand by employers everywhere, higher education ought to be wary about moving to new formats that make it impossible to teach them. Here it is important to recall that, according to *Academically Adrift*, the only students who register significant learning gains while in college are liberal arts students who are assigned at least 40 pages of reading a week and at least 20 pages of writing a semester. MOOCs and other high enrollment online courses simply do not provide teachers the time to provide feedback on writing to students in meaningful ways that will enhance their writing abilities. In my courses, for example (35 students per course) I usually require at least 30 pages of writing divided over three papers. Students receive detailed editorial comments on each page. It typically takes an hour to read and comment on each paper, and I often require students to revise at least one of their papers for a higher grade. Try doing that with 100 or 200 online students, let alone 2,000.

Perhaps MOOCs will lead to a blended system of education on and off campuses that will save money and help facilitate the kind of learning I have been advocating in this book. But in the meantime I believe the future of the humanities remains connected to the kind of hands-on, face-to-face engagement between students and their professors that has served higher education in America so well for so long. Blending such encounters with online delivery systems and digitized access to educational materials should not be done merely to save money or make up for budget shortfalls due to government defunding of higher education, but rather, to enhance both the range of knowledge and the sophistication of skills humanities students will need to be successful as twenty-first-century citizens and workers. As I have argued throughout this book, this means valuing—and continuing to enhance—the rigor of a humanities education by making sure that students are trained in the forms of professional expertise their professors use in their own scholarly work. The subjects and competencies at the center of a humanities education are taught best by professors steeped in historical knowledge of their discipline and trained to think critically about that knowledge. Their professionalism ought to be seen as central to what they teach, not as an impediment to it. For, as we have seen, there is no honest way to separate the subjects humanities professors teach from the theories and methodologies they use to construct those subjects in the first place. Students should not be protected from those theories and methodologies or lulled into thinking that knowledge just naturally occurs. Instead, they should be trained to think theoretically and to apply disciplinary methodologies to analyze and help solve social and cultural problems. The ability to read closely and carefully, to analyze and think critically about the arguments others make, to summarize and synthesize positions, and to develop orally and in writing their own arguments are keys to success that cannot be taught in virtual classrooms or MOOCs in which thousands of students are being fed prepackaged video lectures and quizzed with scant supervision. It is clear that little serious reading and analysis gets done in such contexts, and, worse still, it is impossible in such venues to give student writing the time and attention it deserves.

All of this is particularly important for the future of literary studies. The rise of the digital humanities, to be sure, holds great promise for both transforming and expanding work in the disciplines of English and Comparative literatures. But, as we have already seen, that promise would be squandered if the digitalization of literary studies unfolds in a narrowly technical way that ends up marginalizing the close reading, interpretation, and social and cultural analysis of literary texts by students and their professors. As I noted earlier, one of the attractions of the digital humanities is that they seem of offer a sheerly technical, objective, and practical focus for literary studies that solves what some see as the twin problems of too much theory and the politicizing of literary studies. The digitalizing of literary and cultural studies may well involve teaching students how to write code and develop computerized infrastructures for the presentation and analysis of literary and cultural texts, but it ought to push as well beyond a narrow instrumentalism to serve as a locus for the study of digital culture itself. Here I think Liu is right, that the digital humanities, especially as it unfolds in the context of literary studies, has to have a critical as well as an instrumentalist orientation. For this is what the humanities have always done best: explore the human dimension of our interface with the rational, the technical, the industrial, and the pragmatic.

It is no accident that the most trenchant critique of MOOCs came from a philosophy department. Philosophers, historians, and literary critics are trained to think constructively but skeptically about social, cultural, institutional, and economic reform, to raise questions about their human value. Literary analysis for the sheer sake of literary analysis—formalist and aesthetic criticism—has a profound value we ought to protect, but it is not its only value. Literary studies in the twenty-first century ought to tap into the potential of digitalization at the same time that it critiques digitalization, and it will serve its students best if it supplements a knowledge of historically important texts and authors with the teaching of transferable skills that will make them more productive, innovative, critically aware citizens. For the foreseeable future that kind of education will not come cheaply, nor will it be the product of mass-produced, prepackaged, online courses in which thousands of students are supervised by a single instructor or a group of teaching assistants. It will cost money and take place in actual classrooms where students and their professors are engaged, face-to-face with one another, classrooms in which extensive writing and training in revision is central. The humanities are not threatened by irrelevancy because of the subject areas they cover, but rather, by the systematic defunding of higher education, and the substitution of quick fix, industrialized, online vocational training for embodied, active, engaged learning.

NOTES

1 THE HUMANITIES CRISIS THEN AND NOW

1. http://www.mindingthecampus.com/originals/2009/03/on_february_25_2009_an.html.
2. See Bérubé, 2002.
3. Yale, Saul points out, is an "extreme case, since its humanities programs were historically so popular and since its administration has worked hard to build up its science programs."
4. See http://goo.gl/1M85Zl.
5. Of course it can be argued that such deep budgetary cuts in the humanities, initiated under the guise of economic hard times, are in fact being used to roll back an overly politicized humanities. This argument, for example, is at the center of Christopher Newfield's book, *Unmaking the Public University*. He argues, "Conservative elites who had been threatened by the postwar rise of the college-educated economic majority have put that majority back in its place. Their roundabout weapon has been the culture wars on higher education in general, and on progressive cultural trends in the public universities that create and enfranchise the mass middle class" (5). "[T]he culture wars have coincided with the majority's economic decline for the simple reason that these wars propelled the decline by reducing the public importance and economic claims of the American university and its graduates...the culture wars were economic wars" (6).
6. Indeed, as a recent *New York Times* editorial pointed out ("Who Says Math Is Boring," December 8, 2013), the STEM disciplines are doing just as bad or worse in terms of declining interest. According to the *Times* editorial students are not flocking to math, engineering, science, and computer science programs. Instead, they find them boring. Nearly 90% of high school graduates express disinterest in pursuing majors in these fields. "The number of students who want to pursue engineering or computer sciences is actually falling," the *Times* points out, and rather "precipitously," at that. For example, between 1995 and 2005, according to a study done by the American

College Testing (ACT), students majoring in engineering dropped from 4.5% to 2.9%.
7. The Georgetown survey Weissmann cites pegs humanities and liberal arts graduates' median earnings at 66K versus median salaries in the 80K and 90K range for graduates in the social and natural sciences, and in computing.
8. "Employer Perspectives on Liberal Education," Association of American Colleges and Universities, http://www.aacu.org/leap/students/libedemployerperspectives.cfm.
9. *Occupational Outlook Quarterly* 51, no. 4 (Winter 2007–2008), http://goo.gl/qagNB.
10. "Google Leads Search for Humanities PhD graduates," Matthew Reisz, *The Times Higher Education*, http://goo.gl/WV2mC.
11. "From Technologist to Philosopher: Why You Should Quit Your Technology Job and Get a Ph.D. in the Humanities," *Chronicle of Higher Education*, July 17, 2011.
12. See "Steve Jobs on the Humanities," for a collection of his observations about the centrality of the humanities and the liberal arts for technology innovation, http://4humanities.org/2011/10/steve-jobs-on-the-humanities/. Walter Isaacson stresses Jobs's commitment to the humanities throughout his biography of Apple's founder.
13. For background information on how the survey was conducted see the website of the Association of American Colleges and Universities at http://www.aacu.org/leap/presidentstrust/compact/2013SurveySummary.cfm. The entire report from which I am quoting is available at http://www.aacu.org/leap/documents/2013_EmployerSurvey.pdf.
14. For another recent example of the value CEOs place on humanities graduates, see Vivian Giang's article about the CEO of Logitech, Bracken Darrell, who seeks out English majors wherever he can find them for their communication and interpersonal skills.
15. The authors "predicted 2007 CLA scores" by field of study had business and education/social work students ranked the lowest at 1120 and 1130, respectively, while humanities and social sciences students' scores were 1190 (Figure 4.4, p. 99, e-book edition). Again, the authors found a direct correlation between extended writing assignments and higher scores on the CLA.
16. See Kevin Carey, "'Academically Adrift': The News Gets Worse and Worse," *The Chronicle of Higher Education*, February 12, 2012, http://chronicle.com/article/Academically-Adrift-The/130743/. As Carey notes, Roksa and Arum report that "despite a barren job market, only 3.1 percent of students who scored in the top 20 percent of the Collegiate Learning Assessment, which measures critical-thinking skills, were unemployed. Not infrequently, their

colleges helped them land the jobs they had. Many struck out on their own and were engaged in civic affairs. Those who got married or cohabitated often did so with someone they met in college. For students like these, the college-driven job and mating markets are functioning as advertised. Graduates who scored poorly on the CLA, by contrast, are leading very different lives. It's true that business majors, who were singled out for low CLA scores in *Academically Adrift*, did better than most in finding jobs. But over all, students with poor CLA results are more likely to be living at home with their parents, burdened by credit-card debt, unmarried, and unemployed."

17. This attitude has sometimes thwarted the success of the few programs that have recognized that humanities graduates have much to offer the worlds of business, technology, arts agencies, and philanthropic foundations. The most promising of these efforts was a program in the 1990s developed by the Woodrow Wilson Foundation under the leadership of its then director, Robert Weisbuch. First called "Unleashing the Humanities" and later "The Humanities at Work," the program according to Weisbuch "had persuaded forty non-profits and for-profits to reserve meaningful positions for Ph.D. graduates in the humanities and had placed a large number in well-paying and interesting positions—at places ranging from Verizon to AT Kearney to the Wall St Journal to the National Parks Service." Unfortunately, Weisbuch reports, "only a few humanities graduate programs enlisted their alumni and the influential corporations and others in their areas of influence to revolutionize the possibilities for employment of humanities doctoral graduates," as most faculty members "continued to expect their graduate students to look for jobs much like their own and to consider any other outcome a failure."
18. A "blue ribbon" task force appointed by Florida governor Rick Scott suggested a different approach, proposing what they called "differential tuition." Under this scheme, according to a report in Forbes magazine, "tuition would be frozen over the next few years for bachelor's degree programs identified by the state's legislature as 'high-skill, high-wage, high-demand' but allowed to rise in other programs—history, philosophy, anthropology." See http://goo.gl/sDzhlF.
19. "The Crisis of the Humanities Officially Arrives," *The New York Times, Opinionator*, October 11, 2010, http://goo.gl/cKljhX.
20. See "University at Albany Announces Measures to Rethink, Balance and Reallocate Resources in Face of Reduced State Fiscal Support," University of Albany News Center, http://goo.gl/J6jnnS.
21. "The Crisis of the Humanities Officially Arrives."
22. For example, the *Times* marked the occasion by convening a group of educators just a few days after the Phillips announcement to

discuss the crisis in the humanities. See "Do Colleges Need French Departments?," October 17, 2010, at http://goo.gl/uzju.
23. "Chiseling Away at the Humanities," http://goo.gl/hUJnwJ.
24. "In Tough Times the Humanities Must Justify Their Worth," http://goo.gl/5n0YJq.
25. "Are the Humanities on the Ropes? Maybe Not," http://goo.gl/RuIfd9.
26. "The Liberal Arts Are Not Elitist," *The Chronicle of Higher Education*, February 28, 2010, http://chronicle.com/article/The-Liberal-Arts-Are-Not/64355/.
27. See, for example, Kimball's *Tenured Radicals* (1990) and D'Souza's *Illiberal Education* (1991).
28. Bennett, of course, was the newly appointed secretary of education.
29. "Humanists Seek to Regain Their Public Voice," *The Chronicle of Higher Education*, April 7, 1993, http://goo.gl/u7KWMG.
30. See Carolyn J. Mooney, "A Lull in the 'Political Correctness' Debate?" *The Chronicle of Higher Education*, April 20, 1993, http://goo.gl/5dnf9W.
31. "Sheldon Hackney on the Role of the Humanities," *The Chronicle of Higher Education*, July 21, 1993, http://chronicle.com/article/Sheldon-Hackney-on-the-Role-of/73128/.
32. Martha Nussbaum takes up these issues in a more sustained and complex way 19 years later in *Not for Profit* (2010), both arguing against the idea that a humanities education should be measured by narrow economic criteria, and for the idea that the humanities have a practical value because they teach the kinds of communicative and cross-cultural skills Hackney stresses and that I have been emphasizing. For another, somewhat different argument in favor of the value of a literary education, see Garber, 2011.
33. "Restoring 'Literary Literacy' to the English Curriculum," *The Chronicle of Higher Education*, March 7, 2011, http://goo.gl/SyCNhA.
34. In his conclusion to *Literary Theory* (1983) Eagleton wrote that his advocacy of a focus in literary studies on "the effects which discourses produce" envisioned a return to "what was probably the oldest form of 'literary criticism' in the world, known as rhetoric" (205). On the historical centrality of rhetoric in literary studies see Scholes.
35. See in particular Burke's *A Rhetoric of Motives*.
36. "Making English Majors Marketable," *The Chronicle of Higher Education*, April 23, 2001, http://chronicle.com/article/Making-English-majors/108296/.
37. Her article, under that title, appeared in the February 24, 2009, edition of *The New York Times*, http://www.nytimes.com/2009/02/25/books/25human.html?pagewanted=all&_r=0.

38. As the Harvard report on the humanities illustrates, balancing disinterested appreciation and reasoned, constructive critique, has always been a challenge for humanities educators. Although the report acknowledges there may have been an overemphasis on critique in the humanities during the last few decades ("Mapping the Future," 41), and that we "might recognize a kernel of truth in conservative fears about the left-leaning academy" (42), it nevertheless calls for a balance between appreciation and critique, insisting that critique is both "essential" and "socially constructive" ("In Brief," 4).
39. See "What is Critique? An Essay on Foucault's Virtue," in *eipcp*, a publication of the European Institute for Progressive Policies, May, 2001, http://eipcp.net/transversal/0806/butler/en.
40. Ibid.
41. Ibid.
42. See, for example, James F. English's "Who Says English Is a Dying Discipline?" (*The Chronicle of Higher Education*, September 17, 2012) for a refreshing rejoinder to the idea that English is in a state of crisis (https://chronicle.com/article/Who-Says-English-Is-a-Dying/134410/).

2 Professionalism and Its Discontents

1. "A New Day for Intellectuals," February 13, 2009, http://chronicle.com/article/A-New-Day-for-Intellectuals/21359.
2. See Hirsch, 1988.
3. Ruddick's essay is a specific response to the events of 9/11, but it captures succinctly the general argument against professionalism I have been discussing.
4. It isn't clear what Harpham means here by "increasingly," since literature professors have been professionally trained in PhD programs for most of the twentieth century.
5. Here, by way of example, is a fairly typical English department mission statement from the English department at Skidmore University:

    What is literature? What constitutes a literary education in the twenty-first century? How many ways are there to read and write about the same text, and how do we decide among various interpretations? How does our understanding of a work change when we consider its context, whether biographical, historical, cultural, or political? Why might we ask questions in literature classes about race, class, gender, and sexuality? Why should a student of literature study language? Why should a student interested in creative writing read literature? How does writing enable us to discover and shape our ideas? How does the English major prepare students for living in, and thoughtfully engaging with, the world? The Skidmore English

department invites students to consider such questions and to frame their own. Throughout the curriculum, English majors learn to read closely, think critically, challenge assumptions, practice methods of interpretation and research, analyze the formal qualities of texts, approach texts from various perspectives, place texts in various contexts, and write with clarity, coherence, and precision. As the English major progresses from introductory to capstone courses, students are offered increasingly sophisticated and elaborate writing and analytic tasks and called upon to perform steadily more original, inventive, independent work.
http://cms.skidmore.edu/english/mission.cfm.
6. For example, I recently conducted in my introduction to contemporary critical theory course a theoretical and historical discussion of the concepts of the author and authorship drawing on the classical essays by Roland Barthes ("The Death of the Author") and Michel Foucault ("What is an Author"). Dry and boring? Suppressed my students' enthusiasm? Not at all. We had a lively, exciting discussion about how these concepts had changed over time, and how writing in the digital age was continuing to change them. Students left exhilarated, and a few stayed around after class to tell me so.
7. Of course this is not to say that every English department needs a graduate program. The high production of PhDs at a time when so many jobs are being transformed from tenure-track to adjunct or part-time positions is a significant problem. But there is no reason in the world why the professionalism of literary studies ought to be thought of as a solely graduate and professorial-level pursuit.
8. I'll take up this topic at more length in chapter 5 in my discussion of recent calls for a return to aesthetic criticism in literary studies.
9. See Graff's discussion of this issue on pages 11–12 where he invokes the analyses of this category by Terry Eagleton and Michel Foucault. Graff here acknowledges that criticism can often lead to "poor contextualizing," but he insists all discussion of literature contextualizes it, and that in any case "the remedy for a poor contextualizing of literature is not no contextualizing but better contextualizing" (11).
10. For a concise discussion of why this is the case, see Eagleton (2003), 93–95. "Without preconceptions of some sort," he notes, "we would not even be able to identify a work of art in the first place. Without some form of critical language at our disposal we would simply not know what do look for, just as there is no point in introspection if we have no vocabulary in which to identify what we find inside ourselves" (94).
11. Graff points out that "one salutary lesson of current theory is that though the experience of reading a text may feel like a pretheoretical,

precritical activity, that feeling can arise only because the reader has already mastered the contexts and presuppositions necessary for the text's comprehension" (255).
12. Garber's account of what happened in literary studies since the late 1960s is crisp and cogent, but it emphasizes the impact of continental linguistic theories and philosophies (structuralism, phenomenology, semiotics, deconstruction, etc.) while largely ignoring the impact of political and cultural criticism that came in its wake; forms of literary study that grew out of the women's movement; the Civil Rights movement; gay, lesbian, and queer theory; and postcolonial and multicultural studies. The key point I want to emphasize here is the extent to which both the linguistic and political/cultural turns in literary studies were connected to a broad rethinking of humanism and the institutional and academic structures associated with it, whereas, Garber tends to conflate the work in theory she discusses with humanism. Roland Barthes, Pierre Bourdieu, Raymond Williams, Jacques Derrida Jacques Lacan, and Michel Foucault, for example, get referenced collectively in a single paragraph as representing "the bad child of humanistic work in the 1970s and 1980s" (*Manifesto*, 4). Garber's conflating the work of these critics with "humanistic work" is telling, for their work stands collectively as a radical critique of liberal humanism and its institutional structures (this is especially the case with Derrida and Foucault, of course). One can't begin to think about the work of the critics she cites without recognizing how their work, collectively, constituted a thoroughgoing critique of conceptions of literariness, subjectivity, agency, truth, and power central to the humanities. This was humanistic work that developed a thoughtful, probing, historical, philosophical, and theoretical critique of the discursive formation we call "the humanities." Indeed, it is our recognition that the "humanities" is a concept, a discursive construction, and not a thing itself that is arguably the central hallmark of theory during this period.
13. For another constructive approach to these kinds of issues see Elaine Tuttle Hanson, "The Situation of the Humanities" (2006).

3 Humanism, the Humanities, and Political Correctness

1. *The Chronicle of Higher Education*, December 9, 1992, http://goo.gl/ZlfWEr.
2. Noonan explores at length the extent to which the postmodern critique of subjectivity and agency challenges many of its ideals, and thus constitutes a critical humanism.

3. Brooks goes on to insist that "our teaching needs to demonstrate that oppositions between 'the tradition' (the canon, the great books, and ideas) and new perspectives of analysis can be part of a continuing dialectic that constructs our relation to tradition. To this end, much greater attention should be paid, especially in our graduate teaching, to the 'processes' of the humanities—how traditions are created, how culture is transmitted, and what conditions are necessary for innovation. The creation and transmission of culture are themselves interesting and problematic. They need to be put at the center of both teaching and scholarship. Pertinent here is the fact that several scholars have recently undertaken 'archaeologies' of their own disciplines. Through such archaeologies, we may begin to free ourselves from what have come to appear as immutable curricular forms and professional practices."

4. Gerald Graff rightly points out that the humanist critique of theory in the 1970s and early 1980s was based on a kind of "myth" that humanism itself was not theory. He in fact insists on defining humanism as theory:

> Theory is what is generated when some aspect of literature, its nature, its history, its place in society, its conditions of production and reception, its meaning in general, or the meanings of particular works, ceases to be given and becomes a question to be argued in a generalized way. Theory is what inevitably arises when literary conventions and critical definitions once taken for granted have become objects of generalized discussion and dispute. (252)

If we keep this general notion of theory in mind we can see how "'traditional humanistic' criticism is theoretical" (252). Even though "modern hostility to theory first originated in the romantic critique of industrial society, a critique which associated abstract modes of thought with the nihilistic and corrosive rationalism that had supposedly destroyed the earlier organic unity of culture," the only way traditional humanistic critics such as Matthew Arnold could "restore that unified culture was to propagandize about its desirability; that is, to theorize" (252–253). "Traditional cultural criticism" such as Arnold's is, from this point of view, "unavoidably theoretical" because it takes culture and literature as things "to be theorized" (253). What else is humanism's wholesale rethinking of human nature and rights if it is not a dramatic retheorization of what it means to be human?

5. The idea that post-structuralist theory constitutes a version of antihumanism, of course, has its roots in Foucault's declaration near the end of *The Order of Things* that "man is an invention of recent date. And one perhaps nearing its end" (387). "Man" here stands for the humanist version of the human, steeped as it was in a metaphysical idealism that was the central subject of critique in structuralism

and deconstruction. On the emergence of antihumanism in French philosophy see Ferry and Renaut.
6. For a somewhat different take on the relationship between critical theory and humanism, see Edward Said's *Humanism and Democratic Criticism* (2003). See also *Cultural Critique*, no. 67 (Fall 2007) for a collection of essays on Said's complexly ambivalent relationship to theory and humanism.
7. See *The Foucault Reader*, 76–100.
8. All quotations are from the first edition.
9. According to Davies, it was used, for example, by the early nineteenth-century German educator, Friedrich Immanuel Niethammer "to describe a high-school and university curriculum based on what have been known since the Middle Ages as the 'humanities,'" the "study of ancient Greek and Latin, and of the literature, history, and culture of the peoples who spoke them" (9–10).
10. Burckhardt's Germany, Davies points out, "was developing painfully from an agglomeration of small principalities towards a unified national state," and in Burckhardt's "The State as a Work of Art" emergent "Germany finds her reflection and inspiration…in the writings of Renaissance humanist historians, political theorists and jurists—Guiccardini, Machiavelli, Grotium, Bodin—and in the embattled but fiercely independent states like Florence and Geneva in and about which they wrote" (15–16).
11. Burckhardt can locate this concept of the individual in the Renaissance, Davies points out, only by "striking semantic reversals that from the sixteenth century rendered words like individual (originally 'inseparable') and identity ('sameness') over to meanings almost exactly the opposite of their traditional ones" (16–17).
12. Davies notes how this "desire to find in the fifteenth and sixteenth centuries the headwaters of an essentially nineteenth-century individuality manifest itself even more dramatically" in the French diplomat Comte de Gobineau's *The Renaissance*, which figures Renaissance individualism in ways less related to "civic solidarity" than an "uncompromising selfhood and will to power of individual 'genius' that traffics in a sense of "innate superiority" over what Gonineau calls the "weakness and scruples" of "petty minds and the rabble of underlings" (17).
13. Arnold, Davies notes, along with writers such as John Addington Symonds, "give popular currency in England to ideas, including the idea of humanism itself, first articulated by German-speaking historians and philosophers a generation earlier: ideas developed within a distinctively German tradition and at a particularly critical moment in the historical and cultural formation of modern Germany" (24).
14. As Davies summarizes, "In these nineteenth-century discourses, the figure of the human, though deployed in contexts that might suggest

that it is geographically and historically specific (European and modern), in reality signifies something that is everywhere and always the same" (24).

15. So much so that, as Davies observes, "formulations of the 'human'" invented in the nineteenth century "would have appeared strange, perhaps unintelligible, certainly blasphemously presumptuous to those earlier humanists who are credited with its 'discovery'" (25). So-called "Renaissance humanism," understood as "expressive of an essential humanity unconditioned by time, place or circumstance, is a nineteenth-century anachronism" (25).

16. Marx's early work, up until about 1844, was in fact influenced by humanist speculations about ultimate forms of being and the essence of human nature (in Feuerbach, for example), but as he developed his theory of historical materialism he moved away from this kind of metaphysical language. Davies, for example, points out that after 1844 Marx developed an economic theory of history driven by a form of dialectical materialism that counters the kind of metaphysical idealism that the humanists such as Humboldt, Burckhardt, and Matthew Arnold embraced. By this time Marx had broken with the kind of Hegelian idealism that assumed "people's lives can be transformed simply by reawakening the sense of freedom in their heads and hearts" (11). The key argument for this "espistemological break" in Marx was developed by the French post-structuralist Marxist Louis Althusser in *For Marx* (2006).

17. See Menand, chapter two, for an excellent discussion of how these changes transformed the humanities in the 1980s and 1990s. He is particularly helpful on the historical context for these changes running back to the mid-1940s.

18. For more on this argument see Ajiz Ahmad's "Orientalism and After: Ambivalence and Metropolitan Location in the Work of Edward Said."

19. For another, more recent discussion of the complicity between humanism, racism, and imperialism, see chapter 2, "Roots, Races, and the Return of Philology," in Geoffrey Galt Harpham's *The Humanities and the Dream of America*. Throughout this chapter Harpham emphasizes "the deep investment of linguistic scholarship in the concept of race" (53–54), and how humanists scholars in the nineteenth century "were increasingly committed, not just to articulating cultural differences on the basis of linguistic differences, but also to affirming the supremacy of the groups that had settled Christian Europe" (55–56). See also Davies, 7–10 and 136–137. Writing about the Nazi occupation of Athens in 1941, he notes "from one point of view," the one that underscores the roots of Nazism in nineteenth-century German humanism, "the invading Germans appear not as the destroyers of Greek civilization but as

its liberators, the heirs and custodians of its sacred flame" (9). Terry Eagleton made something like the same point in 1983 in *Literary Theory: An Introduction*, when he noted that reading Goethe did not stop the Germans from trying to exterminate the Jews (35).
20. See Senghor, "Negritude: A Humanism of the Twentieth Century," in *Imperialism: Critical Concepts in Historical Studies*, ed. Cain and Harrison. See also Claudia Alvares, *Humanism after Colonialism*.
21. For an extended treatment of the humanities as a twentieth-century invention, see Harpham (2011) Introduction and chapter 3.
22. For a more extended critical discussion of Appiah's book see my book, *Global Matters*, 61–67.
23. Prominent here would be Franz Fanon's *Black Skin, White Masks* (1952), and *The Wretched of the Earth* (1961), and later, the criticism of C. L. R. James and Edouard Glissant.
24. It should be clear from my discussion of humanism and the humanities that there really never was time when either one was not political. When conservative critics complain that work in the contemporary humanities is political one ought to wonder, so what's new? These complaints ignore the political dimensions of humanism from the Renaissance well into the mid-twentieth century when, as Harpham has shown, the humanities were reinvented in the United States in part to help fight the cold war. See in particular Harpham's *The Humanities and the Dream of America*, chapter 6, "Melancholy in the Midst of Abundance: How America Invented the Humanities."
25. This is already becoming the case in the United States. By 2019 the majority of children in the United States will belong to minority groups, and whites are slated to become a minority population here by at least 2041. See the *New York Times* article, "Numbers of Children of Whites Falling Fast," by Sabrina Tavernise (http://www.nytimes.com/2011/04/06/us/06census.html).
26. As Harpham puts it, "The driving force behind the concretization of the humanities after the war was almost nakedly strategic and political—the desire to strengthen the American nation by producing citizens capable of the confident exercise of the freedoms available in, and protected by, a modern democratic culture" (*The Humanities and the Dream of America*, 15). For an extended version of this argument see Pease.

4 Getting to the Core of the Humanities, or Who's Afraid of Gloria Anzaldúa?

1. Attachment to email communication from Loyola University, Chicago, English department chair to English department faculty, September 1, 2010.

2. Suzanne Bost, for *Encarnación: Illness and Body Politics in Chicana Feminist Literature*.
3. See, for example, the comprehensive biographical and scholarly entry, along with a comprehensive bibliography, on the website *Voices from the Gap*, http://voices.cla.umn.edu/artistpages/anzaldua.php.
4. Of course there is no single *Moby Dick*. It is nearly impossible to count the various editions of *Moby Dick*, though one person is trying on *The Moby Dick Collection* website (http://themobydickcollection.blogspot.com/). And of course there are many abridged editions that skip the difficult chapters on cetology.
5. There is a value, for example, in phenomenology's desire to bracket off all extrinsic contexts in the reading of literary texts, and in a reader-response approach that concentrates on the individual reader's construction of a texts meaning, but there is no reason whatsoever to stop critical analysis at these arbitrary points. They ought to be the prelude to other contextualizations.
6. Derrida makes this point in *Of Grammatology* in his discussion of the "classic" operation of paraphrasing the meaning of a text, which he calls a "doubling commentary." As valuable as it is, this "doubling," he insists, should not serve as a "guardrail" against other forms of critical reading and analysis (158–159).
7. For an extended treatment of the transnational turn in literary studies see my *Global Matters*.
8. See, for example, the requirements at Brown and Cornell.
9. I have chosen to focus my discussion on the history of Columbia's core because of its prominence and importance, and because the debates it reflects are broadly representative. See Keller for a book-length discussion of the core curriculum at two other prominent universities, Harvard, and the University of Chicago. For a closer look at debates about Harvard's core, circa 1945, see *General Education in a Free Society: Report of the Harvard Committee*. For more general treatments of the core curriculum debate in the United States see Atlas, and Menand, chapter one.
10. All the quotations that follow, unless otherwise noted, are from the Columbia University Core Curriculum website page titled *History of the Core*, http://www.college.columbia.edu/core/timeline.
11. In 1928 this utilitarian emphasis was underscored when the Contemporary Civilization sequence was implemented, for one of the key questions it sought to answer was simply, "How do men make a living?"
12. See "Colleges Outline New War Courses," *The New York Times*, September 18, 1918, on the *History of the Core* website.
13. Many on campus who opposed US involvement in the war drove this initiative. Peace studies were meant to counter the focus on study related to successfully waging war.

14. See Coss, "The New Freshman Course in Columbia College," 1919, http://www.college.columbia.edu/core/sites/core/files/The%20 New%20Freshman%20Course%20in%20Columbia%20College.pdf. There was, however, a downside to the interdisciplinary structure of these courses, for faculty would be teaching outside of their areas of specialization. The "difficulty" is that "no one man knows in detail all the subjects which will be treated. Each instructor will teach for a portion of the time in a field which is not his specialty. This means that the teaching staff will be educating itself as well as instructing the students" (248). In 1928 this course was split into two sections. The freshman segment (CC-A) focused on the history of Western civilization from 1200 to the present. According to the core website, "The essential inquiries from the original CC course remained: How do men make a living? How do they live together? How do they understand their world?" CC-B, Introduction to Contemporary Problems in the United States (or CC-B), "emphasized the question of making a living in the United States. This was due in part to the Economics and Government departments abandoning their popular introductory courses in favor of the expanded CC." By 1932 "complications arising from the US economy (the Depression began as the course began) made it necessary to revise the syllabus of CC-B...introduce the most pressing questions about the nation's economic security and survival."
15. For Erskine's rationale for focusing on great books see his "On Reading Great Books," in his book *The Delight of Great Books* (originally published in 1928).
16. James Gutmann, "The Columbia College Colloquium," Columbia University Quarterly 29 (1937): 49. See website link. http://goo.gl/ YFJbD7.
17. "Proposed Secondary Sources for the Humanities A Criticized," Jonathan Katz, *Columbia Spectator*, February 19, 1963. Arguing against Trilling's proposal, professor of French Donald M. Frame insisted, "Students should be pushed into the experience of a direct confrontation with the text." Professor of Spanish Leonardo C. De Morelos agreed: "I like my students to do their own thinking and arrive at their own conclusions about the books they read." Robert L. Belknap, assistant professor of Russian, was more succinct: "If a student wants to know what Plato said, let him read Plato."
18. "A New Direction in Teaching the Humanities," 1963, http://goo. gl/kTgtF4.
19. "Columbia Moves Away from the Unified Courses It Pioneered," by Fred M. Hechinger, *The New York Times*, July 16, 1961, http://goo. gl/xggR3I.
20. Meanwhile, the unity lent to the course by its exclusive organization around "the Western tradition has been seriously thrown off balance

by the new importance of non-Western cultures." There were staffing problems as well, problems that look ahead to complaints today that too many senior faculty are involved in research while graduate students and part-timers are teaching basic undergraduate courses. Senior faculty, according to the article, has "refused to teach" these "interdepartmental courses, leaving their staffing to junior faculty and graduate assistants." The article claims that "the improvement of high-school teaching in recent years brings to the colleges many students too sophisticated not to spot the unseasoned instructor pretending to cope with the controversies of a perplexing world"

21. The recent introduction of majors at Columbia was a strong contributing factor, noted as well by Truman. The disciplines more and more wanted their major to take introductory courses early, in their sophomore year, which drew faculty away from teaching general education courses and cut into student time to take those courses.
22. These changes suggest there have been three general periods in the history of the American university. The first phase is characterized by the emergence of private universities connected to the church, and then public universities with relative autonomy and with a commitment to building national character. A second phase in which the public university becomes intertwined with government, and an emerging third phase in which the university corporatizes and goes global.
23. Bell here is quoting from Reuben Brower.
24. What he seems to be saying about the teaching of composition is interesting, too, that it ought to take place before students get to college so that colleges and universities can do away altogether with what is considered the remedial teaching of writing. One still hears this complaint today, of course, that if only K-12 schools taught writing more effectively colleges and universities would not have to hire so many part-time and adjunct faculty to teach basic writing courses, or have to assign them to tenure-track faculty whose time might be better spent in the literature classroom. Of course this point of view just feeds the very debilitating divide between so-called writing and literature professors in English departments.
25. The Truman report reserved most its criticism for the "B" course, which covered a more contemporary period.
26. For an interesting glimpse at the core circa 1997 see Denby, who chronicles his own experience returning to Columbia to take two core courses at the age of 48.
27. Materials for the Art Humanities and Music Humanities have a similar orientation. There are also University Writing, and Frontiers of Science requirements.
28. "The New Freshman Course in Columbia College," 1919, http://goo.gl/4WFt92.

5 Aesthetics, Close Reading, Theory, and the Future of Literary Studies

1. As we shall see later, the complex web of critical theories dominant in the 1970s, 1980s, and 1990s often get reduced in these essays to the overly broad categories of cultural studies or new historicism. See Best and Marcus for a detailed critique of symptomatic reading.
2. It is important to note that Levine is at pains to present his credentials as a postmodern, "anti-foundationalist" critic. "My 'anti's' are impeccable: I am anti-foundationalist, anti-essentialist, anti-universalist, and I do not believe in the possibility of that view from nowhere that gets one beyond contingency. I welcome new historicism, in lower case, as well as the recognition that all literature needs to be understood in relation to the local and the timebound" (2). He praises critics including the late postcolonial critic, Edward Said; the Marxist critic, Fredric Jameson; the new historicist Shakespeare scholar, Stephen Greenblatt; and queer theorist Eve Kosofsky Sedgwick for having "wonderfully enriched the possibilities of literary criticism" (2). In his view, these critics are able to manage a relative balance between political inquiry and attention to the artistic elements of the literary texts they analyze, but which their followers are not able to sustain. "Their followers," he complains, "reduce critical practice to exercise in political positioning," so that in their criticism "literature is all too often demeaned, the aesthetic experience denigrated or reduced to mystified ideology" (2–3).
3. Levine also criticizes Stephen Greenblatt for treating "literature as a resource... for anthropology" while leaving out "whatever might be distinctive about literature" (8). However, he fails to point us toward a kind of reading of Shakespeare that is both anthropological and literary. It is also troubling that while he blames followers of Jameson, Said, Sedgwick, and Greenblatt for the worst excesses of the kind of politically reductive criticism he finds so troubling (2), he does not cite a single example. Not one, in the text or in his footnotes. Who are these people, the reader wonders? He also makes the sweeping and unsubstantiated claim that "much of the research that now [1994] wins tenure at major universities does not display a primary interest in literature" (3). How can he possibly know this? Where is the research? Where are the statistics, the examples? What does he mean by "a primary interest in literature?"
4. The virtue of Levine's introduction is that it offers a timely reminder about the critic's responsibility to pay attention to the uniquely literary—aesthetic, formal, linguistic—elements of the

texts they write about and teach. In the best moments he calls for a critical practice that melds together aesthetic and ideological criticism. Balancing his sympathy for post-structuralist theory with his commitment to a focus on the aesthetic quality of literary texts, Levine's "argument is that ideology is so delicately and complexly entangled in the textures of literature itself that no discussion of the ideological without attention to the formal can have any but the most reductive relations to what texts are up to, how they get their work done" (4–5).

5. This of course returns us to one of the central questions I've been exploring in this book: In our current atmosphere of crisis, do the humanities in general, and literary studies in particular, define their value in idealist terms (we teach philosophy, history, literature, religion, etc.) or in practical, utilitarian terms, in terms of skills? This is a subject I'll return to later in this chapter when I discuss close reading, but it is important to note here that the commonsense claims Levine makes are actually very contestable.

6. See Graff, chapters 1–7 for a history of the rise of English. As Graff demonstrates in *Professing Literature*, the discipline was in a state of flux between 1915 and 1930, a period in which "linguistic philology ceded further prominence to literary history, the new fields of comparative literature and the history of ideas emerged, and American literature achieved respectability in the wake of war-time patriotism" (121). Literary and aesthetic criticism as we think of it today began to emerge as strong forces only in the years after World War I.

7. See Bérubé (2005) on how the aesthetic actually remained a key topic of concern in contemporary theory during the years Levine covers.

8. Armstrong's key point of departure is to point out that contemporary theoretical critiques of the aesthetic (like Terry Eagleton's *The Ideology of the Aesthetic*) tend to focus exclusively on "a nineteenth-century idealist aesthetic" (2) running from Kant to Hegel that had been discredited long before post-structuralism came along. In her view the anti-aesthetics of post-structuralism, cultural studies, and the new historicism spend altogether too much time trying to discredit an already outmoded, elitist, high culture approach to the aesthetic and no time at all trying to rethink the aesthetic as a critical category of analysis.

9. For her discussion of close reading as slow motion reading see "Shakespeare in Slow Motion."

10. Gallop argues that while "it is generally agreed that it is the big picture that matters" when we are reading this means that "the main idea or general shape of a book is likely to correspond to our preconceptions, but we cannot so easily predict the details," and that reading closely at the level of "detail is, I would argue, the best safeguard

against projection" (16). While I think Gallop is right that we often tend to read superficially for the big picture, I am not convinced that reading in a more detailed way puts a check on "projection," for it seems to me we project meanings onto small details just as much as we do on large patterns.

11. "The sort of close reading I am here advocating," she writes, "derives from the study of language (historically, philology) and rhetoric; it is focused on language rather than on ideas" (18).

12. This conception of close reading cannot, of course insure that readers focus only on what is "in" the text, nor does it guard against ideological or political interpretations of those texts. For example, while we can argue that the aesthetic qualities of a literary text seem for the most part to be qualities of a text, to inhere in them, "close reading" refers to a process of engagement between the text and a reader in which meaning is produced by the nature and quality of a transaction. Of course the aesthetic refers both to form and taste, to the objective existence of beauty and an empirical description of its qualities, which then can lead to judgments about quality and to a justification for taste, although ultimately taste is always going to be subjective compared to an empirical description of formal beauty. But formal beauty is, for the most part, the stuff of what Gallop refers to as the "main ideas and general shape" of a work of art. But is there a kind of formal beauty at the level of detail Gallop has in mind? Sure. A pun has formal beauty, for example, so that the phrase "when in doubt, pun," has a formal quality to it. The pun itself is a form, an intended double meaning or intertextual allusion, which can happen quickly at the level of detail, are also forms. Close reading, then draws our attention to the formal qualities of a literary work, but it draws our attention to a lot more. It produces evidence not simply about the formal or aesthetic qualities of a text but about its meaning. This evidence becomes, in effect, data we can use to interpret the meaning of a text, and these meanings can push beyond the intentional and ultimately have to be grounded in biographical, social, cultural, political, and historical contexts for them to become fully realized. So, while close reading was the mode of reading used by formalist New Critics, it is by no means a method of reading restricted to such an approach to reading. Feminist, Marxist, psychoanalytic, and postcolonial interpretations of texts can and are based on "close reading" every bit as much as formalist ones. A return to "close reading," then, is no guarantee that readers will pay more attention to literature itself or that reading will suddenly be less contaminated by theory, cultural studies, or the new historicism.

13. In making this claim she echoes the deconstructive critic, Barbara Johnson, who insisted that "teaching literature is teaching how to read...how to read what the language is doing, not guess what the

author was thinking, how to take in evidence from a page" (1985, 140). See also Klein, who in the October 2010 issue of *PMLA*, insists that the future of literary criticism ought to follow Jacques Derrida's approach to close reading.
14. For a comprehensive discussion of literal, surface, and symptomatic reading see Best and Marcus. On distance, hyper, and machine reading see Hayles.
15. Of course, as we have seen throughout this study, many traditionalists would argue that literature itself is the sacred icon of literary studies. The split between these two positions is related to the division I've been discussing throughout this book between seeing literary studies as the transmission of knowledge about a particular set of texts, and as the teaching of a set of skills linked to close reading. As we have seen, both Hayles and Gallop are strong advocates of the latter position.
16. See Moretti (2007).
17. For another discussion of the possibilities here see McGill and Parker.

Conclusion: The Humanities and the Public Sphere in the Age of the Internet

1. It is encouraging, for example, to see professional organizations such as the Modern Language Association and American Historical Association begin to rethink the structure of graduate education and the perpetual crisis in the academic job market, and to observe the emergence across the country of engaged and public humanities programs like those I discuss in this chapter.
2. http://www.yale.edu/amstud/publichumanities/index.html.
3. http://www.brown.edu/Research/JNBC/maprogram.php.
4. See, for example, Grafton and Grossman, "No More Plan B: A Very Modest Proposal for Graduate Programs in History," and Berman, et al., "The Future of the Humanities Ph.D. at Stanford."
5. As Charon puts it, narrative medicine does not aim to develop "a civilizing veneer—how cute, a doctor who writes poetry—but is a very practical field. Skills are offered that will allow for more efficacy" (quoted in Thernstrom).
6. See http://www.narrativemedicine.org/index.html and http://medinfo.ufl.edu/~medhum/index.shtml.
7. For another example, see Cathy Davidson's description of Duke University's Haiti Lab in "Why Flip the Classroom When We Can Make It Do Cartwheels?"
8. http://humanities.byu.edu/humanities_plus/.

9. For introductory overviews of the rise of the Digital Humanities with particular emphasis on their place in English departments and literary studies see Kirschenbaum and Jones.
10. Gary Hall observes that the digital humanities may provide a degree of "relief in having escaped the culture wars of the 1980s" into "the space of methodological work" ("Has Critical Theory Run out of Time?" 128).
11. For a somewhat different view on the relationship between the digital humanities and literary criticism, see Parry.
12. See Svensson for a review of debates about this topic.
13. For a counterargument see Scheinfeldt, who argues it is time to drop ideology critique (thinking "about our world in terms of ideologies and our work in terms of theories") in favor of a simple concern with "organizing knowledge," which he links back to philology, lexicology, and especially bibliography "in late 19th/20th centuries" (124).
14. Gary Hall succinctly describes the danger in leaving critical theory out of the digital humanities equation: "Positioning their own work as being either pre- or posttheory in this way in effect gives them permission to continue with their preferred techniques and methodologies for studying culture relatively uncontested (rather than having to ask rigorous, critical and self- reflexive questions about their practices and their justifications for them). Placed in this wider context, far from helping to keep the question concerning the use of digital tools and data-led methodologies in the humanities open (or having anything particularly interesting to say about theory), the rejection of critical- theoretical ideas as untimely can be seen as both moralizing and conservative" ("Has Critical Theory Run Out of Time?" 130).
15. This volume is indispensable for anyone who wants to become familiar with the digital humanities and current debates about the field.
16. On these questions see Tara McPherson, "Why Are the Digital Humanities So White? or Thinking the Histories of Race and Computation"; Amy E. Earhart, "Can Information Be Unfettered? Race and the New Digital Humanities Canon"; and Bethany Nowviskie, "What Do Girls Dig?"
17. For a discussion of the historical tension between the digital humanities and media studies, and proposals regarding linking the two fields, see McPherson (2009).
18. For a similar argument see Bianco who argues digital humanists must "work in and teach the serious know-how of code and critique, computation and cultural studies, collaboration and multimodal composing as so many literacies, capacities, and expressivities attuned to our moment and to the contexts and conditions in which we find ourselves. Let's take up the imperatives of a relational ethics in discussion and in practices and methods through composing creative critical media" (109).

19. For a lengthy analysis of this problem, see Parker. As Fain reports, the GAO released in 2011 a very negative study of for-profits.
20. "Senate Committee Report on For-Profit Colleges Condemns Costs and Practices," by Tamar Lewin, *The New York Times*, July 29, 2012 (http://www.nytimes.com/2012/07/30/education/harkin-report-condemns-for-profit-colleges.html).
21. See "For Profit Higher Education: The Failure to Safeguard the Federal Investment and Ensure Student Success" (http://www.help.senate.gov/imo/media/for_profit_report/Contents.pdf). The report was issued by staff from the Democratic majority of the US Senate Committee on Health, Education, Labor, and Pensions.
22. So-called blended courses aim to keep the classroom experience intact while relying on MOOC technology.
23. For example, see Friedman (2013, 2014), a particularly enthusiastic, and to my mind, naïve enthusiast for the revolutionary potential of MOOCs.
24. See Fowler, "An Early Report Card on Massive Open Online Courses."
25. See Kolowich, "Georgia Tech and Coursera Try to Recover from MOOC Stumble," February 24, 2013.
26. Reported in Fowler, "Survey: MOOC Students Are Elite, Young and Male," November 20, 2013. As Susan Adams pointed out in an article about the Penn GSE report in Forbes (December 11, 2013), the 35 thousand students from two hundred countries surveyed in the report came from the richest 6% of the population, casting more doubt on the democratizing potential of MOOCs.
27. Quoted in Fowler, "Survey: MOOC Students Are Elite, Young and Male."
28. Chafkin, "Udacity's Sebastian Thrun, Godfather Of Free Online Education, Changes Course," n.d.
29. "MOOCs and the Future of the Humanities: A Roundtable (Part 1)" by Ian Bogost, Cathy N. Davidson, Al Filreis, and Ray Schroeder, *The Los Angeles Review of Books*, June 14, 2013, http://goo.gl/PtDuHT.
30. "The purpose of an educational institution is to educate," he writes, "but the purpose of a startup is to convert itself into a financial instrument. The two major MOOC providers, Udacity and Coursera, are venture capital-funded startups, and therefore they are beholden to high leverage, rapid growth with an interest in a fast flip to a larger technology company or the financial market. The concepts of 'disruption' and 'innovation,' so commonly applied to MOOCs, come from the world of business. As for EdX, the MOOC consortium started by Harvard and MIT, it's a nonprofit operating under the logic of speculation rather than as a public service. If anything, it will help the for-profits succeed even more by evangelizing their

vision as compatible with elite nonprofit educational ideals." For another very recent critical discussion of MOOCs see Brady.
31. For more on what MOOCs might—and might not—offer see "Universities Reshaping Education on the Web," by Tamar Lewin, *The New York Times*, July 17, 2012 (http://goo.gl/2xbsjB). See also Bosquet and Vaidhyanathan.

Works Cited

Abraham, Matthew, and Andrew W. Rubin, eds. "Edward Said and After: Toward a new Humanism." Special issue of *Cultural Critique*, no. 67 (Spring 2008).
Adams, Susan. "Are MOOCs Really a Failure?" Forbes. Web. http://www.forbes.com/sites/susanadams/2013/12/11/are-moocs-really-a-failure/.
Ahmad, Aijaz. "Orientalism and After: Ambivalence and Metropolitan Location in the Work of Edward Said." In *In Theory: Nations, Classes, Literatures*. Ed. Aijaz Ahmad. Brooklyn: Verso, 2008.
Althusser, Louis. *For Marx*. London: Verso, 2006.
———. "Marxism and Humanism." Cahiers de L' I.S.E.A. June 1964. Web. http://www.marxists.org/reference/archive/althusser/1964/marxism-humanism.htm.
Alvares, Claudia. *Humanism after Colonialism*. New York: Peter Lang, 2006.
"An Open Letter to Professor Michael Sandel from the Philosophy Department at San Jose State U." *The Chronicle of Higher Education*. May 2, 2013. Web. http://chronicle.com/article/The-Document-an-Open-Letter/138937/.
Appiah, Kwame Anthony. *Cosmopolitanism: Ethics in a World of Strangers*. New York: Norton, 2006.
Armitage, David, et al. "The Humanities Project: Mapping the Future." Harvard University. Web. http://artsandhumanities.fas.harvard.edu/humanities-project.
Armstrong, Isobel. *The Radical Aesthetic*. Oxford: Blackwell, 2000.
Arum, Richard, and Josipa Roksa. *Academically Adrift: Limited Learning on College Campuses*. Chicago: U of Chicago P, 2011. Nook file.
Atlas, James. *Battle of the Books: The Curriculum Debate in America*. New York: Norton, 1990.
Bady, Aaron. "The MOOC Moment and the End of Reform." *The New Inquiry*. May 15, 2013. Web. http://thenewinquiry.com/blogs/zunguzungu/the-mooc-moment-and-the-end-of-reform/.
Bennett, William. "To Claim a Legacy: A Report on the Humanities in Higher Education." The University of Michigan Library, January 1, 1984.
Berman, Russell, et al. "The Future of the Humanities at Stanford." Stanford University. Web. http://goo.gl/5H02u6.

Bérubé, Michael. "Days of Future Past." *ADE Bulletin* 131 (Spring 2002): 20–26.

Bérubé, Michael. "The Humanities, Declining? Not According to the Numbers." July 1, 2013. *The Chronicle of Higher Education.* Web. http://chronicle.com/article/The-Humanities-Declining-Not/140093/.

———. "Introduction: Engaging the Aesthetic." In *The Aesthetics of Cultural Studies.* Ed. Michael Bérubé. Oxford: Blackwell, 2005. 1–27.

Best, Stephen, and Sharon Marcus. "Surface Reading: An Introduction." *Representations* 108, no. 1 (Fall 2009): 1–21.

Bianco, Jamie Skye. "This Digital Humanities Which Is Not One." In Gold, *Debates in the Digital Humanities,* 96–112.

Bivens-Tatum, Wayne. "The 'Crisis' in the Humanities." *Academic Librarian.* November 5, 2010. Web. http://blogs.princeton.edu/librarian/2010/11/the_crisis_in_the_humanities/.

Bosquet, Marc. "Good MOOCs, Bad MOOCs." *The Chronicle of Higher Education.* July 25, 2012. Web. http://chronicle.com/blogs/brainstorm/good-moocs-bad-moocs/50361.

Bost, Suzanne. *Encarnación: Illness and Body Politics in Chicana Feminist Literature.* New York: Fordham UP, 2009.

Brainard, Jeffrey. "Are the Humanities on the Ropes? Maybe Not." *The Chronicle of Higher Education.* February 28, 2010. Web. http://chronicle.com/article/Are-the-Humanities-on-the/64404/.

Brooks, Peter. "The Humanities as a Cultural Combat Zone." *The Chronicle of Higher Education.* December 9, 1992. Web. http://chronicle.com/article/The-Humanities-as-a-Cultural/70500/.

Burke, Kenneth. *A Rhetoric of Motives.* New York: Prentice Hall, 1950.

Carey, Kevin. "'Academically Adrift': The News Gets Worse and Worse." *The Chronicle of Higher Education.* February 12, 2012. Web. http://chronicle.com/article/Academically-Adrift-The/130743/.

Chace, William M. "The Decline of the English Department." *The American Scholar.* Autumn, 2009. Web. http://goo.gl/B3z0sp.

Chafkin, Max. "Udacity's Sebastian Thrun, Godfather Of Free Online Education, Changes Course," n.d. Web. http://www.fastcompany.com/3021473/udacity-sebastian-thrun-uphill-climb.

Charon, Rita. *Narrative Medicine: Honoring the Stories of Illness.* New York: Oxford UP, 2006.

Chopp, Rebecca. "Against the Grain: Liberal Arts in the 21st Century." October 25, 2012. Swarthmore College President's Office. Web. http://goo.gl/PsfQJC.

Cohen, Patricia. "In Tough Times, the Humanities Must Justify Their Worth." *The New York Times.* February 24, 2009. Web. http://www.nytimes.com/2009/02/25/books/25human.html?_r=1&scp=1&sq=in%20tough%20times%20the%20humanities%20must%20justify&st=cse.

Conant, James Bryant. *General Education in a Free Society: Report of the Harvard Committee.* Cambridge, MA: Harvard UP, 1945.

Coss, John J. "The New Freshman Course at Columbia College." July 1919. http://www.college.columbia.edu/core/sites/core/files/The%20 New%20Freshman%20Course%20in%20Columbia%20College.pdf.
Culler, Jonathan. "The Closeness of Close Reading." *ADE Bulletin* 149 (2010): 20–25.
———. *Literary Theory: A Very Short Introduction*. Oxford: Oxford UP, 1997.
Davidson, Catherine. "Can We Replace Professors with Computer Screens?" June 18, 2012, Co.EXIST. Web. http://www.fastcoexist.com/1680030 /can-we-replace-professors-with-computer-screens.
———. *Now You See It: How Technology and Brain Science Will Transform Schools and Business for the 21st Century*. New York: Penguin Books, 2012.
———. "Why Flip the Classroom When We Can Make It Do Cartwheels?" May 9, 2012. Co.EXIST. Web. http://www.fastcoexist.com/1679807 /why-flip-the-classroom-when-we-can-make-it-do-cartwheels.
Davidson, Catherine, et al. "MOOCs and the Future of the Humanities: A Roundtable by Ian Bogost, Cathy N. Davidson, Al Filreis and Ray Schroeder." *The Los Angeles Review of Books*, June 14, 2013. Web. http:// goo.gl/MzeYOj.
Davies, Tony. *Humanism*. Oxford: Routledge, 1997.
Delbanco, Andrew. "A New Day for Intellectuals." February 13, 2009. Web. http://chronicle.com/article/A-New-Day-for-Intellectuals/21359.
Denby, David. *Great Books: My Adventures with Homer, Rousseau, Woolf, and Other Indestructible Writers of the Western World*. New York: Simon and Schuster, 1996.
Derrida, Jacques. *Of Grammatology*. Trans. Gayatri Chakravorty Spivak. Baltimore: Johns Hopkins UP, 1976.
Donoghue, Frank. *The Last Professors: The Corporate University and the Fate of the Humanities*. New York: Fordham UP, 2008.
———. "Can the Humanities Survive the 21st Century?" *The Chronicle of Higher Education*. September 5, 2010. Web. http://goo.gl/ogdKk0.
Drucker, Johanna. "Humanistic Theory and Digital Scholarship." In Gold, *Debates in the Digital Humanities*, 85–95.
Editorial Board. "Who Says Math Is Boring." *The New York Times*. December 8, 2013. Web. http://goo.gl/2u0coZ.
Eagleton, Terry. *After Theory*. New York: Basic Books, 2003.
———. *The Ideology of the Aesthetic*. Oxford: Blackwell, 1990.
———. *Literary Theory: An Introduction*. Minneapolis: U of Minnesota P, 1983.
Earhart, Amy E. "Can Information Be Unfettered? Race and the New Digital Humanities Canon." In Gold, *Debates in the Digital Humanities*, 309–318.
Ellis, John M. *Literature Lost: Social Agendas and the Corruption of the Humanities*. 1999. New Haven: Yale UP, 2009.
———. "Why Students Flee the Humanities." March 9, 2009. Web. http:// goo.gl/HHPRpC.

English, James F. "Who Says English Is a Dying Discipline?" *The Chronicle of Higher Education*. September 17, 2012. Web. https://chronicle.com/article/Who-Says-English-Is-a-Dying/134410/.

Erskine, John. *The Delight of Great Books*. 1928. Whitefish MT: Kessinger Books, 2005.

Fain, Paul. "GAO Takes Another Crack." *Inside Higher Ed*. November 23, 2011. Web. http://goo.gl/iYBGXf.

Ferry, Luc, and Alain Renaut. *French Philosophy of the Sixties: An Essay on Antihumanism*. Paris: Gallimard, 1985.

Forster, Chris. "I'm Chris. Where am I wrong?" *HASTAC*. Web. September 8, 2010. http://hastac.org/blogs/cforster/im-chris-where-am-i-wrong.

Fish, Stanley. "The Crisis of the Humanities Officially Arrives." *The New York Times*. October 11, 2010. Web. http://opinionator.blogs.nytimes.com/?s=the+crisis+of+the+humanities+officially+arrives.

———. *Save the World on Your Own Time*. New York: Oxford UP, 2008.

———. "Will the Humanities Save Us?" January 6, 2008. *The New York Times*. Web. http://goo.gl/RqTbcM.

Foucault, Michel. "Nietzsche, Genealogy, History." In *The Foucault Reader*, ed. Paul Rabinow. New York: Pantheon, 1984.

———. *The Order of Things: An Archaeology of Knowledge*. New York: Random House, 1970.

Fowler, Geoffrey A. "An Early Report Card on Massive Open Online Courses." *The Wall Street Journal*. October 8, 2013. Web. http://online.wsj.com/news/articles/SB10001424052702303759604579093400834738972.

———. "Survey: MOOC Students Are Elite, Young and Male." November 20, 2013. Web. http://goo.gl/mvxi6B.

Friedman, Thomas L. "Revolution Hits the Universities." *The New York Times,* January 26, 2013. Web. http://www.nytimes.com/2013/01/27/opinion/sunday/friedman-revolution-hits-the-universities.html?ref=thomaslfriedman&_r=0.

———. "Breakfast Before the MOOC." *The New York Times*, February 18, 2014. Web. http://goo.gl/cNnO0I.

Frodeman, Robert. "Experiments in Field Philosophy." *The New York Times*. November 23, 2010. Web. http://opinionator.blogs.nytimes.com/2010/11/23/experiments-in-field-philosophy/.

Garber, Marjorie. *A Manifesto for Literary Studies*. Seattle: U of Washington P, 2004.

———. "Shakespeare in Slow Motion." *Profession* (2010): 151–164.

———. *The Use and Abuse of Literature*. New York: Pantheon, 2011.

Gallop, Jane. "The Ethics of Reading: Close Encounters." *Journal of Curriculum Theorizing* 16, no. 3 (Fall 2000): 7–17.

———. "Close Reading in 2009." *ADE Bulletin* 149 (2010): 15–19.

Gehlaus, Diana. "What Can I Do with My Liberal Arts Degree?" *Occupational Outlook Quarterly* 51, no. 4. (Winter 2007–08). Web. http://goo.gl/qagNB.

Giang, Vivian. "Logitech CEO: 'I Love Hiring English Majors.'" *Business Insider.* June 20, 2013. Web. http://goo.gl/fDKlQo.
Gilroy, Paul. *The Black Atlantic.* Boston: Harvard UP, 1993.
Gold, Matthew K. *Debates in the Digital Humanities.* Minneapolis: U of Minnesota P, 2012.
Graff, Gerald. *Professing Literature: An Institutional History.* Chicago: U of Chicago P, 1987.
Graff, Gerald, and Paul Jay. "Fear of Being Useful." *Inside Higher Ed.* January 5, 2012. Web. http://www.insidehighered.com/views/2012/01/05/essay-new-approach-defend-value-humanities.
Grafton, Anthony, and Jim Grossman. "No More Plan B: A Very Modest Proposal for Graduate Programs in History." American Historical Society. Web. http://www.historians.org/perspectives/issues/2011/1110/1110pre1.cfm.
Griswold, Alison. "Majoring in the Humanities Might Soon Cost You More in Florida." Forbes. January 18, 2013. Web. http://goo.gl/OtQrn2.
Gutmann, James. "The Columbia College Colloquium." Columbia University Quarterly no. 29, 1937. http://www.college.columbia.edu/core/sites/core/files/The%20Columbia%20College%20Colloquium.pdf.
Hall, Gary. "Has Critical Theory Run Out of Time for Data-Driven Scholarship?" In Gold, *Debates in the Digital Humanities,* 127–132.
———. "There Are No Digital Humanities." In Gold, *Debates in the Digital Humanities,* 133–138.
Hackney, Sheldon. "Sheldon Hackney on the Role of the Humanities." *The Chronicle of Higher Education.* July 21, 1993. Web. http://chronicle.com/article/Sheldon-Hackney-on-the-Role-of/73128/.
Hansen, Elain Tuttle. "The Situation of the Humanities." *ADE Bulletin* 138–139 (Fall–Spring 2006). 18–22.
Harkin, Tom, et al. "For Profit Higher Education: The Failure to Safeguard the Federal Investment and Ensure Student Success." July 29, 2012. Web. http://www.help.senate.gov/imo/media/for_profit_report/Contents.pdf
Harpham, Geoffrey Galt. *The Humanities and the Dream of America.* Chicago: U of Chicago P, 2011.
Hayles, N. Katherine. "How We Read: Close, Hyper, Machine." *ADE Bulletin* 150 (2010). 62–79.
Heller, Scott. "Humanists Seek to Regain Their Public Voice." *The Chronicle of Higher Education.* April 7, 1993. Web. http://chronicle.com/article|/Humanists-Seek-to-Regain-Their/71422/.
Hirsch, E. D. *Cultural Literacy: What Every American Needs to Know.* New York: Vintage, 1988.
Horowitz, Damon. "From Technologist to Philosopher: Why You Should Quit Your Technology Job and Get a Ph.D. in the Humanities." *Chronicle of Higher Education.* July 17, 2011. Web. http://chronicle.com/article/From-Technologist-to/128231/.

Isaacson, Walter. *Steve Jobs: A Biography.* New York: Simon and Schuster, 2011.

Jay, Gregory. "The Engaged Humanities: Principles and Practices for Public Scholarship and Teaching." *Journal of Community Engagement and Scholarship* 3, no. 1 (Spring 2010): 51–63.

Jay, Paul. *Global Matters: The Transnational Turn in Literary Studies.* Ithaca: Cornell UP, 2010.

Johnson, Barbara. "Teaching Deconstructively." *Writing and Reading Differently: Deconstruction and the Teaching of Composition and Literature.* Ed. G. Douglas Atkins and Michael L. Johnson. Lawrence: UP of Kansas, 1985. 140–148.

Jones, Steven E. *The Emergence of the Digital Humanities.* New York: Routledge, 2013.

Keller, Phyllis. *Getting at the Core: Curricular Reform at Harvard.* Cambridge: Harvard UP, 1982.

Kirschenbaum, Matthew. "What Is Digital Humanities and What's It Doing in English Departments." *ADE Bulletin* 150 (2010): 1–7.

Klein, Richard. "The Future of Literary Criticism." *PMLA* 125, no. 4 (October 2010): 920–923.

Kolowich, Steve. "Georgia Tech and Coursera Try to Recover from MOOC Stumble." February 24, 2013. Web. http://chronicle.com/blogs/wiredcampus/georgia-tech-and-coursera-try-to-recover-from-mooc-stumble/42167.

Levine, George, ed. *Aesthetics and Ideology.* New Brunswick: Rutgers UP, 1994.

———. "Introduction: Reclaiming the Aesthetic." In Levine, *Aesthetics and Ideology*, 1–28.

Lewin, Tamar. "Universities Reshaping Education on the Web." *The New York Times.* July 17, 2012. Web. http://goo.gl/5qhnFJ.

———. "Senate Committee Report on For-Profit Colleges Condemns Costs and Practices." *The New York Times.* July 29, 2012. Web. http://goo.gl/v9W0Qm.

Liu, Alan. "Where is the Cultural Criticism in the Digital Humanities?" In Gold, *Debates in the Digital Humanities*, 490–510.

McGill, Meredith L., and Andrew Parker. "The Future of the Literary Past." *PMLA* 125, no. 4, (October 2010): 959–967.

McPherson, Tara. "Introduction: Media Studies and the Digital Humanities." *Cinema Journal* 48, no. 2 (Winter 2009): 119–123.

———. "Why Are the Digital Humanities So White? or, Thinking the Histories of Race and Computation." In Gold, *Debates in the Digital Humanities*, 139–160.

Menand, Louis. *The Marketplace of Ideas.* New York: Norton, 2010.

Mooney, Carolyn J. "A Lull in the 'Political Correctness' Debate?" *The Chronicle of Higher Education.* April 20, 1993. Web. http://chronicle.com/article/A-Lull-in-the-Political/70989/.

Moretti, Franco. *Graphs, Maps, Trees: Abstract Models for Literary History*. Brooklyn: Verso, 2007.
Newfield, Christopher. *Unmaking the Public University: The Forty-Year Assault on the Middle Class*. Boston: Harvard UP, 2011.
Ngai, Sianne. *Ugly Feelings*. Boston: Harvard UP, 2007.
Noonan, Jeff. *Critical Humanism and the Politics of Difference*. Montreal: McGill UP, 2003.
Nowviskie, Bethany. "What Do Girls Dig?" In Gold, *Debates in the Digital Humanities*, 235–240.
Nussbaum, Martha C. "Do Colleges Need French Departments?" *The New York Times*. October 17, 2010. Web. http://www.nytimes.com/roomfordebate/2010/10/17/do-colleges-need-french-departments/cultivating-the-imagination.
———. "The Liberal Arts Are Not Elitist." *The Chronicle of Higher Education*. February 28, 2010. Web. https://chronicle.com/article/The-Liberal-Arts-Are-Not/64355/.
———. *Not for Profit: Why Democracy Needs the Humanities*. Princeton: Princeton UP, 2010.
"Our Mission." The Foundation for Critical Thinking. Web. http://www.criticalthinking.org/pages/our-mission/599.
Parker, Chris. "For-Profit Colleges Only a Con Man Could Love." The Village Voice. August 1, 2012. Web. http://goo.gl/1RZ64R.
Parry, David. "The Digital Humanities or a Digital Humanism." In Gold, *Debates in the Digital Humanities*, 429–437.
Pease, Donald. *The New American Exceptionalism*. Minneapolis: U of Minnesota P, 2009.
Perloff, Marjorie. "Restoring 'Literary Literacy' to the English Curriculum." *The Chronicle of Higher Education*. March 7, 2011. Web. http://chronicle.com/article/RestoringLiterary-Literacy/76829/.
Ramsay, Stephen. "Who's In and Who's Out." 2011. Web. http://stephenramsay.us/text/2011/01/08/whos-in-and-whos-out/.
Reisz, Matthew. "Google Leads Search for Humanities PhD Graduates." *The Times Higher Education*. May 19, 2011. Web. http://goo.gl/WV2mC.
Robbins, Bruce. "The Scholar in Society." *The Chronicle of Higher Education*. June 8, 2007. Web. http://chronicle.com/article/The-Scholar-in-Society/17462.
Ruddick, Lisa. "The Near Enemy of the Humanities Is Professionalization." *The Chronicle of Higher Education*. March 23, 2001. Web. http://chronicle.com/article/The-Near-Enemy-of-the/15135/.
Said, Edward. *Culture and Imperialism*. New York: Vintage, 1993
———. *Humanism and Democratic Criticism*. New York: Columbia UP, 2004.
Saul, Scott. "The Humanities in Crisis? Not at Most Schools." *The New York Times*. July 3, 2013. Web. http://www.nytimes.com/2013/07/04/opinion/the-humanities-in-crisis-not-at-most-schools.html?_r=0.

Scheinfeldt, Tom. "Sunset for Ideology, Sunrise for Methodology." In Gold, *Debates in the Digital Humanities*, 124–126.

Schmidt, Ben. "How Are College Majors Changing?" Web. http://benschmidt.org/Degrees/.

Schmidt, Jeff. *Disciplined Minds: A Critical Look at Salaried Professionals and the Soul-battering System That Shapes Their Lives*. Lanham, MD: Rowman & Littlefield, 2001.

Scholes, Robert. *The Rise and Fall of English*. New Haven and London: Yale UP, 1998.

Segal, Carolyn Foster. "Chiseling Away at the Humanities." *The Chronicle of Higher Education*. February 28, 2010. Web. http://chronicle.com/article/Chiseling-Away-at-the/64346/.

Senghor, Léopold. "Negritude: A Humanism of the Twentieth Century." In *Imperialism: Critical Concepts in Historical Studies*. Ed. P. J. Cain and Mark Harrison. London: Routledge, 2001. 220–229.

Svensson, Patrick. "Beyond the Big Tent." In Gold, *Debates in the Digital Humanities*, 36–49.

Swartzendruber, Tim. "Making English Majors Marketable." *The Chronicle of Higher Education*. April 23, 2001. Web. http://chronicle.com/article/Making-English-majors/108296/.

Tavernise, Sabrina. "Numbers of Children of Whites Falling Fast." *The New York Times*. April 6, 2006. Web. http://www.nytimes.com/2011/04/06/us/06census.html.

Thernstrom, Melanie. "The Writing Cure." *The New York Times Magazine*. April 18, 2004. Web. http://www.nytimes.com/2004/04/18/magazine/18NARRATIVE.html?pagewanted=all.

Trilling, Lionel. "A New Direction in Teaching the Humanities." 1963. http://www.college.columbia.edu/core/sites/core/files/A%20New%20Direction%20in%20Teaching%20the%20Humanities.pdf.

"University at Albany Announces Measures to Rethink, Balance and Reallocate Resources in Face of Reduced State Fiscal Support." *University of Albany*. October 10, 2010. Web. http://www.albany.edu/news/9902.php?WT.svl=news.

Vaidhyanathan, Siva. "What's the Matter with MOOCs?" *The Chronicle of Higher Education*. July 6, 2012. Web. http://chronicle.com/blogs/innovations/whats-the-matter-with-moocs/33289.

Weisbuch, Robert. Private email to Gerald Graff, October 23, 2011.

Weissmann, Jordan. "The Best Argument for Studying English? The Employment Numbers." *The Atlantic*. June 25, 2013. Web. http://www.theatlantic.com/business/archive/2013/06/the-best-argument-for-studying-english-the-employment-numbers/277162/.

Williams, Raymond. "Culture is Ordinary." In *Resources of Hope: Culture, Democracy, Socialism*. Ed. R. Gable. London: Verso, 1958. 3–18.

INDEX

Academically Adrift (Arum and Roksa), 16
aesthetics
   Armstrong and, 125–7
   beautiful/sublime and, 120
   close reading and, 132–6
   Contemporary Civilization courses and, 97, 111
   contemporary theory and, 126
   criticism and, 118–31, 161, 171
   culture and, 46, 73–4, 126–7, 153
   "democratic aesthetic," 127
   formalism and, 117–18
   German idealism and, 126
   humanism and, 67, 88–9
   humanities education and, 14, 128–31, 157
   Kant's theory of, 27, 125, 127–8
   Levine and, 118–27, 131
   literary studies and, 41, 44–6, 49–51, 53, 91, 112–17, 121–4
   literature and, 124–7, 134, 145
   Ngai and, 127–31
   political and, 41, 44, 116
   positions on, 128
   return to, 125–8
   Schiller and, 127
   Sedgwick and, 121–3
   subject matter and, 111–13
Althusser, Louis, 66–7
American Academy of Arts & Sciences, 11
American Historical Society, 147
Anzaldúa, Gloria, 85–8, 93–4, 107
Appiah, Kwame Anthony, 74–5, 93
Aristotle, 97, 109

Armstrong, Isobel, 118, 127–9, 131, 188n8
Arnold, Matthew, 51–2, 62–4, 72–4, 98, 180n4, 181n13, 182n16
Arnold, Thomas, 62
art history, 26, 88
artificial intelligence (AI), 13–14
Arum, Richard, 16, 174n16
"Asking Literary Questions" (Garber), 47
Association of American Colleges and Universities, 15
Austen, Jane, 89, 109–10, 121
authenticity, 35–7, 74–5
authority, 9, 25–7, 52, 57, 121–3

bachelor's degrees, 9–11, 19, 175n18
Barthes, Roland, 138, 178n6, 179n12
Baudelaire, Charles, 85–6, 88, 121
Bell, Daniel, 104–8, 113
Bennett, William, 19, 21, 74, 120
Bérubé, Michael, 10–11
"Best Argument for Studying English? The Employment Numbers" (Weissmann), 11
Bianco, Jamie Skye, 191n18
Bible, 109, 122
Bivens-Tatum, Wayne, 8
Black Atlantic, The (Gilroy), 71
Bloom, Harold, 90
Bogost, Ian, 167–8
Borderlands/La Frontera (Anzaldúa), 86, 93
Bradlaugh, Charles, 63

Index

Brigham young University (BYU), 153
Brooks, Peter, 55–9, 62–3, 70, 72
Brown University, 150
budget cuts, 1, 4–5, 7, 17–18, 162, 168–9
Burckhardt, Jacob, 62–3, 181n10–11, 182n16
Burke, Kenneth, 22, 109
Butler, Judith, 26–8

canon
  aesthetics and, 126, 128–31
  Bennett and, 19, 21
  close reading and, 98
  Contemporary Civilization courses and, 109, 111
  criticism and, 90–1, 98, 155
  culture and, 72, 84
  Delbanco and, 34–5
  English courses and, 125
  formation of, 6, 91, 93
  Gallop and, 137
  history and, 90–1, 99, 102, 145
  humanities and, 3, 8, 19, 90–4, 107–9
  Lit Hum A and, 99
  literature and, 34–5, 44, 48, 50, 52, 64, 70, 72, 125, 141
  multiculturalism and, 86–8, 111
  Perloff and, 21–2, 87, 107
  professionalization and, 34–5
  revision of, 86–8
  tradition and, 52, 57, 146
Canterbury Tales (Chaucer), 63
Carnegie, Andrew, 13
Cervantes, Miguel de, 98, 109–10
Chace, William M., 9, 42–3
Chafkin, Max, 166
Charon, Rita, 150–1
Chaucer, Geoffrey, 63–4, 90, 121
Cheney, Lynne, 19, 74, 120
Chicano/a studies, 6, 77
"Chiseling Away at the Humanities" (Segal), 19
Cicero, 97

Civil Rights movement, 52, 77, 95, 109, 179n12
Civilization and Its Discontents (Freud), 27
CLA, 16–17, 175n16
close reading
  aesthetics and, 113–15, 117–18, 131–2
  canon and, 98
  Charon and, 151
  digitalization and, 161, 170
  Gallop and, 136–8
  Garber and, 46, 136–7
  Hayles and, 139–41
  humanities and, 16, 80, 131–2, 150, 161
  hyperreading and, 139–40
  literary study and, 46, 101, 113–14, 134–5, 170
  New Criticism and, 5–6, 132–3, 136–8
  protocols of, 5–6
  recent advocates of, 133–5
Cohen, Patricia, 19, 23
Cohen, Philip, 22
Cold War, 79, 105
Columbia University, 2, 95–100, 102–5, 107–8, 111, 113, 151
Contemporary Civilization courses
  Introduction to (CC-A), 96–7, 103–4, 110, 185n14
  Introduction to Contemporary Problems in the US (CC-B), 97, 185n14
contextualization
  aesthetics and, 126, 131–5
  canon and, 98–9
  Columbia and, 99–100
  Felski and, 50
  Garber and, 47–8
  Gutmann and, 98
  history and, 47, 85, 99, 120, 135
  literature and, 45–8, 53, 91–2, 108, 115, 117, 135, 144
  marginalization and, 45–6
  natural and, 100–1

New Criticism and, 133–4
professionalization and, 45–8, 53
reading and, 47–8, 50, 134
tradition and, 84
Trilling and, 100–1
core revision committee, 84–8, 99, 107–8
Cornell University, 10
Cosmopolitanism: Ethics in a World of Strangers (Appiah), 74
Coss, John J., 96, 111
critique
  aesthetics and, 125
  anti-intellectualism and, 40
  critical theory, 4, 20, 25, 27–8
  of criticism, 43
  culture and, 161
  digital humanities and, 157–8, 161–2
  Enlightenment and, 27–8
  humanism and, 25–7, 55–6, 58, 66–7, 69, 71, 76, 79–80, 144
  humanities and, 16, 21, 26–7, 34, 58, 87, 118, 146–7
  liberal arts and, 16
  literature and, 118, 134–5, 137
  tradition and, 2
Culler, Jonathan, 25, 47, 133–4, 137
Culture and Imperialism (Said), 72
curation, 4, 25–7, 34–5, 50, 87, 91, 98, 104, 120, 138, 145, 155, 162

Dante, 64, 74, 98, 109
Darwin, Charles, 63, 109
data mining, 156, 161
Davidson, Cathy, 30, 167–8
Davies, Tony, 62–3, 65, 181n9–14
"Decline of the English Department" (Chace), 9
Delbanco, Andrew, 25–6, 34–5, 40, 43, 87, 98, 104, 120
Derrida, Jacques, 179n12, 184n6, 189–90n13
Diasporic history/literature, 75, 79, 93

Dickens, Charles, 89, 98
Dickinson, Emily, 110
digital humanities, 5, 148, 154–62, 170
Donoghue, Frank, 8, 12–13, 42, 57
Dostoevsky, Fyodor, 98, 109–10
Drucker, Johanna, 156–9
D'Souza, Dinesh, 19

Eagleton, Terry, 22, 38, 50, 59, 62, 87
Edman, Irwin, 98
Eliot, George, 121
Eliot, T. S., 74, 110
Ellis, John M., 9, 42–3
Emerson, Ralph Waldo, 110, 121
employment, 17, 19, 23, 116, 131, 148–50, 162
English studies
  canon and, 72
  core curriculum and, 82–6
  drop in number of majors, 9–12, 41
  humanities education and, 2, 9
  literary studies, 33, 35, 51–2, 83–4, 90, 93, 124–5, 136
  New Criticism and, 132
  professionalization and, 5, 35, 39–40
  reading and, 47, 136–7
  rhetoric and, 22–3
  see also literary studies
Enlightenment, 27, 34, 65, 68, 71, 73, 78, 97, 127
Erdrich, Louise, 121
Erskine, John, 97

Faulkner, William, 110
Felski, Rita, 48–50
feminism, 3, 68–71, 76–7, 86, 116, 126–7, 155
Fish, Stanley, 18, 23, 116
formalism, 29, 91, 114, 117–18, 137, 155, 171
Forster, Chris, 161
Foucault, Michel, 26–8, 60–1

Freud, Sigmund, 27, 97, 109
Frodeman, Robert, 151–3

Gallop, Jane, 133, 136–9
Garber, Majorie, 45–9, 133–7
Gates, Henry Louis, 138
gay rights movement, 77
Gehlaus, Diana, 12
Georgetown Center on Education and the Workforce, 11–12, 174n7
Gilroy, Paul, 71
globalization, 13, 20–1, 23–4, 75, 79–81, 105, 111
Goethe, Johann Wolfgang von, 63–4, 98, 110
Gold, Matthew, 158
Google, 12–13, 157
Graff, Gerald, 38, 42–3, 48, 50, 52, 65, 70, 87, 91, 99, 102, 132
"great books" 91, 96–9, 102–4, 107–9, 137, 143–4, 155
"great tradition" of Western texts, 57, 74, 146
Greek literature, 62–4, 74, 79, 95
Greenblatt, Stephen, 124, 138, 187n2–3
Gutmann, James, 98

Hackney, Sheldon, 20–2, 80, 176n32
Hall, Gary, 158–9, 191n14
Harkin, Tom, 164
Harpham, Geoffrey Galt, 37–43, 45, 47–8, 50–1, 79–80, 91, 177n4, 182n19, 183n24, 183n26
Hawthorne, Nathaniel, 110, 119
Hayles, Katherine, 139–41
Hegel, G. W. F., 27, 109, 182n16, 188n8
Heller, Scott, 20
Hemingway, Ernest, 89, 110, 145
Hirsch, E. D., 34, 74
historicism, 3, 45–6, 102, 117, 125, 129, 134–5, 138
Hobbes, Thomas, 98, 109

Homer, 63–4, 85–6, 88
homosexuality, 77, 86, 121, 123, 179n12
Horowitz, Damon, 13–14
humanism
  aesthetics and, 67, 88–9
  authenticity and, 36
  critique and, 25–7, 55–6, 58, 66–7, 69, 71, 76, 79–80, 144
  English studies and, 41
  historical narrative of, 59–61
  humanities and, 8, 12, 17, 19, 30–1, 51
  identity and, 88
  literary studies and, 41, 43, 48
  multiculturalism and, 72–7
  practical skills and, 23
  professionalization and, 53
  religion and, 63–4, 77
  sciences and, 19
  tradition and, 3, 19, 23, 25–7, 55–6, 68, 72–6, 79, 117
Humanism (Davies), 62
humanities
  aesthetics and, 14, 128–31, 157
  canon and, 3, 8, 19, 90–4, 107–9
  in classroom, 162–71
  close reading and, 16, 80, 131–2, 150, 161
  critique and, 16, 21, 26–7, 34, 58, 87, 118, 146–7
  digital, 154–62
  future of, 143–5
  multiculturalism and, 6, 20, 147
  practical skills and, 3–5, 14, 19, 144, 147–8, 153, 155, 160, 162, 169
  professionalization and, 3, 20, 23–4, 33–5, 39, 42, 83–4, 95, 99, 143–4
  religion and, 14, 81, 111–12, 131, 146
  specialization and, 29–30, 96, 98, 103–7, 143–4, 148, 150
  toward engaged and public humanities, 145–54

tradition and, 2, 19–21, 34, 55–9, 66, 80–1, 115, 143
Humanities and the Dream of America (Harpham), 37
"Humanities in Crisis? Not at Most Schools" (Saul), 10
Humboldt, Alexander von, 62
Hurston, Zora Neale, 145
Huxley, T. H., 63–4
hyperattention, 140
hyperreading, 140
  see also close reading

Imagining America Curriculum Project, 152–3
Immigration and Nationalization Act (1965), 52
individualism, 14, 20, 27, 62–4, 66, 70, 78, 181n11–12
information visualization, 156–7
"intellectual authority," 57
"It Takes More Than a Major" (report), 15

Jameson, Frederic, 138, 187n2–3
Jay, Gregory, 152–3
Jobs, Steve, 14
Johnson, Barbara, 189n13

Kant, Immanuel, 27, 51, 109, 125, 127, 188n8
Kaplan University, 164
Keats, John, 89, 121, 163
Kimball, Roger, 19, 74, 120
Klein, Naomi, 168
Klein, Richard, 189–90n13

La Raza, 77
Last Professors, The (Donoghue), 8, 12
Latin studies, 74, 95
Latino/a literature, 77, 108
Leavis, F. R., 74
Levine, George, 118–27, 131, 135, 187–8
Lewin, Tamar, 164

literary studies
  aesthetics and, 41, 44–6, 49–51, 53, 91, 112–17, 121–4
  canon and, 34–5, 44, 48, 50, 52, 64, 70, 72, 125, 141
  critique and, 118, 134–5, 137
  English studies and, 33, 35, 51–2, 83–4, 90, 93, 124–5, 136
  humanism and, 41, 43, 48
  multiculturalism and, 3, 6, 86, 93, 125, 179n12
  practical skills and, 51, 53, 132, 137–8
  professionalization and, 37, 42, 48–9, 52–3, 120, 137
  religion and, 46–7, 90, 92
  tradition and, 43–4, 50–2, 55, 63–4, 84–5, 125
  see also English studies
Literary Theory: A Very Short Introduction (Culler), 25
Literature Lost: Social Agendas and the Corruption of the Humanities (Ellis), 9
Liu, Alan, 140, 159–62, 170
Lives of the Painters (Vasari), 63

Macbeth (Shakespeare), 89
Machiavelli, Niccolò, 63, 109
machine reading, 138–41
Manifesto for Literary Studies (Garber), 45, 48, 134
marginalization, 3, 19, 45–6, 55, 91, 117, 126, 145, 148, 154, 158, 170
Marx, Karl, 27, 60, 63–4, 66–8, 70, 76, 109, 127, 132, 182n16
"Marxism and Humanism" (Althusser), 66–7
Massive Open Online Courses (MOOCs), 162–71
masterpieces, 17, 109–10
masters degrees, 149
Mayer, Marissa, 12
Merchant of Venice, The (Shakespeare), 119

Miller, J. Hillis, 138
Milton, John, 64, 74, 79, 90, 98, 121
Modern Language Association (MLA), 124, 147, 159
Modern Languages and Literatures, 83–4, 86
modernism, 64–5, 71, 110, 130
modernity, 63, 71–2, 132
Moretti, Franco, 140
multiculturalism
  aesthetics and, 116, 128
  Anzaldúa and, 86
  criticism of, 74
  Garber and, 179n12
  globalization and, 111
  humanism and, 72–7
  humanities and, 6, 20, 147
  literature and, 3, 6, 86, 93, 125, 179n12
  marginalization of, 3

narrative competence, 151
National Association of Colleges and Employers (NACE), 12
National Secular Society, 63
Native American culture, 77, 108, 110
New Criticism, 6, 43, 46, 51, 98, 132–6, 138
New Historicism, 3, 6, 45, 60, 126, 138, 145, 187n1–2, 188n8, 189n12
Newfield, Christopher, 173n5
Ngai, Sianne, 118, 127–31
Nietzsche, Friedrich, 8, 27, 60–1, 109
Noonan, Jeff, 56, 179n2
Nussbaum, Martha, 19, 50, 57, 59–60, 65, 78–80, 92, 94

Paradise Lost (Milton), 90, 98
particularization, 23
passivity, 101
Perloff, Marjorie, 21–2, 29, 38, 50, 52, 87, 106

PhDs, 9, 13–14, 148–51, 177n4, 178n7
philology, 124–5, 188n6, 191n13
Plato, 90, 97–8, 109, 185n17
"poetics of culture," 124
political correctness, 2–3, 9–11, 18, 20–1, 50, 56, 58–9, 66, 73, 75, 118, 129, 144, 147
positivist orientation of computation, 156–8
postcolonial theory, 3, 52, 71–2, 76–7, 93, 125, 127, 155, 157
postmodernism, 60, 90, 110, 130, 179n2, 187n2
Pound, Ezra, 110
practical skills
  close reading and, 132–3
  critique and, 26
  Gallop and, 137
  humanities and, 3–5, 14, 19, 144, 147–8, 153, 155, 160, 162, 169
  literature and, 51, 53, 132, 137–8
  narrative competency and, 151
  teaching of, 1, 22–3
Prince, The (Machiavelli), 63
Princeton University, 8, 165
Professing Literature: An Institutional History (Graff), 42
professionalization
  aesthetics and, 129–30
  Bell and, 105–7
  canon and, 99
  Columbia and, 96, 102–7, 113
  contextualization and, 45–8
  critical thinking and, 25
  criticism of, 29, 43, 51, 99, 102, 106, 115–16, 121, 130
  debates regarding, 5, 95
  humanities education and, 83–4, 95, 99, 143–4
  humanities faculty and, 3, 20, 23–4, 33–5, 39, 42, 95
  Levine and, 121
  literary studies and, 37, 42, 48–9, 52–3, 120, 137

theories, 2
Trilling and, 102

queer theory, 3, 155, 179n12, 187n2

Radical Aesthetic, The (Armstrong), 118, 127
Ramsay, Stephen, 159
recession, impact on humanities education, 1, 7, 10, 16–17
religion/religious studies
  aesthetics and, 129, 131
  Columbia Plan and, 97
  core courses and, 88
  critique and, 26
  humanism and, 63–4, 77
  humanities and, 14, 81, 111–12, 131, 146
  literature and, 46–7, 90, 92
  Paradise Lost and, 90
  secular and, 64
  theory and, 28–9
  traditionalists and, 146
Renaissance, 55, 62–5, 68, 73, 79, 181n10–12, 182n15
Renaissance man, 103–4
Republic (Plato), 98, 109
revisionists, 146–8
rhetoric, 1–2, 4, 8–9, 13–14, 21–2, 29, 34, 46, 50–1, 76, 87, 94, 99, 115, 122, 124–5, 134–5, 165
Richards, I. A., 138
Roksa, Josipa, 16, 174n16
Ruddick, Lisa, 35–7
Rust, Edward B. Jr., 12

Said, Edward, 72, 138, 181n6, 187n2–3
San Jose State University, 164–6
Saul, Scott, 10–11
Save the World on Your Own Time (Fish), 116
Scheinfeldt, Tom, 191n13
Schiller, Friedrich, 127

Schmidt, Ben, 9–11
Schmidt, Jeff, 36
science, technology, engineering, and mathematics (STEM), 7, 11–13, 173n6
Scott, Rick, 175n18
secular individualism, 62–4
Sedgwick, Eve Kosofsky, 121–4, 187n2–3
Segal, Carolyn Foster, 19, 187n2
"Shakespeare in Slow Motion" (Garber), 46
Shakespeare, William, 14, 63–4, 74, 85–6, 90, 109–10, 121–2, 187n2–3
Skidmore University, 177n5
social science, 11, 14, 19, 23, 30, 35, 39–40, 51, 69, 103, 111–12, 123, 137, 143–4
Sophocles, 63, 98, 109
specialization
  aesthetics and, 115, 131
  Columbia Plan and, 96, 98, 100
  core courses and, 84–6, 91
  higher education and, 23
  humanities and, 29–30, 96, 98, 103–7, 143–4, 148, 150
  increased emphasis on, 96
  professionalization and, 115
Spivak, Gayatri, 138
St. John's College, 99
Stanford University, 153
State Farm Insurance Companies, 12
State University of New York, Albany, 18
Stern, Fritz, 99, 103, 106
Swartzendruber, Tim, 22
Symonds, John Addington, 62, 181n13

tenure, 168, 178n7, 186n24, 187n3
"tenured radicals," 11, 19
"To Reclaim a Legacy: A Report on the Humanities in Higher Education" (Bennett), 19

tradition
  aesthetics and, 127–30, 132–4, 137
  core curriculum and, 106–9
  criticism and, 43, 106
  history and, 61
  humanism and, 3, 19, 23, 25–7, 55–6, 68, 72–6, 79, 117
  humanities and, 2, 19–21, 34, 55–9, 66, 80–1, 115, 143
  intervention and, 63
  literature and, 43–4, 50–2, 55, 63–4, 84–5, 125
  multiculturalism and, 73, 86–9
  reading and, 139–42
  society and, 105
  Western, 6, 74, 84–6, 90, 92–4, 97, 102–3, 105, 110
traditionalism, 23, 44, 52, 70, 74–6, 109
Trilling, Lionel, 99–103, 106–8, 113, 123
tuition, 11, 150, 163–4, 175n18
Twain, Mark, 110

Ugly Feelings (Ngai), 118
University of California, Berkeley, 11
University of California, Irvine, 167
University of California, Santa Barbara, 140
University of Chicago, 99, 184n9
University of Florida, 151
University of Pennsylvania, 166
University of Phoenix, 164
University of Texas, 22, 153
University of Washington, 150, 153
University of Wisconsin-Milwaukee, 153
Unmaking the Public University (Newfield), 173n5

Vasari, Giorgio, 63
Vietnam war, 95
visual arts, 14, 70, 98, 112
visualization, 140, 156–7

Weisbuch, Robert, 175n17
Weissmann, Jordan, 11–12, 174n7
"What Can I Do with My Liberal Arts Degree?" (Gehlaus), 12
Whitman, Walt, 89, 110
Williams, Raymond, 73, 179n12
Winckelmann, Johann Joachim, 62
women's movement, 52, 68–70, 77, 86, 95, 109
Woolf, Virginia, 109–10, 121
World War I, 2, 95–6, 104
World War II, 77, 88, 97

Yale University, 10, 149

GPSR Compliance

The European Union's (EU) General Product Safety Regulation (GPSR) is a set of rules that requires consumer products to be safe and our obligations to ensure this.

If you have any concerns about our products, you can contact us on

ProductSafety@springernature.com

In case Publisher is established outside the EU, the EU authorized representative is:

Springer Nature Customer Service Center GmbH
Europaplatz 3
69115 Heidelberg, Germany

www.ingramcontent.com/pod-product-compliance
Lightning Source LLC
LaVergne TN
LVHW041630060526
838200LV00040B/1523